The Opera Stage
of Sarah Caldwell

The Opera Stage of Sarah Caldwell

A Directing Philosophy in Practice

KRISTINA BENDIKAS

McFarland & Company, Inc., Publishers
Jefferson, North Carolina

Library of Congress Cataloguing-in-Publication Data

Names: Bendikas, Kristina, author.
Title: The opera stage of Sarah Caldwell : a directing philosophy in practice / Kristina Bendikas.
Description: Jefferson, North Carolina : McFarland & Company, Inc., Publishers, 2020. | Includes bibliographical references and index.
Identifiers: LCCN 2020011065 | ISBN 9781476680408 (paperback) ∞
ISBN 9781476639253 (ebook)
Subjects: LCSH: Caldwell, Sarah, 1924–2006—Criticism and interpretation. | Opera producers and directors—Massachusetts—Boston. | Opera—Production and direction—Massachusetts—Boston—History—20th century. | Opera—Stage setting and scenery—Massachusetts—Boston—History—20th century. | Opera—Massachusetts—Boston—20th century. | Opera Company of Boston.
Classification: LCC ML422.C225 B46 2020 | DDC 782.1092—dc23
LC record available at https://lccn.loc.gov/2020011065

British Library cataloguing data are available
ISBN (print) 978-1-4766-8040-8
ISBN (ebook) 978-1-4766-3925-3

© 2020 Kristina Bendikas. All rights reserved

No part of this book may be reproduced or transmitted in any form or by any means, electronic or mechanical, including photocopying or recording, or by any information storage and retrieval system, without permission in writing from the publisher.

The front cover image is of Sarah Caldwell (Photofest)

Printed in the United States of America

*McFarland & Company, Inc., Publishers
Box 611, Jefferson, North Carolina 28640
www.mcfarlandpub.com*

Table of Contents

A Note on Opera Titles — vi
Preface — 1
Introduction — 5

1. Beginnings — 25
2. The Company — 41
3. The Repertoire — 66
4. Preparation and Rehearsal — 84
5. Spaces — 99
6. Experiments — 119
7. Final Years — 138

Conclusion — 147
Appendix A: The Conductor — 157
Appendix B: Operas Staged by Caldwell — 166
Chapter Notes — 171
Bibliography — 185
Index — 195

A Note on Opera Titles

While researching Caldwell's productions I was struck by the variability of opera titles in different sources. As I began writing the narrative, I thought it important to establish consistency by keeping them in their original languages. However, as the manuscript began to take shape, I started to question that choice. Would readers wonder why I was writing about *Prodaná nevěsta*, when it was given (well, mostly) in English? Would they be confused if I used *Il barbiere di Siviglia* when writing about her production with the Opera Company of Boston, and then switched to *The Barber of Seville* when referencing its reiteration at the New York City Opera (although both were sung in Italian)? And should I try to explain why her English language production of Schönberg's *Moses and Aaron* (which in German would be *Moses und Aron*) appears in one source as *Moses and Aron* and in another as *Moses und Aaron*?

Setting aside a potentially fascinating inquiry into the linguistic and cultural influences on the nomenclature of opera titles, I concluded that to impose consistency where there was none would be to side-step Caldwell's own ambivalence in the matter. Over the course of her long career she maintained, at least in theory, that operas for an English-speaking audience should be performed in English. Yet, while she presented some in English translation, others (including her groundbreaking premieres of Berlioz's *Les Troyens* and Verdi's *Don Carlos*) were given in their original languages. Ultimately, my choices reflect the duality of hers. I used English titles for the majority of operas, but kept those that are not typically translated, or need no translation (such as *Der Freischütz* and *La Traviata*) in their original languages. Titles that appear in citations, end notes, and the bibliography have been reproduced exactly.

Preface

I first became aware of Sarah Caldwell in the mid–1970s, when I was a teenager, studying voice and piano, and hoping that one day I would become an opera singer. She was about to become the first woman to conduct the Metropolitan Opera Orchestra for a production of Verdi's *La Traviata* (starring my idol Beverly Sills) and was interviewed on the *CBS Evening News with Walter Cronkite*. At the time, I was more interested in Sills, but I never forgot the initial impression Caldwell made upon me. She was an unadorned, middle-aged woman with a sonorous voice and a clear vision of the potential of opera: "To me," she said, "opera doesn't exist unless it is a combination of music and theater. It has to be exciting theater, wonderful music. If you bring them together and make them function, together, then you have a performance."[1] The news segment did not delve into how she did that, however. It was just a brief story about her as an anomaly: a conductor who happened to be a woman. Only years later did I understand what an anomaly she truly was: an impresario, a conductor, and a stage director who happened to be a woman. And I realized that no one had closely analyzed her work within the context of American opera history.

I rediscovered Caldwell while working on my dissertation about the French director/designer Jean-Pierre Ponnelle, whose career in the United States paralleled hers. My interest in her directorial philosophy and methods began to take hold as I read reviews about her work in Boston. The idea for a book, however, remained on the proverbial back burner, and in 2008, two years after Caldwell's death, two books about her were published, which seemed to put an end to the need for a third. That turned out not to be the case. The first, *Sarah Caldwell: The First Woman of Opera*, was a general overview of her career, enlivened with anecdotes about her eccentricities. The second, *Challenges: A Memoir of My Life in Opera*, was a transcription of Caldwell's recollections about her career that she had recorded shortly before her death. The books were published in close succession, and coincidently, used the same cover image of Caldwell. Neither included any significant analysis of her career as a stage director.

Waiting to write the present work proved serendipitous because additional resources that were crucial to my analysis had become available. In particular, the Howard Gottlieb Archival Center at Boston University established the Sarah Caldwell Collection, which includes extensive records of the Opera Company of Boston such as financial and legal records, production records, photographs, musical scores, as well as audio and video recordings of performances. In addition, I was able to access additional material at the Boston Symphony Orchestra Archives and the New England Conservatory Archives, which shed light on productions she did with her mentor Boris Goldovsky at Tanglewood and with the New England Opera Theater before she established the Opera Company of Boston. This volume also draws from hundreds of reviews of the Opera Company of Boston's productions from journals, periodicals, and major newspapers, including the *Boston Globe*, *Boston Herald*, *Christian Science Monitor*, *New York Times*, *Opera*, *Opera News*, and *The New Yorker*. Those reviews represent first-hand observations of Richard Dyer, Bernard Holland, Andrew Porter, Winthrop Sargeant, Harold C. Schonberg, and other leading critics of the day. In addition, autobiographies and biographies of singers who worked with Caldwell, including Plácido Domingo, Beverly Sills, Joan Sutherland, Shirley Verrett, and Jon Vickers, contained indispensable perspectives on her philosophy and methods.

This book does not purport to be a biography of Caldwell, nor does it include detailed musical analyses of scores (which would be outside my scope of expertise). Rather, it is an investigation into her choices as an opera director, her influences, her philosophy and methods, in order to situate her work within the history of opera in America. It begins by introducing the reader to her initiation into the world of opera under the supportive tutelage of Boris Goldovsky. That is followed by an overview of the Opera Company of Boston, in order to provide context for her productions and an understanding of the demands that leading the company placed on her. The chapter on her repertoire explores the breadth of her choices and the risks that they represented for her personally and professionally. The next three chapters focus on her process: her research and work with singers, her creative use of unusual performance spaces, and her experiments. The final chapter sums up her work after the Opera Company of Boston and the conclusion provides a reflection on her place in American opera in the 20th century. For those readers interested in Caldwell's conducting career, there is an appendix that gives an overview of it through the lens of contemporary critical reception, which I hope will encourage a closer examination of her work in that capacity.

During my research for this book I had the pleasure of meeting a number of people who worked with Caldwell. I am grateful for the time they took to share their insights and reflections. Others contributed to this project in various and no less important ways. In particular, I would like to thank Nathalie Anderson, J. Michael Deegan, Suzanne Hayden, Freda Herseth, Victoria Leacock Hoffman, Joan Kufrin, Vincent Lubrano III, James T. Morgan, Lisi Oliver, Deirdre Taylor Paster, Paul Peabody, Helen Pond, William Fred Scott, Eszter Szalczer, Albie Walton, and Thomas Whitman.

Introduction

In 1958, at the age of 34, Sarah Caldwell formed The Opera Group, Inc. (a.k.a. the Boston Opera Group, or just Opera Group, renamed the Opera Company of Boston in 1965) and led it for over 30 years. A decade later, she was named the Artistic Director of the short-lived American National Opera Company, and went on to establish Opera New England, an outgrowth of the OCB that toured to smaller cities throughout the region for 16 years. She brokered international cultural exchanges. One resulted in a production of Verdi's *La Traviata* in Beijing; another brought Mozart's *The Magic Flute* to the Philippines. Her global reach brought hundreds of Soviet and American artists together in the Making Music Together (MMT) festival in Boston 1988, then repeated the feat in 1991, in what had just recently become the former Soviet Union. As a stage director, she followed in the footsteps of her mentor, Boris Goldovsky, and her idol, the legendary German director, Walter Felsenstein, in merging music and drama. She was quick to embrace new stage technologies in her productions, including supertitles and film, and she delighted in the magical spectacles that she created together with set designers. Yet, she was no slave to modern technology nor did she have predilections towards revisionist conceptions. Her priority was to develop a *mise en scène* based on the musical score, as the composer originally envisioned it.

Between the short seasons of the Opera Company of Boston, and more frequently after its demise in 1990, she served as a regular guest conductor of the Ural Philharmonic Orchestra in Yekaterinburg, Russia, and led orchestras in the United States, Canada, Israel, The Netherlands, South Africa, Sweden, Venezuela, and the People's Republic of China. She made history as the first woman to conduct at the Worcester Festival in 1949, the first woman to conduct at the Ravinia Festival in 1976, and as noted above, the first woman to conduct the Metropolitan Opera Orchestra that same year. When she was in her 70s, she reached out to the renowned musicologist Laurence Picken because she was interested in his discovery of music from the court of Tang

China. Their association led her to produce the documentary *On the Road to Tang Through Cambridge* (2004), an overview of Picken's work, including performances of reconstructed music from the Tang period. And she became the director of the Ancient Asian Music Project at the Library of Congress, working to preserve music from the Tang court uncovered by Picken and his collaborators.[1] These endeavors are only a few highlights of a career that was recognized with 22 honorary doctorates and a National Medal of Arts in 1996, the highest honor the American government bestows upon artists.

The level of national attention that Caldwell received during her lifetime peaked in the mid-1970s, when she made her conducting debut at the Metropolitan Opera. As a result, when she is remembered, she is remembered primarily as a conductor (for example, she is listed only as an opera conductor on the National Medal of Arts website). Certainly, she was a musician by training, the primary conductor for her own company, and served many orchestras as a guest conductor. Yet, her passion and her greater influence on American opera history was through stage directing. The Opera Company of Boston presented over 130 productions and she staged almost every one. She co-directed three and only once turned over the staging of a production entirely to someone else[2]—but still conducted the performances. In contrast to the majority of opera stage directors, she worked almost exclusively with her own company where she unleashed her boundless imagination and formidable musical sensibilities, turning former vaudeville theaters, movie palaces, concert halls, and sports facilities into temporary opera houses where audience members and singers often occupied the same spaces.

Caldwell began her career as an impresario believing that "in a country where you could sell green toothpaste, you could certainly sell opera."[3] Her optimism never wavered, but her company's fortunes did. Almost from its beginning, financial difficulties beset it. Some were those faced by all arts organizations, but others resulted from a mismatch between her expansive artistic vision and her ability to finance it. Still, she was able to persist and continued to produce operas because she was able to show Bostonians what opera could be and should be. As a plain, obese person with a labored walk, she did not give the impression of being polished fundraiser. Yet, she possessed a winning combination of audacity and charm that earned her many admirers and many donations. When she wanted to work with someone, she found a way. She convinced Igor Stravinsky to be the honorary Chair of the Officers of the fledging Opera Group. She made late night calls to singers and designers to coax them to Boston and refused to take "no" for an answer. She flew all the way to England just to introduce herself to Laurence Picken, unannounced. At his front door, she said simply, "I was told you weren't on the phone, so I've come from Boston to see you."[4] When she wanted to engage the legendary Czech set designer Josef Svoboda, she tracked him down in New York City and watched his boxes being unpacked, disappointed to find that a box she thought held special projection equipment he used for his *Laterna Magika* effects was actually full of toilet paper.[5]

She surrounded herself with ambitious young artists who were willing to work long hours for little money because she inspired them though her own passion and work ethic. In lieu of a decent (or even regular) paycheck she gave them the training they needed to become highly successful elsewhere (and many did). Friends and former OCB colleagues who I interviewed for this book spoke about how hard they worked, how demanding she could be at times, and yet how funny and generous also. All of them were inspired by her unfailing enthusiasm for opera. Opera was Caldwell's passion, her life, and the joy that she took in creating it was infectious and transformative.

Before the middle of the 20th century, opera in America was generally a grand spectacle imported from Europe, performed for an elite audience more interested in it as a social occasion than as art. Caldwell was one of the first American opera stage directors who expanded its reach to all sectors of society. She appealed to sophisticated audience members by expanding the repertoire, producing operas for the first time in their entirety, and by including never before heard musical elements. Yet, she also popularized opera for uninitiated attendees by incorporating gimmicks that made her productions wildly popular with her audiences. One of those gimmicks was the inclusion of celebrities in her productions. Offenbach's comic *Orpheus in the Underworld* delighted audiences with appearances by Fred Gwynne (Herman Munster in the 1960s situation comedy *The Munsters*), Margaret Hamilton (the Wicked Witch of the West in the 1939 film *The Wizard of Oz*), and comedians Sid Caesar and Imogene Coca. In her New York City Opera debut production of Henze's *The Young Lord*, Rudolf Bing, General Manager of the Metropolitan Opera, joined in as Sir Edgar, a pantomimed role. The entertainer and arts advocate Kitty Carlisle Hart portrayed the Duchess de Krackenthorpe in *The Daughter of the Regiment*, the humorist Victor Borge portrayed Frank in Strauss' *Die Fledermaus*, and the Ringling Brothers Circus clown Emmett Kelly, Sr., was a highlight of the circus scene in Smetana's *The Bartered Bride*.

Another of Caldwell's signature gimmicks was to involve animals in the stage action. In Rossini's *Semiramide* Joan Sutherland made a spectacular entrance as the Queen of Assyria, accompanied by 20 doves that flew into the auditorium. The orgy scene in Schönberg's *Moses and Aaron* was to have live animals—including a 1200-pound ox, a donkey, three goats, and three sheep—but the noise they made backstage during rehearsals forced her to limit the number that ultimately appeared on stage during the performance. Fortunately for Caldwell, the dressing room she shared with the two horses that made their entrance in the final scene of Puccini's *Girl of the Golden West* were, according to her, "extraordinarily well-behaved."[6] She asked for scrawny cats to add atmosphere to Berlioz's *Benvenuto Cellini*, but since the animal trainers could only supply ones that were well-fed, that idea had to scrapped. Finally, the beginning of Act III in Smetana's *The Bartered Bride* included not only jugglers and acrobats, and a famous clown, but also performing dogs. No wonder she was once proclaimed "Boston's Barnum."[7]

Caldwell was, however, much more than an operatic ringmaster. She was an inventive director who was an early proponent of beautiful singing supported by believable acting. In the early 20th century, opera singers tended to use a presentational style of acting, expressing emotion through stock gestures rather than finding motivations that could lead to individualized expressions of psychological realism. Only gradually did the ideal of the singer-actor take hold. Goldovsky promoted that ideal at Tanglewood and Caldwell insisted upon it as fervently as her mentor had. Moreover, she was an astute musician, able to analyze opera scores and therefore, able to conceptualize and realize *mise en scènes* that blended music and drama. Although she considered herself principally a stage director, she conducted with skill and earned many accolades as a guest conductor with orchestras around the world (see Appendix A). After seeing her touring production of Verdi's *Falstaff* in 1967 Winthrop Sargeant wrote in *The New Yorker*, "Not only is she a great director, one must also place her among the finest operatic conductors currently before the public."[8] Still, critics noted that she could be uneven or seemingly disinterested at the podium. Clearly, conducting was not her passion. She did it out of necessity because she believed that the best way to achieve her goal of uniting music and drama was through one person. When she did relinquish the baton, she did so to an exceptional group of collaborators. Arthur Fiedler, long-time conductor of the Boston Pops, conducted *Die Fledermaus* in 1961; Laszlo Halasz, the first music director of the New York City Opera, conducted *Die Meistersinger von Nürnburg* in 1962 and *Madama Butterfly* in 1964; Richard Bonynge conducted *I Puritani*, *Semiramide*, and *Don Giovanni*, all starring Joan Sutherland; Bruno Maderna, who conducted the 1961 world premiere of Nono's *Intolleranza 1960* in Venice, did so in Boston in 1965; and Robert Shaw conducted Berlioz's *The Damnation of Faust* (1978). Guest conductors also included Vincent La Selva, who conducted *La Bohème* in 1966 and *Tosca* in 1967, before founding the New York Grand Opera Company in 1973; the Hungarian composer and conductor János Kulka conducted *Bluebeard's Castle* in 1967 and again in 1969; and Gunther Schuller conducted the world premiere of his opera, *The Fisherman and His Wife* (1970). Finally, Caldwell worked regularly with Osbourne McConathy, who not only conducted regularly, but also prepared performance editions for the company, and William Fred Scott (a Caldwell protégé), who conducted for the Opera Company of Boston, Opera New England, and shared the conducting credits with Caldwell on a recording of Bellini's *I Capuleti e i Montecchi*.[9]

Under Caldwell's artistic leadership the Opera Company of Boston introduced the world premieres of Middleton's *Command Performance* (1962), Schuller's *The Fisherman and His Wife* (1970), and Di Domenica's *The Balcony*, as well as more than a dozen American premieres. Season after season she enticed world class singers, including Plácido Domingo, Nicolai Gedda, Donald Gramm, Tito Gobbi, Marilyn Horne, Magda Olivero, Louis Quilico, Anja Silja, Beverly Sills, Joan Sutherland, Renata Tebaldi, Tatiana Troyanos, Shirley Verrett, and Jon Vickers to work with her. Renowned designers, too, including Heinrich Rudolf and Josef Svoboda came to Boston because of Caldwell. The significance of her company led Governor Dukakis to declare 1978 "Opera Company of Boston Year in the State of Massachusetts," and by doing so recognized the organization as "vital and necessary to the maintenance of the cultural preeminence of the state."[10]

Caldwell drew artists to Boston because she put into practice a directing philosophy that served the art form rather than her ego. Goldovsky had instilled in her the view that opera could be—indeed must be—not only musically, but also dramatically exciting and cohesive. When she came to study at the New England Conservatory, she became captivated by his approach. He became her mentor and guided her development during her studies, over the course of their collaborations at Tanglewood, and at his own company, the New England Opera Theater. Later she discovered the work of Walter Felsenstein, founder of the Komische Oper in East Germany. She spent time watching him in rehearsal and incorporated his approach as well. Felsenstein's insistence upon musical research, his attention to details of character motivation, his work with actors in exploring the offstage life of characters— all were evident in her process. However, the economic conditions under which she toiled were quite different from those he experienced. He worked in a rarified atmosphere in which he could dictate his own rehearsal and performance schedule without worrying about the financial state of his theater. It was possible for him to extend a rehearsal period and not worry about the expense of keeping unionized musicians over time or having to explain the cost to a Board of Directors. Moreover, he could cancel a performance if one of the singers, even in a small role, became ill (and he famously did). Caldwell could not possibly recreate the conditions at the Komische Oper, the practical and financial impediments were too great. Nevertheless, she strove to apply what she could and became the first and only American director to utilize Felsenstein's methods in staging opera. Moreover, she brought him to American audiences to introduce them first-hand to his philosophy and practice of directing.

In 1970, Caldwell's Eastern Opera Consortium, a collaboration between the Opera Company of Boston and seven area colleges (Boston College, Boston University, College of the Holy Cross, Northeastern University, Tufts University, the University of Massachusetts Boston, and the University of Rhode Island), sponsored a visit by Walter Felsenstein. Over the course of two weeks spent mostly in New England, he gave interviews, conducted workshops, and introduced his opera films, including Beethoven's *Fidelio*, Offenbach's *The Tales of Hoffmann*, and Verdi's *Otello*. Attendees were able to hear him discuss his theories and watch him work on arias with young singers in his characteristically intense manner. In one session, he spent over an hour analyzing a single phrase, and at another, he devoted two hours to a young baritone, drawing out the pivotal importance of Iago's "Credo in un Dio crudel" in the second act of Verdi's *Otello*. It was Felsenstein's last of only three visits to the United States and therefore a rare and important dissemination of the theory and practice of one of the leading figures in 20th-century theater and opera.

Caldwell was both passionate and playful about opera: "It's like being in another world for a little while and that's interesting, that's fun. That's really being alive."[11] Producing operas was her life and her joy. For her it was "magic time," but not everyone was captivated with her process. Her passion drove her to work at a level of intensity that drained the energy and patience of those around her. She gained a reputation as a relentless perfectionist, absent-minded, and heedless of time. Her unconventional habits and attitudes towards her appearance led to "Sarah Stories," anecdotes that were told and retold by members of the company and the press: she slept in the theater aisles, wore slippers to conduct, dressed in whatever kind of garment was at hand, and neglected her personal hygiene. Some of the stories were true, others were embellished, and a few were quite cruel. She was painfully aware of their derogatory nature of these stories: "[T]hey make great reading if you don't have to live with them. It did turn me into a bit of a cartoon."[12] In light of those public humiliations, she was exceedingly self-conscious. She dreaded appearing on stage to take a curtain call with her cast because she knew people would judge her work against her appearance. The media suggested that she did not care what people thought about how she looked, but that was not true. She did care about what people thought, but ultimately, she cared more about her work. Opera was her obsession and it drove her year after year to push the boundaries of her own creativity, to expand the canon, to share her excitement with her audiences and, not infrequently, to forget all else, because for her, nothing else mattered.

Caldwell fulfilled three interdependent roles within the Opera Company of Boston. The operas she selected were ones she wanted to direct, but also ones she wanted to conduct. At the same time, she had to consider her choices through the lens of an impresario, mindful of her audiences and always conscience of the fiscal precipice near which the company perpetually teetered. In particular, her roles as director and conductor were almost inseparable. Shunning preconceptions about operatic characters led her to question accepted revisions to the score. The restoration of musical passages led her to stage insightful dramatic moments. She could then underscore those moments with the orchestra during the performance with a precision and understanding not always possible when the roles of director and conductor are separated. She was adamant that a good director must be a trained musician, and when that person embodies both skills, the best results happen.[13] "I have very little patience," she said, "with people who argue that one must put more emphasis on musical values or emphasis on dramatic values ... because without all of the elements this thing which we call opera cannot exist."[14] She was not merely a conductor who also directed operas, nor a director who also conducted, but someone who was both. While each are worthy of consideration, her greatest contributions to late 20th-century opera were through her work as a stage director and that role is the primary focus of this book.

Caldwell's career spanned the second half of the 20th century, decades during which the modern opera director ascended to an unprecedented level of importance. She began her opera studies in the 1940s, scarcely a half century after the emergence of the modern stage director—the person who conceptualized and visualized the opera score and coordinated all the production elements. That emergence owes much to the influence of Richard Wagner, whose attempt to achieve a coherence of aural and visual elements (*Gesamtkunstwerk*) in his own operas made him one of the first modern directors. By the time he died, theater design was beginning to change from a realist style to a more suggestive style, advocated by theorist and designer Adolphe Appia specifically for Wagner's operas. Appia argued that suggestive *mise en scènes* would liberate the music from the encumbrance of three-dimensional sets. However, Wagner's widow, Cosima, would have none of it, preferring to retain the realistic style that the "master" had dictated. During the first two decades of 20th century opera staging of Wagnerian productions and others stagnated, while in the spoken theater, powerful figures like Max Reinhardt and Vsevelod Meyerhold advanced the art of stage directing and the influence of the stage director in Europe.

After World War II, a "director's theater" or "*Regietheater*" evolved in Europe and in America. This new approach rejected existing para-textual indications for staging and historical authenticity in favor of radical re-imaginings of the *mise en scène* to explore contemporary issues. In Europe, two of the most influential directors at that time were Walter Felsenstein, whose philosophy and process Caldwell alone embraced and introduced to American audiences, and Wieland Wagner (the composer's grandson) whose visual canvas freed Wagner's archetypes from the constraints of theatrical realism. In later decades, directors Patrice Chéreau, Jean-Pierre Ponnelle, and Franco Zefferelli were among an elite group who dominated the opera world with their forceful concepts and pioneering visualizations that raised the opera director to a level of importance equal to or exceeding that of the conductor.

In post-war America, Rudolf Bing, who became the General Manager of the Metropolitan Opera in 1950, was among the first to acknowledge that opera production in America lagged behind Europe in theatrical sophistication. Therefore, early in his tenure at the Metropolitan Opera, he hired directors from the theater, including Margaret Webster, Tyrone Guthrie, Peter Brook, and Alfred Lunt, to inject new life into its productions. While their interpretations certainly revitalized operatic "chesnuts," it was the next generation that radicalized them in America. Frank Corsaro followed by Peter Sellars were among the next wave of American directors who applied theatrical values to opera, and drew diverse and passionate reactions from audiences and critics. They regularly "revisioned" operas, usually by updating the *mise en scènes* or situating the stories in unexpected locations, in order to create a recognizable visual world for audiences far removed from the historical period of the composition.

The upheavals in opera production in the second half of the 20th century paralleled significant changes in the roles of women in public life. Caldwell's career spanned the decades when women in America made great strides towards gender equality. After the end of World War II, when women who had taken jobs held by men before the war began to question a return to their former domestic roles, Caldwell was honing her directing and conducting skills with Goldovsky at Tanglewood. Soon after Simone de Beauvoir's groundbreaking *The Second Sex* was translated into English (1952), she established her own company and became only the second female opera impresario in America (after Carol Fox at the Lyric Opera of Chicago). By the time Betty Friedan gave voice to the growing discontent of educated American women in *The Feminine Mystique* (1963), she was emerging as a cultural force in Boston. Finally, in the 1970s, the decade that the Equal Rights Amendment was approved by the House and the Senate, she reached the pinnacle of her artistic powers. Although the ERA eventually failed to be ratified by the required number of state legislatures, years of public debates by influential leaders like Bella Abzug and Gloria Steinem introduced many women (this author included) to think more deeply about the rights and roles of women in society. This was a decade when I came of age as a feminist and when I first learned about Sarah Caldwell. Yet, just as the Equal Rights Amendment had a half century of history prior to its reintroduction, the history of American women as impresarios, conductors, and stage directors began before Caldwell entered the opera scene. There were women who succeeded, despite all odds, in each of these male-dominated fields. Her role models were few, but their achievements and the obstacles they faced provide an important backdrop against which to view her career.

Opera history has been graced with many important and talented women. Many were singers, but in 19th-century America, there were women who made their mark as impresarios. Typically, they were associated with Women's Clubs and, in an era when women were not always able to be visible in certain roles, they worked behind the scenes to produce and coordinate musical performances. Clara Louise Kellogg, an American soprano who sang on extensive tours throughout the United States, was someone who also distinguished herself as an impresario. She established the English Opera Company in 1876, a company that presented operas in English translation.[15] Women of high social standing could be very influential in their communities, supporting musical entertainments at a time when public musical performances by women instrumentalists were rare. Jeanette Thurber, a wealthy patroness of music founded the American Opera Company in 1886, shortly after she established the National Conservatory of Music of America in New York City, which was led for several years by the Czech composer Antonin Dvořák. Although neither the English nor the American opera company lasted for very long, Kellogg and Thurber may be credited with laying a foundation for future women opera impresarios.

The city of Chicago was the location of another early example of a singer-turned-impresario emerged, at least briefly. When the Chicago Opera Association replaced the short-lived Chicago Grand Opera Company (1910–1914), its general manager and chief underwriter, Harold F. McCormick, appointed Mary Garden as General Director and gave her a free hand to determine its sixth and final season (1921–1922). She made liberal use of McCormick's promise to pay for her selections, including the world premiere of Sergei Prokofiev's *A Love for Three Oranges*, conducted by the composer.[16] The company lost over $1 million that season, but opera in Chicago remained secure and even receptive to future women leaders. In 1952, Carol Fox, at 26 years of age, co-founded the Lyric Theater of Chicago with Lawrence V. Kelly (who later founded the Dallas Civic Opera) and the conductor Nicola Rescigno. By 1956, the Lyric Theater became the Lyric Opera of Chicago and Fox became its General Director, a position she held until shortly before her death 1981.[17] After Fox, the Lyric Opera of Chicago continued to be led by a woman, Ardis Krainik, who had been with the company since its founding. She served as its General Director from 1982 until her death in 1997.

The Chicago examples are, however, anomalies for women in opera. Throughout the 20th century in America, few women have held leadership roles in opera companies, especially in major ones. According to *Opera America* data,[18] in 1990 (the first year it complied statistics on women in leadership roles at opera companies in America) Ardis Krainik was the only female General Director at the time for a Level 1 (over $10 million annual budget) company. Beverly Sills was not included since she had just stepped down from her role as General Director of the New York City Opera. At the same time, there were only two Artistic Administrators (Marianne Fletcher at the San Diego Opera and Sarah Billinghurst at the San Francisco Opera) at a Level 1. The number of women leaders increased slightly for Level 2 ($3–$10m) and Level 3 ($1–$3m) companies and almost tripled for Level 4 (under $1m) companies. In later updates of the *Opera America* study, that inverse correlation remained. In 2015, Susan T. Davis (General Director of Florida Grand Opera), Francesca Zambello (Artistic Director of the Washington National Opera Company as well as the Artistic and General Director of the Glimmerglass Opera) and three Artistic Administrators were the sole women in these top positions in Level 1 companies. More women held leadership positions at Level 2 and 3 companies and the figures more than quintupled at Level 4. Still today, whether one looks at companies in the United States or around the world, there are few impresarios who happen to be women—which makes Caldwell an historically important exception.

Almost as rare as the number of women impresarios was the number of women who were able to establish careers as conductors in the 20th century. Perhaps not surprisingly, women were rarely in front of the orchestra, because for much of the century they were underrepresented in the orchestra. They made gains during World War II, sometimes replacing their male counterparts, but in 1947, only eight per cent of musicians in major American orchestras were women.[19] The Philadelphia Orchestra hired its first woman, a harpist, in 1930. The Boston Symphony Orchestra admitted its first woman, a bassoonist, in 1945. The New York Philharmonic was recalcitrant, hiring its first woman, a double bassist, in 1966. The conductor Thomas Beecham's quip "The trouble with women in an orchestra is that if they are attractive they will upset my players, if they are not, they will upset me" demonstrates, through a thin veneer of humor, that there was active resistance to hiring women.

In light of the obstacles that women musicians encountered when seeking employment in orchestras in the first half of the 20th century, it is not surprising that a few of them decided they could be more productive, not to mention employed, if they formed their own orchestras. From the turn of the century until World War II, at least two dozen all-female orchestras led by women conductors flourished across the United States. Among the first on the podium was Frédérique Petrides, a violinist who founded the Orchestrette of New York, which she led from 1932 to 1943. Another was Ethel Leginska, a concert pianist turned conductor, who formed the Boston Philharmonic Orchestra and the Women's Symphony of Boston. Leginska appeared at Carnegie Hall a number of times as a pianist and debuted there as a conductor with the New York Symphony Orchestra in 1925.[20] Finally, there was Antonia Brico, who struggled to make a living as a guest conductor in America and abroad despite receiving critical acclaim. Frustrated by being unable to secure a permanent post, she established the Women's Symphony Orchestra of New York in 1934.[21] In 1937, she became the first woman to conduct an opera performance by a major New York opera company, leading the New York Hippodrome Opera in a production of Humperdinck's *Hansel and Gretel*. The following year, she made her debut with the New York Philharmonic, the first woman to conduct that orchestra.[22] A decade later, she formed the Denver Businessmen's Orchestra, which later became the Brico Symphony, a semi-professional (mixed sex) orchestra that she led until her retirement in 1985. That orchestra continues to the present day under its new name, the Denver Philharmonic Orchestra. While most women conductors of the period worked with all women orchestras at some point, there were two notable exceptions. Emma R. Steiner, a Maryland native with little formal training, forged a career as a conductor and composer, and served as guest conductor of the Anton Seidl Orchestra in 1894, in a program of her own compositions.[23] Lastly, the most well-known female conductor of the period, Nadia Boulanger, devoted much of her career to teaching composition to distinguished pupils such as Aaron Copland and Philip Glass. Yet, she became the first woman to conduct the Boston Symphony, the Philadelphia Orchestra, and the New York Philharmonic in Carnegie Hall in the late 1930s.[24]

Unfortunately, the pioneering work and accomplishments of these women did little to open doors for other women aspiring to conducting careers even as the middle of the century approached. When Margaret Hillis graduated from Indiana University in 1947 (just after Caldwell began her studies at Tanglewood), she was told bluntly that a woman's prospects as a symphonic conductor were very slim.[25] She turned to choral conducting and was engaged by the Chicago Symphony Chorus, which she led for 37 years. Most women who pursued conducting careers tended to find steady employment more often in community and academic settings, and greater acceptance in choral conducting rather than orchestral conducting. Beatrice Brown was an exception. She held a permanent position as the music director and conductor of the Scranton Philharmonic (Pennsylvania) from 1963 to 1970 and then the Ridgefield Symphony Orchestra (Connecticut) from 1970 to 1995.

By the 1970s, women were finally gaining more acceptance as orchestral musicians and slowly paving the way to the podium. In that decade, they made up about one quarter of the musicians in 31 major American orchestras. However, their participation levels were inversely proportionate to the prestige of the orchestra, i.e., the bigger the budget, the fewer women engaged.[26] Even when women were able to get the training, support, and experience that conductors needed, fewer women than men with the same educational credentials made it to the podium, and fewer still ever conducted in front of the most prestigious orchestras. Among those few who did achieve higher profile positions was Judith Somogi. Somogi, mentored by Leopold Stokowski, was the first woman to lead the New York City Opera Orchestra in 1974 and the first to receive a permanent appointment as head of an orchestra when she became music director of the Utica Symphony.[27] Eve Queler, conductor of the Opera Orchestra of New York, which she formed in 1972 to present rarely performed works in concert form, was another, and finally, the aforementioned Antonia Brico, Margaret Hillis, and Beatrice Brown. In 1971, the *Musical America Annual Directory* listed 218 conductors, but only three (1.3 percent) were women. By 1982, there was a significant rise in the number of conductors, with 424 listed, but only 13 (3 percent) of them were women. Moreover, there was still evidence of a disparity in the prestige of the orchestras that employed women. In 1990, as Caldwell was nearing the end of her career, only a handful of women held associate positions with major orchestras, only four were principal conductors and none held permanent positions with the "big five" (Boston, Chicago, Cleveland, New York, Philadelphia).[28]

Although women were able to study conducting in college and conservatory music programs, they were not welcome everywhere. For years, Pierre Monteux, the former principal conductor of the Boston Symphony Orchestra, taught an intensive four-week summer conducting class (the Domain School of Conducting) at his home in Maine. Yet, Monteux would not accept women because, as his wife explained to a reporter in 1952, "he does not believe that women should be conductors."[29] Fortunately for Caldwell, his successor at the BSO and the founder of Tanglewood, Serge Koussevitzky, did not hold the same views. Typically, women had more difficulty finding mentors to guide their careers beyond their formal studies to obtain opportunities and gain experience. Beatrice Brown, who studied under Leopold Stokowski and Serge Koussevitzky, once remarked how important it was to have a mentor to provide not only teaching guidance, but also emotional and career support.[30] Margaret Hillis was not as lucky. She recalled that in the 1940s "there was no master teacher of conducting who would take a woman student."[31] Caldwell's experience was very different from that of Hillis. Once she began attending the New England Conservatory of Music and studying with Boris Goldovsky, she acquired a mentor who guided her career and opened doors that may have been closed to other women.

In the field of opera directing, like producing and conducting, men have been dominant. Again, Caldwell had few role models from whom she could seek inspiration or examples. One of the first women to direct operas in America was Margaret Webster, an actress, producer, and director who in 1946, together with Eva Le Gallienne and Cheryl Crawford (co-founder of the Stanislavski inspired Group Theater), had founded the American Repertory Theater. Although Webster was a seasoned director in spoken theater, when Rudolf Bing hired her to direct Verdi's *Don Carlos* at the Metropolitan Opera in 1950, she was struck by the stark difference between the two art forms. For instance, she discovered, to her dismay, that opera rehearsal time was shorter, and that musical imperatives, not psychological motivation, dictated movement and placement of the singers. The singers, too, were taken aback when she required them to participate in a group reading of the libretto to emphasize the drama as the primary focus of the opera.[32] If they had any reservations about accepting a woman as the stage director, those may have been superseded by their shock at her unconventional (at least for opera) directorial approach.

Bing had chosen Webster to direct at the Met over prominent male directors of spoken theater, but that is not to say that she was his first choice, or that he supported the advancement of women. He had initially chosen Tyrone Guthrie, a British theater director known for his Shakespearean productions, but Guthrie was already engaged to direct elsewhere. His selection of Webster had nothing to do with promoting her sex, nor with eliciting deeper character portrayals or enhancing the drama of opera. Rather, he thought that her experience in staging crowd scenes in Shakespeare's plays could translate into the effective handling of the choruses in opera.[33] Webster exceeded his expectations and was invited back to stage Verdi's *Aida* (1951) and *Simon Boccanegra* (1960). The New York City Opera also engaged her to stage Walton's *Troilus and Cressida* (1955), Verdi's *Macbeth* (1957), Vittorio Giannini's *The Taming of the Shrew* (1958), and Richard Strauss' *The Silent Woman* (1968). Webster's successes in New York were artistically and historically important, but her pioneering example failed to lead to more opportunities for women directors in opera.

When Caldwell began staging operas there were only a handful of women directors in either opera or theater. Margarete Wallmann, a German born ballet dancer turned opera director worked in major European opera houses from the early 1950s to 1990, but never in America. Helene Weigel, who with Bertolt Brecht founded The Berliner Ensemble, succeeded him as the sole Artistic Director of the company after his death. She was followed in that position by Ruth Berghaus, a leading choreographer and stage director. The annals of American opera companies, however, list the names of only a few women stage directors, even in recent years. They include Sally Stubblefield (the first woman to direct an opera at the New York City Opera in 1945) and Cynthia Auerbach, who was a freelance director for the New York City Opera and Artistic Director of the Chautauqua Opera. In addition, Pamela Rosenberg, who began her career as a stage director before serving as the General Director of the San Francisco Opera (2001–2005), is a rarity in that dual role. More recently, Mary Zimmerman, Susan Stroman, and Julie Taymor, all with strong ties to Broadway, have had successful careers in theater and opera. Finally, Francesca Zambello a stage director as well as Artistic Director of the Washington National Opera and General Director of the Glimmerglass Opera has emerged as multi-talented leader.

The number of women impresarios, conductors, and opera stage directors remained small during the decades when Caldwell succeeded in those roles. Yet, the situation did not prompt her to any political action. She did not actively engage in protests against sexual discrimination, nor did she publically advocate for greater representation in opera leadership roles for women. She seemed, if not oblivious to the social struggles around her, at least disinterested in them. Perhaps, she did not identify with feminist efforts to shatter the proverbial glass ceiling, because she felt that she had not encountered it herself. Indeed, she had strong role model early in life. Her mother had been a pianist who taught choral music in Kansas City, Missouri, schools. She had graduated from Northwestern University, and later studied at Juilliard and Columbia University. Given that her mother was a divorcée with an unusually high level of education and financial independence for a woman in the early 20th century, it is not surprising that Caldwell did not see obstacles in her own path or feel sympathy for others who faced them. In fact, when asked about bias in her career, she was dismissive: "I don't feel I've had a problem. From the start, I have felt accepted."[34] Of course, as noted earlier, Boris Goldovsky was her mentor for a number of years, starting when she enrolled at the New England Conservatory of Music. His influence may have shielded her from the sexual discrimination faced by other women and afforded her opportunities that she might not have had otherwise. Moreover, once she had established herself at the helm of her own company, she had control over the direction of her career and her artistic choices. That position of leadership gave her autonomy; it enabled her to work in a manner and on a repertoire that would have been impossible had she followed a career as a freelance director or guest conductor, so it is very likely that she felt that she did not have a problem. However, an examination of media sources reveals that she was not always accepted.

In the 1960s, Caldwell emerged as a promising director, conductor, and impresario of the Opera Company of Boston and became the subject of profile stories in popular magazines. Rather than focusing on her talents and skills, however, they began to shape a public image of her as an eccentric genius and unnatural woman. A *Life Magazine* article began: "An amazing woman named Sarah Caldwell made one of her absent-minded forays into New York City last month...." The writer seemed to relish telling how she wore neither hat nor gloves on a cold day and in her haste to leave the writer's office to take a phone call, left behind a dark blue bundle that turned out to be her best suit. Even though the majority of the article was complimentary, it suggested that her uncommon talents could only be the result of abnormality. The narrative concluded with Caldwell conducting a dress rehearsal when she was approached by a little girl. The girl's sitter had not shown up, so she had to come to the theater with her mother who was singing in the chorus. The writer noted that "Sarah bundled the child into her lap and went right on alternately conducting, raking her fingers through her ruined hair and humming to herself."[35] The image of Caldwell showing maternal warmth to the child seemed designed to mitigate the previous descriptions and demonstrate that she was at least *capable* of acceptable female behavior.

As noted earlier, Caldwell was obese and that fact combined with her unapologetic attitude about her appearance seemed to unsettle the media. A

1964 *Time Magazine* article began: "Sarah Caldwell was neglecting herself again. Her hair was stringy and matted, her clothes unbelievably shabby. She was keeping alive on a daily ration of one dozen hamburgers, with suitable amounts of coffee and Cokes. On nights when she worked till dawn, she would wrap herself up in her overcoat, ease her 300 lbs. down into one of the aisles of her theater, and sleep."[36] The focus on her appearance was relentless. That same year, a feature article in *Opera News*, reported that she was clad in a "commodious Japanese robe for rehearsal and a gargantuan black velvet mantle for conducting."[37] Elsewhere in the article, she was described as directing the performers like a "lady Buddha on the stage apron." Disparaging descriptions continued into the 1970s in a profile written by Robert Jacobson. It described how Caldwell needed something to wear for a performance, and that a seamstress with her company "found an old pair of draperies, pinned them at Sarah's ample shoulders, and she went into the pit with her customary sneakers under her makeshift gown."[38] These "Sarah Stories" were repeated by leading critics in articles that appeared in the 1970s in *The New Yorker*[39] and the *New York Times*[40] just prior to Caldwell's historic debut as the first woman to conduct the Metropolitan Opera Orchestra.

In the present day, the term "body shaming" describes negative statements and attitudes about a person's appearance and in retrospect, it can be applied to what Caldwell faced. Her weight, in particular, but also her eating habits, her manner of dress, and personal hygiene were fodder for criticism and speculation, repeated for amusement and ridicule within the Opera Company of Boston and in the press. There is no denying that Caldwell was obese, absent-minded at times, and that she paid little attention to fashion or personal grooming (although she did like to have her hair done for performances). Yet, Caldwell, like other women of the day, was caught in the classic double bind: had she been an attractive women, she would not have been taken seriously (one musician reportedly confessed that "if she'd been a babe, we'd have walked right over her"[41]). As an unattractive woman, or at least one apparently indifferent to her looks, she was subjected to body-shaming. *Time Magazine* was a perpetual participant. In a brief overview of her production of *The Barber of Seville* in 1974, she was described as "that kooky rotund lady" who "waddles to the podium."[42] The frequency of such unflattering descriptions escalated in the publicity surrounding her invitation to be the first woman to lead the Metropolitan Opera Orchestra in a production of Verdi's *La Traviata* in 1976. The announcement created a flurry of media attention. Newspapers, magazines, and even the *CBS Evening News with Walter Cronkite* ran a story on the much-anticipated event. There were reports that tickets were being scalped for $40 at a time when the top price for a single ticket was $35. At the height of the Women's Liberation Movement Caldwell was thrust into the spotlight as a heroine who was tearing down another barrier to equal rights for women. Every other woman conductor was interviewed about how she had achieved success in a male-dominated profession. The tone and content of the media attention to Caldwell (and her colleagues) undermined her conducting accomplishments, which should have been celebrated on that historic occasion.

Caldwell was clearly uncomfortable being viewed as a feminist and tried to neutralize the attention on herself: "[I]t's a little late to speak of women in the arts, because this is not a new phenomenon. I don't think of myself as a 'woman conductor,' but as a conductor and I hope my abilities will speak for themselves."[43] Yet, in the weeks leading up to her debut, before her conducting abilities could speak for themselves, she was fashioned into an object of ridicule. *Time Magazine* devoted its feature article to her in November 1975 with a piece entitled "Music's Wonder Woman." It began by recounting her professional successes, but by the fourth paragraph comments about her appearance surfaced: "[Caldwell] is going to be hard to miss elsewhere around the U.S. and not just because she carries close to 300 lbs. on a 5-ft. 3-in. frame." "Her energy would be impressive for a basketball star; for a beach ball of a woman, it is phenomenal." "Sarah gets around surprisingly well for a 300-pounder. Often she resembles a great mother whale with a school of pilot fish circling her."[44] As a popular magazine, *Time* appealed to a fascination with Caldwell as an anomaly while at the same time, it voiced a disapproval of her physical appearance. As Kate Millet wrote in her 1970 book *Sexual Politics*, across history and cultures, patriarchy has exerted "a variety of cruelties and barbarities" to force women's bodies to confirm to its norms.[45] That objective continued into late 20th-century American society (and arguably to the present) with more subtle, but still effective means to shape women's bodies and maintain the status quo of male domination. Caldwell was not feminine as defined in a patriarchy, and therefore, she was subjected to public ridicule that undermined her artistic credibility. Although in Caldwell's case, the attention to her appearance was negative, even when such attention is positive, it can sabotage success. Victoria Bond told of conducting the Pittsburgh Youth Orchestra early in her career, and seeing the following in a newspaper: "She's no bigger than a bass fiddle, but she's in charge of the orchestra." Bond responded, "That was all very flattering, but it undermined my sense of authority."[46] Conducting an orchestra, which in the 1970s was still a powerful symbol of male domination, was threatening.

Of course, the argument that beauty is solely a social construct devoid of the influence of natural laws is not universally accepted. Further, it has been noted that men, too, are held to socially constructed standards. Male conductors, for instance, may fare better during the hiring process with orchestral boards of directors if they can demonstrate "the Leonard Bernstein syndrome," a combination of talent, and sex appeal that will attract audiences to performances.[47] It is plausible that Bernstein's vast popularity was boosted by his handsome features, especially since they were so effective on television (his *Young People's Concerts*, 1958–1972, were widely popular). Certainly, Esa-Pekka Salonen, the former conductor of the Los Angeles Symphony, seems to have possessed the expected attributes. After a 25-year career with the orchestra, the *Los Angeles Times* noted with satisfaction in 2009, that he had "made classical music sexy—and very important."[48] The difference may be that while male conductors have been hired and celebrated for their good looks, they have not been subjected to public ridicule when they did not possess them. For Caldwell, and other conductors of her generation who happened to be women, it was a no-win situation.

The media was apparently baffled by Caldwell and frustrated by its own inability to define her or confine her to expectations of the feminine ideal. It even got tripped up when it tried to be accommodating and progressive. An *Opera News* article attempted to explain Caldwell to its readers: "Miss Caldwell, unlike a male afflicted with feminism or—as the national press like to imply—a diligently sublimating female, is gifted by nature with the most power-making attributes usually associated with men, modified by the maternal, seductive powers of a woman. As such, she is irresistible to man and woman alike. The fact that she also happens to be a superbly skilled musician and conductor is almost beside the point."[49] Apparently, the only way to explain the extraordinary talents of a woman who refused to conform to contemporary social norms of the feminine was to suggest that she was not really a woman at all!

The foregoing discussion of Caldwell's treatment by the press, especially prior to her debut at the Metropolitan Opera, does not purport to constitute a comprehensive content analysis of the media coverage. Rather, it is intended to provide social context for Caldwell's work and to demonstrate that she had indeed encountered resistance to her aspirations, despite her statements to the contrary. Fortunately, there were critics who recognized the prejudices expressed in the media. Richard Dyer of the *Boston Globe* wrote in 1976 that the publicity around Caldwell's premiere at the Metropolitan Opera was offensive because of the numerous unflattering references to her appearance.[50] Dyer who reviewed her productions throughout most of her career in Boston was someone who reviewed her work, not her appearance, and so it was in Boston that her talents did speak for themselves more fully.

When confronted with sexual discrimination some women rally to meet their foes head on and even very publicly. Caldwell was not among that group. Perhaps she gave the insulting descriptions little thought, or decided not to dignify negative attention with a response. Whatever her reasons, she refused to respond or engage with the media. She endured the humiliations with a stoic silence and remained distant from the Women's Movement. Her lack of interest in engaging in feminist issues reflects a lack of engagement with them in her work. There is no definitive evidence that a feminist viewpoint influenced her selection of repertoire, her concepts, or stage realizations. Her sex and gender were invisible in her directing. Only her rehearsal style, which was highly collaborative and non-linear, could be seen as embodying a communication style more associated with female leaders, in contrast to the more autocratic style practiced by many of the male stage directors of her era. That style will be discussed in more detail in the chapter on her rehearsal methods.

Since her death, Caldwell's career as a pioneering American opera stage director, conductor, and impresario for over three decades has received little scholarly attention, and prior to this work, has not been the subject of any extended analysis. It is my hope that at the conclusion of this study the reader will be better able to determine whether her stage productions, at least, deserve a more prominent place in American opera history, or whether they should remain peripheral examples of modest influence compared to the achievements of her (male) contemporaries.

Chapter 1

Beginnings

During a childhood and youth in Maryville, Missouri, Caldwell was immersed in music, owing mainly to the influence of her mother, a pianist and choral teacher. She was a child prodigy on the violin and by the age of 10 was giving public recitals. After her parents divorced, her mother married Henry Alexander and the family moved to Fayetteville, Arkansas, where he had accepted a job as a professor of government (later political science) at the University of Arkansas. Upon graduation from high school, Caldwell studied Music and Psychology for two years at the University of Arkansas, then at Hendrix College, a small liberal arts college north of Little Rock. In 1943, she received a scholarship to attend the New England Conservatory of Music in Boston. There she studied the violin under Richard Burgin, concertmaster of the Boston Symphony Orchestra. Her aspiration had been to become a concert violinist until she met Boris Goldovsky. He became her teacher and mentor and had a profound and lasting influence on her development as a stage director.

Goldovsky had studied piano at the Moscow Conservatory, the Berlin Academy of Music, and the Franz Liszt Academy of Music in Budapest before coming the United States. He arrived at the age of 22 to finish his musical education at the Curtis Institute of Music in Philadelphia, where his mother, a violinist, was a faculty member. There he studied under Fritz Reiner before joining the faculty at the New England Conservatory. Although he had worked as an opera coach, he was, as he put it, "a hearty despiser" of opera and viewed it as a "ponderous and stilted art form."[1] He came to that conclusion after comparing opera performances to theater performances he had seen in his youth at the Moscow Art Theatre under the guidance of the legendary director Constantin Stanislavski. Stanislavski had championed modern realism and developed the acting technique still taught today throughout the world. The Stanislavski "System" is an actor training approach that emphasizes background research and character motivation as a means to develop true-to-life portrayals. Stanislavski not only applied this system to spoken theater, but also to productions in his Opera Studio, where he coached singer-actors to seek information from the musical score just as actors in spoken plays work do the text.

Goldovsky's view of opera changed while he was serving as an accompanist at the Curtis Institute, where he observed Ernst Lert directing rehearsals. Lert was a composer and music historian as well as a stage director and an avid practitioner of making staging choices informed by both the music and the libretto. He inspired Goldovsky with his logical approach to staging and with an expectation of realism that was wholly consistent with the aims of Stanislavski's System. Later, when Goldovsky became the head of a new opera department at the Cleveland Institute of Music, he discouraged the presentational style of acting prevalent at the time, and in its place promoted justifiable dramatic action that supported the music. In his memoir, *My Road to Opera*, he confessed his frustration with the "old school" style. "But," he said, "my eyes had been opened—by Ernst Lert—and I refused to close them."[2] Through his apprenticeship under Lert, Goldovsky had learned how to developed dramatic conceptions from the libretto and hints in the music. He also came to espouse the notion that all the elements of opera needed to be "integrated into a totality that was as real and true as the things that happen to us in our daily lives."[3] Realism characterized his approach and, subsequently, Caldwell's, too.

Initially, Caldwell, like Goldovsky, had possessed a dim view of opera. She echoed the sentiment of her mentor when years later, she confessed that "like all instrumentalists I had a great contempt for opera."[4] However, while a student at the New England Conservatory, she had an epiphany. When a colleague heard her complain about the quality of operatic acting, she challenged Caldwell to attend a few classes led by Goldovsky. There she witnessed the power of operatic music performed with dramatic integrity and became interested in learning more. During her second year at the NEC, she audited one of his opera classes and followed that up by enrolling in two additional classes with him in Opera Conducting. Soon afterwards, she served as Music Assistant to Goldovsky on a production of Humperdinck's *Hansel and Gretel*.[5] Her conversion was complete; she decided on a career in opera.

At the time, Caldwell had minimal knowledge of the opera repertoire and lacked experience in conducting and staging. Nevertheless, she recalled, Goldovsky had expressed faith in her potential: "[He] took very kindly to me as a student and said something to me then that really made it all possible. He said there was nothing to be afraid of. The fact that I didn't know anything about opera, I hadn't studied conducting and I knew very little about

Boris Goldovsky with students from the graduating class of 1952 (Caldwell took this class in 1943) at the New England Conservatory, Boston, Massachusetts (reprinted from the NEC yearbook, *The Neume*, page 30, courtesy New England Conservatory Archives).

the technical aspects of the theater didn't matter. He said that everything was learnable."[6] In 1946, she applied to the Berkshire Music Center's Opera Department at Tanglewood,[7] in western Massachusetts and was accepted on a full scholarship from the Koussevitzky Music Foundation to study further with Goldosky.

The Berkshire Music Center at Tanglewood is a summer training academy that has had a profound and far-reaching influence on American music. Historically, "The Berkshires" was a largely an agricultural area worked by settlers awarded land by the Massachusetts Bay Colony. In the 19th century, agriculture gradually gave way to manufacturing and railroad companies competed to connect Massachusetts with the recently opened Erie Canal, which connected the Atlantic Ocean through New York State to the Great Lakes. When the Boston and Albany Railroad line was completed in 1841, the area's natural beauty began to attract tourists. Wealthy families began to travel by rail from New York or Boston, arriving at the Pittsfield-North Adams station where carriages then took them to their ultimate destinations for weekends or even whole summers away from the heat of their bustling cities. At first, they stayed at resorts, but soon the wealthier ones built elaborate summer houses—which they referred to as "cottages"—for their vacation comfort. The area was attractive not only to tourists. At mid-century two literary giants also made it their home for a time. Hermann Melville wrote his epic novel *Moby Dick* at his home in Pittsfield, and Nathaniel Hawthorne penned *The House of Seven Gables* and *Tanglewood Tales* during a winter he spent in a small red cottage on the expansive estate of William Aspinwall Tappen. Tappen was a rather typical new resident of the area, a railroad magnate who had purchased a large piece of land situated between Lenox and Stockbridge in 1849, complete with lakeside cottages that he rented out. Initially he had christened his estate "Highwood" but, delighted by Hawthorne's story, he changed it to Tanglewood, the name by which it is known today.

The decades of wealth and leisure that the so-called "cottagers" enjoyed came to a sudden standstill with the crash of the stock market 1929, followed by the Great Depression. Many previously affluent residents were forced to sell their estates for a fraction of their value, convert them into resorts, schools, or donate them to charitable organizations if a buyer could not be found. The economic difficulties of the period were, however, no deterrent to Massachusetts native Henry Kimball Hadley, the associate conductor of the New York Philharmonic. He believed that The Berkshires remained a prime market for a summer music festival and his idea piqued the interest of an energetic local socialite and transplanted New Yorker named Gertrude Robinson Smith. Miss Robinson Smith decided that a summer festival was not only desirable, but necessary to ensure the availability of suitable quality entertainment for the remaining cottagers and to provide musical edification for the local residents. She took the project in hand and completed all the arrangements for the first Berkshire Festival by August of 1934. It consisted of three outdoor concerts given by the New York Philharmonic under the direction of Hadley. Two years later, the New York Philharmonic withdrew from the Berkshire Festival, replaced by the Boston Symphony Orchestra and Serge Koussevitzky.

Although Hadley had originated the idea of the festival and Miss Robinson Smith's unwavering determination had made it a reality, it was Serge Koussevitzky who became inextricably identified with it. He was a Russian-born conductor, initially trained as a bass player, who had studied and conducted in Leningrad, Rome, and Berlin before settling in Paris where he had made his mark as a champion of modern music. His inaugural Tanglewood concert in 1936 included *Pacific 231*, written only the year before by the French composer Arthur Honegger, and Alexander Scriabin's

Symphony no. 4, opus 54, known as the *Poem of Ecstasy*, a nod to both contemporary music and Koussevitzky's Russian roots.[8] Throughout his career, he championed works from Benjamin Britten, Aaron Copland, Samuel Barber, Leonard Bernstein, Igor Stravinsky, and Maurice Ravel.

Whereas the festival had proved promising under Hadley's direction, under Koussevitzky, it became a sensation. The summer series was extended to six concerts over two weekends. The following year, 38,000 people attended the concerts in the newly constructed "shed," an open-air pavilion seating 5,000 patrons with extra seating on the lawn. By 1939, the attendance figure jumped to 95,000.[9] Tourists not only flocked to the concerts, they also attended public rehearsals where they took pictures of Koussevitzky on the podium in what one stunned observer could only describe as overt hero worship.[10] Koussevitzky was the iconic star of the Tanglewood and his popularity enabled it to flourish. The conductor's professional reputation drew music enthusiasts and his personal élan brought in donations. The most spectacular gift was 210 acres of land, a portion of the Tappen estate that the family gave to the Boston Symphony Orchestra. That gift enabled Koussevitzky to realize a goal he had long held dear: the creation of The Berkshire Music Center in 1940.

The Berkshire Music Center ("Tanglewood") was a rare summer school experience for young artists. In its inaugural year, it welcomed 312 aspiring musicians who each paid $100 tuition to study for six weeks with faculty members hand-picked by Koussevitzky. Both the school and the Berkshire Festival were immediate artistic and financial successes, but the following year the involvement of the United States in World War II brought both to a virtual standstill. Koussevitzky was still able to hold a six-week session in 1942, but gas rationing the next year curtailed all efforts to continue. In 1944 and 1945, the Berkshire Festival consisted of only a single concert.

When World War II ended, the immediate jubilation and relief that Americans felt was followed by a period of readjustment. In many regions, the end of the war brought not only social changes, but also economic ones. In the Berkshires, the textile industry, which had sustained the local economy in the early part of the century, was hard hit during the depression and continued to falter during the war. Consequently, after the war, residents of western Massachusetts turned to tourism to bolster the local economy and Tanglewood became its centerpiece. Koussevitzky was more than ready to revive the festival and school. Under his leadership, it became a center of artistic activity and a successful economic draw as well. The school reinstated its curriculum and admission become more competitive. Whereas in 1940 a total of 312 students were admitted from the 599 that applied, in 1946, the year Caldwell entered, 410 were admitted—a quarter of them on the Servicemen's Readjustment Act of 1944, better known as the G.I. Bill—from over 1,000 applicants.[11]

In late June 1946, the opening ceremony for the music school included, as it had since its beginning, a performance of Virgil Thomson's *Alleluia*. Koussevitzky then addressed the group with words that conveyed his vision: "Today, in a period of an unprecedented crisis in history, when men find no common contact and means of understanding each other ... music is an element of unity among men. More than any other art, music has the driving force, the facility and freedom of crossing social, political, geographical, racial and religious barriers, and speaks a language accessible to all...."[12] That day, the inspiring words of the venerable 72-year-old founder of the Berkshire Music Center were heard by the future impresario, conductor, stage director, advocate and ambassador for opera in America, the 22-year-old Sarah Caldwell.

Tanglewood was important to the development of American opera artists in the middle of the 20th century. It provided an intensive training experience on American soil for singers, musicians, composers, and conductors on the verge of professional careers. As a result of their study in its programs, generations of talented young artists, coached by world class faculty, have gained invaluable performance experience. Tanglewood's influence spread to America's orchestras, opera companies, and music schools, by alumni that included conductors Leonard Bernstein and Seiji Ozawa, composer Lukas Foss; and singers Shirley Verrett, David Lloyd, Thomas Stewart, and Donald Gramm (all of whom later performed with the Opera Company of Boston). Also among the alumni are numerous instrumentalists and teachers whose names may not have made headlines but who have, nonetheless, helped shape the American music scene. Caldwell remembered it as a place of importance and intensity where "one had the impression that what was happening at Tanglewood in the summer was the most important thing that was happening in music—and it was."[13] It was a transformative experience for her. She spent nine summers there, first as a student then as a member of the faculty, to learn the craft of directing and conducting opera. She received training from Goldovsky and the support of Koussevitzky to develop her artistic aspirations (a rarity for a woman in the 1940s).

Tanglewood was not a school where students competed for grades or honors. There was no set curriculum of courses and no diplomas or certificates were awarded for having completed its programs. Rather, it was an intense six-week period of advanced study by musicians, mostly in their twenties, who studied with practitioner-teachers. There they established lifelong friendships and professional connections that shaped their future careers. In 1946, applicants applied for one or more of five departments that included Conducting, Advanced Orchestra and Chamber Music, Composition Choral Singing and Ensemble Playing, as well as Opera. That year, the opera department consisted of 42 students who chose classes from Opera Dramatics, Song Repertoire, Coaching and Stage Directing, Scenic Division or Costume Division (later combined), Libretto Writing (offered until 1951), opera and chamber music. Although the names of the divisions changed from year to year, the process consisted of studying opera scenes that were then sung, conducted, and directed by students under the supervision of Goldovsky. Students rehearsed during morning and afternoon sessions, attended mid-day lectures on various subjects concerning the theory and practice of opera, and spent evenings attending concerts and presentations by the students and members of the Boston Symphony Orchestra.[14]

Caldwell was able to study and learn an extensive opera repertoire. During her first summer, she worked with other students to prepare excerpts from *The Marriage of Figaro*,[15] *Aida, Don Giovanni, Cavalleria Rusticana, The Bartered Bride, La Bohème, The Old Maid and the Thief, I Pagliacci, Eugene Onegin, Falstaff, Marriage by the Lantern, Ariane et Barbe-bleue*, and *Boris Godunov*. Her specific assignment was to conduct selections from Verdi's *La Forza del destino* and Puccini's *Il Tabarro*. Goldovsky wanted his students to work on numerous individual scenes rather than on an entire opera so that he could focus their efforts on the detailed work of score analysis and acting as needed in a variety of operas.[16] At Tanglewood, he worked with the students as he did at the New England Conservatory, coaching young singers, conductors, and stage directors towards a cohesive product of dramatic viability and musical integrity. The information for prospective Tanglewood students about the opera program captured his approach and his life-long agenda: "The chief aim of the summer's work will be the exploration of all paths consistent with dramatic truth and believable characterization in operatic performances."[17] He remained committed to these goals throughout his career, passing them on to his many students, including his star *protégée*, Sarah Caldwell.

In order to eliminate the challenge for young students of performing in a foreign language and to make the operas more comprehensible to the audiences, Goldovsky had them performed in English. He was not alone in preferring English for performances in America, but his position was not without controversy. There were those who wanted to hear operas in the original language (even if that meant not fully understanding the libretto), and those who thought that opera should be performed in the language of the audience. The controversy was almost as old as opera in America, and resurfaced numerous times. In 1908, Henry Krehbiel, music editor of the *New York Tribune*, argued that opera in America would remain experimental until "the vernacular becomes the language of performances and native talent provides both works and interpreters."[18] His position was echoed in the *New York Times* by Metropolitan Opera soprano Jane Noria (the stage name of Josephine Ludwig), who wrote an opinion piece entitled "A Plea for the Development of a National Opera," in which she cited a question she said that she had heard many times: "Why should we go to hear opera we don't understand?"[19] In 1924, *New York Times* music critic Olin Downes acknowledged that English versions were necessary at times for the sake of educating the "rank and file of the American public" which for Downes was not the audience of the Met.[20] In the 1940s, he ran a series of columns that revived the debate once again, but only served to underscore the vigor of the opposing views on the subject.[21] Goldovsky's position was consistent with that of his Tanglewood predecessor Herbert Graf. Graf had robustly dismissed all arguments in favor of the original language and accused Americans of succumbing to a "European complex"—the snobbery of wanting to hear operas in a foreign language as a means to broadcast social status over the musical or theatrical values of attending performances.[22]

Although Caldwell tended to follow Goldovsky's lead early in her career with respect to language choices, she did not equate the development of opera in America with the need to perform in English. While she maintained that performance in the vernacular was desirable, she experimented with performing operas in their original languages and even—in the case of *The Trojans* and *Médée*—multiple languages. Overall, she seemed to base her choice on the quality and availability of translations and singers rather than on any philosophical tenet. The decades long controversy over the language of performance was finally resolved when the Canadian Opera Company debuted the use of *Surtitles* (its trademarked term for an English language translation of the libretto projected above the stage) in 1983. A few months later, the New York City Opera debuted *Supertitles* followed closely by the Opera Company of Boston, which debuted them in January 1984 in a production Weber's *Der Freischütz*. Conveniently, supertitles reconciled Caldwell's desire to create accessible operas for a broad audience with her desire for authenticity in performance. She used them regularly thereafter.

Goldovsky was a generous and diligent teacher and was fully supported by Koussevitzky, who approved of his method of training young singers in performing a variety of individual opera scenes, but whose enthusiasm for new works (and possibly his desire to enhance the reputation of the school) led him to request the performance of a complete opera in 1946. He opted for Benjamin Britten's *Peter Grimes*, a work that had been commissioned by the Koussevitzky Music Foundation in 1944. The opera, about a fisherman suspected in the deaths of his young apprentices, had won immediate acclaim when it premiered at Sadler's Wells in London the year before. Eric Crozier, the stage director of the London production, directed the opera department's students in collaboration with Fritz (Frederic) Cohen. Leonard Bernstein conducted. Britten himself observed rehearsals and attended the performances. The premiere was a typical Koussevitzky publicity feast that lured Olin Downes from New York City to The Berkshires. Downes had strong reservations about the tortured verse of the libretto (by Montagu Slater) and the thin characterizations of all but Grimes. However, he countered those reservations with unqualified praise of the score and its execution (although he made no particular reference to Bernstein), the 33-year-old composer, and the cast. Finally, he lavished praise on Koussevitzky for his risky undertaking of a difficult opera with students. It was, he wrote, "astonishingly brilliant on the part of the orchestra, the chorus and, in the sum of it, the gifted and intelligent solo interpreters, whose sincerity was contagious." Koussevitzky's gamble had paid off. He had put Tanglewood squarely on the New York critics' map and each summer thereafter they came to see what he would do.[23]

In her first summer at Tanglewood, Caldwell was not directly involved in the major production. That changed the following year when Koussevitzky decided to present another American premiere. This time he chose the almost forgotten 18th-century *opera seria Idomeneo* by Mozart, directed by Goldovsky and assisted by Caldwell as the Chorus Director. Thus, in 1947, in addition to presenting scenes from *Così fan tutte, Rigoletto, Carmen, Don Giovanni, Der Rosencavalier, L'Enfant Prodigue, I Pagliacci, Fidelio, The Marriage of Figaro, La Favorita, The Magic Flute, Lohengrin, Il Trovatore, Madama Butterfly, Falstaff, Wozzeck, Aida, La Damnation de Faust,* and *Turandot,* the opera department students presented *Idomeneo*.

The libretto of *Idomeneo* recounts the myth of the Greek warrior who is caught in a storm on his return from the Trojan War and swears to Neptune that if he arrives safely he will sacrifice the first person he meets in Greece. That person turns out to be his son Idamante. Mozart completed it before he turned 25 years of age, but it was only performed four times during his life. An early biographer, Otto Jahn, wrote in 1856 that *Idomeneo* "has been given from time to time on different stages, without exciting as much interest in the general public as the better-known works of Mozart; the judgment of connoisseurs, on the other hand, has always distinguished it."[24] Yet, it was an opera that was rarely seen until the early 20th century. When it was performed, producers at the beginning of the 20th century (perhaps feeling themselves justified by Mozart's own request for brevity from his librettist, Giambattista Varesco) took it upon themselves to try to reshape the drama. Goldovsky was one of them. He agreed with earlier judgments of the work as fundamentally flawed.[25] Therefore, he excised all the subplot material and eliminated a number of arias, a process that he characterized as "an elaborate cutting and restitching job."[26] He wanted to have it sung in English, but there was insufficient time to develop a translation, so it was sung in the original Italian.

Goldovsky's extensive editing with the intent of improving the opera was not an unusual undertaking. In the 1940s, there was little confidence in the viability of *Idomeneo* as a dramatic work, and the alterations made for the Tanglewood premiere were accepted as a matter of necessity. The few archival photographs that exist of this historic premiere depict a setting of generalized antiquity: Ionian columns on steps around a rocky base was the primary décor. A cloth drop suggesting a waterfall was a fixture of the background. Costumes likewise conveyed a sense of stylized antiquity on a budget with singers in long or short tunics, but sporting haircuts and make up fashionable in the 1940s. Overall, the performance was received positively and critics agreed with Goldovsky that his editing had improved the work. Jay Rosenfeld wrote in the *New York Herald Tribune* that "the original plot was very long and taxed one's credulity. Goldovsky's version has a reasonable and terse continuity. The material he has retained is all valuable and is good Mozart."[27] Of course, to assume that certain operas have not benefited musically and dramatically from judicious editing is to give undo credit to composers who, like other artists, are not necessarily their own best critics. Still, in later decades heavy-handed editing came to be considered an act of hubris. After Jean-Pierre Ponnelle's production of *Idomeneo* at the Cologne Opera in 1974 received critical acclaim for revealing its "performance worthiness" as originally conceived, it was safer from such radical tampering. Whether Caldwell agreed with Goldovsky's editing of *Idomeneo* at the time remains unknown. However, over the course of her career, she became known for her opening up of opera scores, the completely opposite approach taken by Goldovsky.

After two summers at Tanglewood as a student, Caldwell was invited back as a member of the faculty, with assignments that followed the similar pattern of previous years. She assisted Goldovsky and conducted excerpts from operas as varied as Leoncavallo's *Cavalleria Rusticana* and Handel's *Orlando*. The full-length opera in 1948 was *The Turk in Italy*, Rossini's comic tale of spousal jealousy. It was presented in English with the translation and recitatives prepared by Goldovsky and Caldwell, but both staged and conducted by Goldovsky. The following summer they shared both staging and conducting credits for the American premiere of Britten's comic opera *Albert Herring*. She capped off the summer by both staging and conducting Ralph Vaughan Williams' tragic one-act opera *Riders to the Sea*.[28]

Opportunities for Caldwell expanded in the summer of 1950 while Goldovsky was away on leave. She conducted the first American performance of Jacques Ibert's *Le Roi d'Yvetot*, a four-act comic fantasy, and later staged the one-act comic opera, *The Jumping Frog of Calaveras County*, conducted by its composer, Lukas Foss. That year she also conducted and staged Mozart's early comic opera, *La Finta Giardiniera*, about a woman who forgives her lover after he tries to kill her. The original Italian version of the opera by Pasquale Anfossi had not yet been discovered and there was no definitive version, so she made some revisions to create her own. The program notes explained her choices: "In order to make it acceptable to the modern theater going public," she wrote, "certain alterations have had to be made; the music, in mood, and in text, has been carefully preserved and edited; the plot has been revised to maintain theatrical unity, and new dialogues have been composed to carry the revised narrative."[29] Although she demonstrated her capacity and independence that summer apart from her mentor, his influence on her was still evident in her decision to alter the score. It was highly commended in a local newspaper, *The Berkshire Eagle*, as "not only one of the Center's highlights in its short career but one of which it could be proud under any circumstances whatsoever."[30] Years later Caldwell remembered that summer as her favorite year at Tanglewood both socially and artistically, remarking with satisfaction that she and the cast had rehearsed *La Finta Giardiniera* for 11 hours every day.[31]

Caldwell's Tanglewood experience over the five summers she had already spent there was formative, owing much to Goldosky's support of her ambitions, but also, though more indirectly, to Koussevitzky's. When he died in 1951, just a few weeks prior to the start of the season, he left behind a legacy that touched everyone who had come to Tanglewood, whether as a student, faculty member, or a visitor. He had made an indelible mark on American music through the Berkshire Festival and Music Center, his leadership of the Boston Symphony Orchestra, and by introducing audiences to new works. Through his Koussevitzky Music Foundation he had commissioned numerous compositions and presented over 100 world premieres with the Boston Symphony Orchestra. As the founder of the Berkshire Music Center, he had been an inspiring leader to many students, including Caldwell. There she learned not only directing and conducting skills, but also a broad canon from which she drew many works for her own company. Koussevitzky's acceptance of her ambitions made it possible for her to continue her training.

At the time when women were rarely encouraged or supported in their aspirations to be conductors or directors, his approval of her studies helped make her career possible.

That summer Tanglewood produced two full-length operas: Tchaikovsky's *The Queen of Spades* (conducted and directed by Goldovsky) and Strauss' *Ariadne auf Naxos* starring Leontyne Price (conducted by Caldwell with directing credits shared by her and Goldovsky). The following year she returned to assist him in the presentation of Mozart's *La Clemenza di Tito*, a rarely performed *opera seria* about the Roman emperor Titus whose penchant for clemency during his short reign triumphed even when an assassination plot against him is revealed. It had never before been presented in the United States and rarely in Europe in modern times, having been all but dismissed by critics as a feeble effort by Mozart at the end of his life. At this American premiere, Caldwell took to the podium. She conducted the score without cuts. Goldovsky staged the production in an English translation prepared by himself and Caldwell and retitled *Titus*, in which spoken dialogue replaced the recitatives. It was performed on a multilevel platform stage with minimal scenery, against a plain background on which slides depicting Rome were projected. Despite careful preparations, it was not a success. Critics described it as an important historical revival, but beyond that they dismissed it as an attempt to present a "fundamentally a weak piece."[32] The next summer she staged André Grétry's *Richard the Lion-hearted*, an 18th-century *opéra comique* about the captivity and rescue of England's twelfth-century king. The performance was reviewed in the *New York Times*, which praised Tanglewood's opera department for continuing its tradition of presenting little known operas.[33] That tradition continued in Caldwell's career long after her years at Tanglewood.

In 1946, the same year Caldwell had arrived at Tanglewood as a student, Boris Goldovsky had formed the New England Opera Theater in Boston, to provide professional performing experience to graduates from the New England Conservatory and Tanglewood. Its mission was to present operas in English, to introduce new works or revive older works, and to teach performers how to approach operas as works that integrated music and drama—as the name of the company implies. Caldwell joined Goldovsky from its inception, first as "Musical Assistant to Mr. Goldovsky" and once as "Properties Supervisor." Thereafter, she became the "Chorus Director and Musical Assistant to Mr. Goldovsky" for the remaining eight years of her tenure with the company.[34] The New England Opera Theater was a small, low-budget organization, but it served as a forerunner of regional opera companies and was an important training ground for young American singers. It presented operas ranging from *Albert Herring* to *Carmen* to *Idomeneo*, often repeating the Tanglewood repertoire at local Boston venues including Jordan Hall, the Boston Opera House, the Majestic Theater, and Harvard Square Theater. One of its most successful endeavors was the tour of Mozart's *La Finta Giardiniera* in 1953, as it had been conducted and staged by Caldwell at Tanglewood three years earlier. The only change was that it toured under its English title, *Merry Masquerade*. Once again, the production received the acclaim it had garnered at Tanglewood. It was performed in 37 cities in 14 states,[35] but Caldwell was not brought along to conduct, nor did she get credit on the program for the staging. Audiences, she was told, would not accept a woman in that position.[36]

The New England Opera Theater garnered little media attention beyond the Boston area until 1955 when Goldovsky decided to stage and conduct the American premiere of Berlioz's mammoth work, *The Trojans*, an opera about the fall of Troy as related in Virgil's *Aeneid*. Originally, the

Gimi Beni (The Podesta) and Edith Evans (Ramiro) in a scene from Caldwell's 1971 revival of one of her early successes, Mozart's *La Finta Giardiniera*. She presented it in English with the subtitle *A Gay Intervention* (photograph by Albie Walton).

opera was in two parts, beginning with "The Capture of Troy" and followed by the "Trojans at Carthage." It begins with a celebration by the Trojans who believe that the Greeks have abandoned their efforts to seize the city and left a wooden horse, the symbol of the city, as parting gift. Despite warnings by the prophetess Cassandra, the people bring the statue into the city, only to be slaughtered by the Greek soldiers who emerge from it. "The Trojans at Carthage" tells of the tragic love affair between Queen Dido and the Trojan hero Aeneas who eventually leaves to found the city of Rome and the empire that would in turn destroy Carthage. The opera's scale alone made it a unique attempt for such a modest company and an unusual choice for Goldovsky. It runs about five hours when performed complete, requires a large orchestra and large cast of singers and dancers to costume and rehearse. Its extensive production requirements are among the reasons it is rarely presented in its entirety.

Caldwell fulfilled her customary role as Chorus Director and Assistant to Goldovsky. Together, they, with Richard Sloss, spent 18 months translating the French libretto into English. Then as he had done with *Idomeneo* and *La Clemenza di Tito* at Tanglewood, Goldovsky edited it. He cut the opera down to two hours by condensing the first two acts into one, but then expanding the last three acts into four. Among the substantial cuts were the love scene between Cassandra and Coroebus, the ballet from the "Trojans at Carthage," and Dido's first aria "Chers Tyriens." In doing so, Goldovsky "endeavored to leave out only such dramatic material, which he felt did not either advance the action or help to establish character."[37] The scene changes, however, required four intermissions, bringing the performance time back up to almost three and a half hours. The response of critics was lukewarm; they acknowledged the historical importance of the presentation.

A large-scale undertaking like *The Trojans* was not typical for the New England Opera Theater. Afterwards, it returned to its primary mission of cultivating young singers, with Goldovsky coaching his pupils in developing dramatic and musical integrity in their roles. He seemed to prefer coaching rather than producing large spectacles. Caldwell's experience with this opera must have been particularly profound and possibly frustrating. Goldovsky had presented the opera much condensed, which may not have been the way she wanted to present it. Almost 20 years later she returned to *The Trojans* and presented it in its entirety to great acclaim (see Chapter 5).

Caldwell's apprenticeship under Goldovsky continued for a number of years, but at the same time, she was working independently. She taught choral conducting at the Longy School of Music of Bard College in Cambridge. In 1949, she joined Boston University's College of Music and taught there until 1960, first as an Instructor in Vocal Ensemble, and later as Assistant Professor in Vocal Ensemble. In 1955, she was appointed Head of the Boston University Opera Workshop and immediately presented the American premiere of Hindemith's *Mathis der Maler*, an opera about the 16th-century German painter Matthias Grünewald's struggle for artistic freedom. She staged and conducted it in an auditorium with an orchestra pit that could not accommodate the 60 musicians required. In order to overcome this difficulty, she situated the orchestra behind a scrim and used amplification to relay the voices back to her. That arrangement not only solved the space problem, it also enabled her to balance the sound of the orchestra and the student singers for the audience. The experiment was so successful that Caldwell and co-director Francis Sidlauskas produced Bizet's *Carmen* the following year with the orchestra removed to another room in the building and the sound relayed to the singers only by amplification.[38] These early experiments with the placement of musicians and singers foreshadowed her later attempts to more radically alter performance spaces. She went on to present Martinu's *Comedy on the Bridge*, Middleton's *Life Goes to a Party*, Ibert's *Angélique*, Puccini's *Il Tabarro*, *Gianni Schicchi* and *Madama Butterfly*, Bizet's *Carmen* in its original version with spoken dialogue, and Stravinsky's *The Rake's Progress*, conducted for the first time in America by the composer.

Caldwell was establishing herself as an independent operatic force, and that eventually led to a rupture with Goldovsky. He wanted to maintain the New England Opera Theater as a training center for performers early in their careers. He was not interested in hiring star performers nor in offering additional large-scale productions like *The Trojans* with any regularity. Caldwell, by contrast, had a more expansive vision that became characteristic of her mature productions. She described their schism this way: "Whatever versatility is attributed to me stems directly from Boris. He trained me. But we developed differently.... [H]e was reluctant to rock the boat, to press trustees beyond a certain point.... I was fascinated with the idea of building a professional company at home."[39]

In 1957, Caldwell and Charles Forester, a public relations professional who also happened to be enrolled in one of her opera classes, decided to draft a prospectus for a new opera company. An undated draft of that proposal to establish The Opera Group stated that Goldovsky "assures us of his complete good will and support and the backing of the NEOT [New England Opera Theater] as well as its Leadership Training Program. He has indicated his interest in directing occasional productions for the new company."[40] Actually, that did not appear to be the case. Goldovsky made his displeasure known to her and ties between them were severed. Although the details of the dispute have never been disclosed by either Goldovsky or Caldwell, it is likely that he felt betrayed by her desire to form a company of her own. She had been very close to him and his wife. When she was studying at the New England Conservatory, they took her in to live with them and, in exchange, she helped care for their two children. He had mentored her throughout her years at Tanglewood and with the New England Opera Theater, and may have wanted her to succeed him. The NEOT remained active and toured regionally until Goldovsky's retirement in 1984, but Caldwell never worked with him again. She tried on several occasions over the years to reconcile with him, but without success. Still, in interviews, she always praised him and spoke gratefully about his mentorship and encouragement. Finally, in 1993, she hosted a party for him that included many of his former pupils, and in a gesture of good will, he accepted the invitation. Their professional separation, however, remained irreconcilable.

Goldovsky's influence on Caldwell was significant and lasting. He introduced her to opera and guided her in developing both a philosophy and approach to unifying the dramatic and musical elements of opera into a cohesive whole. She readily acknowledged her indebtedness to his mentorship; he had shaped her vision and practice of opera. Yet, she also recognized that they had different goals. After she formed her own company, she mentored many young talented singers and other artists, just as Goldovsky had for her and so many others over his career. In the late 1950s, however, her confidence, her ambition and her vision converged. She broke with him and formed her own company. And while much of her subsequent work benefited from her apprenticeship with Goldovsky, the remainder soon became identifiable as Caldwell's own.

Chapter 2

The Company

Caldwell presented her most significant stage realizations with the Opera Company of Boston. Its history, therefore, is not just the history of a company, but of her career. Since she was not only its primary stage director, but also its conductor and impresario, her philosophy, vision, ambitions, processes, abilities, and limitations defined the company. In short, the OCB was Caldwell and Caldwell was the OCB. In contrast to a freelance director, hired by different companies only to direct, or a director within a company who has only directorial responsibilities, she fulfilled multiple roles that overlapped and affected the fortunes of the company in every respect. She was not without artistic support staff members, but it was she who chose the operas, directed them, conducted the orchestra, hired singers, musicians and artistic personnel, led fundraising efforts, and performed a host of other activities in the management of the company that were necessary to its survival. Her responsibilities at times diverted her energies away from directing, but that is not to say that her directing would have been better or even different had she limited herself (or been able to limit herself) to stage directing. Rather, it merely underscores the fact that her directorial choices, achievements, and failures cannot be separated from her other responsibilities.

The Opera Company of Boston was not the first professional opera company in that city. Bostonians had long been great patrons of the visual and literary arts, but the introduction of the performing arts had a much more complicated history. Its first taste of opera was in 1750 when a group of citizens decided to present Thomas Otway's *The Orphan*, a Restoration tragedy about an ill-fated love triangle. The spectators received the production enthusiastically, but the response of city authorities was to pass the "Act to Prevent Stage Plays and Other Theatrical Entertainments" into law, effectively preventing the recurrence of what had been, in their estimation, a lapse in moral judgment.[1] By the 19th century, however, the demand for theatrical and musical entertainments outweighed official opposition and in 1841 the first Boston Museum opened, housing museum artifacts on the first floor and a theater for concerts and plays on the second. This combination allowed Bostonians to find amusement in "a meeting place where those who did not wish to be regarded as theatergoers could visit without a blush."[2] Yet, a blush remained evident. A visitor to the city in 1876 observed: "I would consider Boston the most cultivated [of cities]; but the people are narrow and too pretentious for their knowledge. Puritanism has frozen art in New England; it's a miracle that it hasn't killed it altogether in the last one hundred years."[3]

Fortunately, Puritanism did not freeze art in New England, but it did influence it for a long time—and some would argue, continues to do so today. In the span of about a quarter century the Museum of Fine Arts (1876), the Boston Public Library (1895), Symphony Hall (1900), Jordan Hall (1903),[4] and the Isabella Stewart Garner Museum (1903) had all been built following the path of Huntington Avenue that came to be known as "The Cultural Mile." Clearly, Bostonians revered the certain arts, but the absence of an opera house to celebrate an art form rooted in ancient Greek tragedy was conspicuous in a city that prided itself in being the "New Athens."

At the turn of the 20th century, New York, Chicago, San Francisco, Philadelphia, and New Orleans were all thriving opera centers. Boston, though it lagged behind, was not without opera activity and even had to its credit The Boston Ideal Opera Company, a homegrown organization that operated (under different names) until 1905. When a void opened again, a wealthy entrepreneur and arts lover from Maine stepped forward to answer the call for an opera company in Boston to rival those established elsewhere in America. Eben Jordan, Jr., had financed the building of the New England Conservatory's Jordan Hall then turned his attention to building an opera house. He opted for a site on Huntington Avenue, between the Museum of Fine Arts and Symphony Hall on "The Cultural Mile." He committed to building the opera house at a cost of $700,000 and guaranteed the expenses of performances there for three years.[5] His singular purpose and his financial backing sped the project along so quickly that it was completed in one year.

The new building was a solid brick structure of substantial size, with just over 2,700 seats in the auditorium and 54 boxes, and a proscenium opening measuring 48 feet wide by 86 feet deep. By way of comparison, the "Old Met" in New York City, which had opened in 1883, accommodated 3,625-seated patrons and had a stage measuring 101 feet wide by 86 feet deep. There was an ample lobby on the first floor and more space on the second floor for crowds to mingle. Its style and decor were typical of New England understatement. The main interior colors were gray, ivory, and antique gold with the only extravagance of rich color being the dark red for the box hang-

The first Boston Opera House on Huntington Avenue. It was completed in 1909 and demolished less than fifty years later (Detroit Publishing Company photograph collection, Library of Congress).

ings, proscenium curtains, and valances. Bostonians approved of the building as a tasteful edifice in which function took proper precedence over form or, as Arthur Whiting, a Massachusetts author and composer described it, "the first Unitarian Opera House."[6] The new addition to Huntington Avenue fit in not only visually, but also nominally. Just as the city's recently completed and somewhat austere concert hall had come to be known simply as "Symphony Hall," Bostonians rejected any flowery appellate for the new structure, preferring to call it simply "the Opera House."

On opening night, November 8, 1909, the newly formed Boston Opera Company, under the direction of Henry Russell, the English founder of the San Carlo Opera Company from which it derived, performed Ponchielli's *La Gioconda*, conducted by Arnaldo Conti and starring Lillian Nordica. That performance was well received by the audience and critics and was followed by an ambitious season that included 18 other operas[7] and a number of concerts interspersed within. After the initial ground swell of interest, however, attendance dropped during the next few seasons, despite the appearance of stars including Mary Garden and Olive Fremstad. In 1914, Russell took the company on an extensive tour to Paris, but its favorable critical reception there did not increase its popularity in Boston. Jordan Jr. soon found himself in a desperate financial situation. Economic uncertainties at home, exacerbated by the start of World War I soon drove the Boston Opera Company into bankruptcy. It was resurrected for two seasons as the Boston Grand Opera Company, but that too collapsed in 1917.

That an opera company would incur financial problems in a time of war merely confirms that like any other business, it is subject to the vicissitudes of local and international politics and economics. Nevertheless, since companies in other cities were able to survive that difficult period, one is tempted to speculate on why it succumbed so quickly. The building was new and inviting. Russell had hired well-known singers and presented a varied repertoire in productions that earned praise for their musical and dramatic quality. Still, the initial excitement diminished quickly. Audiences remained passive when in attendance, or stayed away all together.[8] The financial strain on Jordan Jr. and the importance of opera as a cultural institution in the city, prompted Mayor John F. Fitzgerald to suggest that the city exempt the Opera House from civic taxes, but neither that offer nor the suggestion that Boston actually purchase the building was adopted.[9] As a result, the company folded and Boston was again without a resident company.

During and between the first and second world wars, opera activity in Boston languished until Goldovsky formed the New England Opera Theater in 1945. The rebirth of opera activity in the city at that time was consistent with a resurgence of interest in the art form across America. After World War II, the country experienced an economic and cultural golden age that stimulated an increase in opera activity for the next two decades. The number of opera producing organizations, the number of opera performances, and the number of people attending opera performances increased rapidly. At colleges and universities, the number of opera training programs grew from 167 in the mid-1950s to 409 only 10 years later,[10] providing unprecedented opportunities for American born artists. The number of professional companies also increased throughout the period. In 1964–65, there were 27 companies with budgets over $100,000, but by 1974–75, there were 54. Five years later (1979–80), that number rose to 109.[11] Most companies were small to medium sized regional ones that attracted spectators who wanted to enjoy opera productions at affordable prices. They included the Kentucky Opera (1952), Tulsa Opera (1953), Houston Grand Opera (1955), Santa Fe Opera (1956), Dallas Civic Opera (1957), and the Lyric Opera of Kansas City (1958). As

Virgil Thomson observed in 1962, even garage mechanics were taking their wives to see operas by Gershwin, Moore, Menotti, and Stravinsky.[12] In addition, for those Americans who did not have easy or affordable access to live opera, radio broadcasts, recorded music, and even television brought the art form into living rooms around the country. It was as if the nation as a whole suddenly embraced the arts and with the formation of the National Endowment for the Arts in 1965 recognized their worth for all citizens.

As national opera enthusiasm swelled, Caldwell and Charles Forester began a series of meetings with potential supporters to determine the viability of establishing a permanent company in Boston and soon ushered in a new era of opera activity. In the spring of 1958, the *Boston Globe* published an announcement stating that Opera Group, Inc. had been formed. Caldwell became the Artistic Director and Igor Stravinsky, the Honorary Chairman. Prominent Bostonians gave their prestige to the endeavor: Linda Cabot Black, President; Mrs. Constantine A. Pertzoff, Vice President; John Lowell, Treasurer; Dean Nicholson, Secretary; and Mrs. Thomas D. Cabot, Chairman of the Friends of The Opera Group.[13] "It is our intent," a press statement read, "to present productions of theatrical and musical integrity with a company of artists of the first rank. We present to ourselves the practical challenges of becoming eventually self-sustaining. To do this we must win the support not only of opera and music lovers but of those who love musical theater as well."[14] Caldwell's ambition was "to develop a company with its own special stamp, thus having here in Boston the first truly American opera company, not an imitation of other great companies ... but a company that is truly American."[15]

That desire for a national artistic voice in opera was not new. American theater had demonstrated similar aspirations. In the 19th century, America had not yet developed its own playwrights or works of dramatic merit. By contrast, in Europe, great modern works of dramatic literature were being written, supported by the formation of independent, experimental theaters such as the Théâtre Libre, the Moscow Art Theatre, and the Freie Bühne. While the plays that evolved from these experiments soon made their way across the ocean in translation, American theater artists wanted to develop their own dramatic voices. The formation of native companies that encouraged young playwrights to write about American culture became the Little Theatre Movement, a regional flowering of small theaters that nurtured native talent, just as regional opera companies did decades later. It began in 1910 with the establishment of the Chicago Little Theatre, then the Boston Toy Theatre, and the Provincetown Players, which launched the career of America's first great playwright, Eugene O'Neill. By 1917, there were about

50 Little Theatres in the United States. By 1925, there were about 2000. The momentum of the nationalist theater movement gained so much strength that in the 1930s a group of artists under the leadership of Leopold Stokowski persuaded Congress to enact a federal charter for a national theater. The charter, signed by Franklin Roosevelt on July 3, 1935, created The American National Theatre and Academy: "A people's project organized and conducted in their interest, free from commercialism, but with the firm intent of being as far as possible self-supporting. A national theater should bring to the people throughout the country their heritage of the great drama of the past and the best of the present, which has been too frequently unavailable to them under existing conditions."[16] The endeavor, which was put on hold for creation of a Federal Theatre Project (1935–1939) that employed thousands of artists during the depression, was revived after World War II. It took up where the Little Theatre Movement had left off and led to the development of new theaters, the growth of university theater programs, and subsequently to the writing of American plays.

In a manner similar to American spoken theater, American opera struggled to break free from its European roots and establish its own identity, but the very term "American opera" was problematic. One writer has observed that when it came to culture, "American opera was perceived by Americans themselves as equivalent to 'bad opera.'"[17] The term also had political connotations at a time when anything that could be viewed as a threat to established ideals and cultural norms was labeled "anti–American." Thus, not only was Caldwell's rhetoric around an American company designed to appeal to the patriotism of those in a financial position to help her attain her goal, it was also consistent with Cold War era rhetoric more broadly. Of course, if we accept the definition of American opera as encompassing operas written by Americans and/or on American themes and/or using American musical idioms, then she was tapping into a relatively short, but worthy history. By the time she had established The Opera Group there was a growing number of operas by composers including Thomson, Gershwin, Barber, Bernstein, Menotti, and Moore[18] who by then had written works that dismissed any notion of American operas as second rate.

The Opera Group took its place amid a group of adventurous new companies that were introducing audiences to an expanded canon and theatrically inspired staging ideas. It made its debut in June 1958 at the seventh annual Boston Arts Festival, performing on the lakeside stage in the Public Garden. The selection was the American premiere of *Voyage to the Moon*, a fantasy opera by Jacques Offenbach loosely based on the Jules Verne novel *From the Earth to the Moon*, about the earthly Prince Caprice, whose visit to the moon and love interest in the daughter of the king of the Moon cause comic havoc. *Voyage to the Moon* was not a new opera, nor an American one, but it was timely choice, linked thematically to the "space race" between the Soviet Union and the United States that was underway at the time. The performance, staged and conducted by Caldwell, starred Norman Kelly as Dr. Blastoff, Donald Gramm as the Earth King, James Billing as King Cosmos and David Lloyd as the young prince—each of whom went on to sing multiple roles with the Opera Company of Boston.

In this first Opera Group production, there were elements characteristic of Caldwell's preparation for other operas throughout her career, especially her attention to finding source material. She went to the Boston Public Library and there she found leather bound copies of the libretto in which there were of color renderings of the sets and costume designs used at the premiere at the Théâtre de la Gaîté in 1875. An inscription in one volume shows that it belonged to Mr. and Mrs. H.M. Rogers, and the date, December 7, 1910, which may be when the volumes were donated to the library.[19] Caldwell, along with a poet friend, translated the libretto into English, then revised and edited it into a free adaptation ("manipulated" was the word she used).[20] The opening night performance received a lukewarm critical reception from the *Boston Globe* and *Boston Herald*, but it was a success with those in attendance. The *Boston Globe*'s Kevin Kelly wrote, "The roar you may have heard along Charles st. [sic] about 11:30 was not from a space ship; it was a standing ovation from the large Festival crowd."[21]

A few months later, Caldwell capitalized on the popularity of her company's debut and held a successful fund-raising gala that included a performance of Puccini's *La Bohème* in the Fine Arts Theater on Norway Street (dubbed by Caldwell "The Little Opera House"). In what appeared to be a level of enthusiastic support reminiscent of the beginnings of Jordan Jr.'s Boston Opera Company in 1909, it even had to turn away a number of potential patrons for their first subscription season:

> The trustees and members of the corporation of The Opera Group, Inc. wish to thank the hundreds of workers throughout Metropolitan Boston whose diligent efforts have made it possible for our first season to be completely sold out. Over eight thousand people have become members of The Opera Group, and will attend this season's three productions. The first is *La Boheme* [sic] which is now currently at the Little Opera House and will play for sixteen performances. We regret that it has been necessary to return over three hundred membership applications, received after the Invitation to Membership was closed. Every effort will be made to accommodate these and many other applications at the beginning of our next season. The Opera Group is most grateful for the community-wide endorsement it has received.[22]

The Opera Group was clearly off to a promising start and the positive response to the fund-raising campaign, like the reaction of Bostonians to *Voyage to the Moon*, was indicative of the nationwide enthusiasm for opera that led not only to the formation of new companies like Caldwell's, but also to companies presenting new operas and operas in new ways. The Central Opera Service reported that from the mid–1950s until the mid–1970s the performance of contemporary foreign works increased 69 percent.[23] Alan Rich in the *New York Herald* celebrated the decade of 1960s as a time of "real ferment and real experimentation."[24] That was true for the maturing Opera Group as well.

In the mid–1960s, The Opera Group became the Opera Company of Boston [25] and established itself as a leading regional company that drew the attention of national critics and publications. President Lyndon B. Johnson invited the company to the White House in 1967 to present its first triumph, Offenbach's *Voyage to the Moon*, for President Cevdet Sunay of Turkey who was there on an official visit. The following year it was invited back to perform the opera again, just before the launch of Apollo 8, the first manned spacecraft to orbit the moon. In Boston, the OCB had already attracted leading artists including, Plácido Domingo, Tito Gobbi, Marilyn Horne, Beverly Sills, Joan Sutherland, Renata Tebaldi, and designers including Rudolf Heinrich, Ming Cho Lee, and Josef Svoboda. It presented American premieres by Nono, Rameau, and Schönberg, and its first world premiere, American composer Robert Middleton's chamber opera *Command Performance*. The OCB began to expand the opera canon with works (see later chapters) that earned Caldwell the reputation of a daring and imaginative stage director. Within a decade of forming her company, she was ensconced in Boston, but she was not content to remain a regional influence. She sought to reach a national audience by establishing a touring company.

The American National Opera Company (ANOC) was formed shortly after the Metropolitan National Opera Company (the touring arm of the Metropolitan Opera) had folded after only two years of operation. Caldwell secured a National Council on the Arts grant of $350,000 to form the new company. The amount was to pay over 100 singers, musicians, administrators, and a 63-piece orchestra. The plan was to go into rehearsal in July 1967, open in Indianapolis in mid–September, and tour 70 cities with three operas (Verdi's *Falstaff*, Berg's *Lulu*, and Puccini's *Tosca*) until December, closing with a five-day engagement in Boston. Those three operas would then form the season for the Opera Company of Boston. After a rehearsal period for the final two works (Wagner's *Die Meistersinger von Nürnberg* and a double bill of Mascagni's *Cavalleria Rusticana* and Leoncavallo's *I Pagliacci*), the tour would resume, then continue to the West coast.[26] In an inventive, but ultimately disastrous marketing strategy, the cities were able to choose which of the three operas they want to see performed.

The tour began auspiciously with the Shakespearean inspired *Falstaff* at the Clowes Memorial Hall in Indianapolis. The set design, by Oliver Smith, was a two level revolve depicting the Garter Inn and Ford's house in 15th-century Windsor. According to one reviewer, the production "breezed along gracefully enough until it bumped into awkward moments."[27] The awkward moments, according to Smith, occurred when Caldwell added slapstick elements to the staging, a tendency towards comedic excess that she displayed periodically. For example, Falstaff fell fall flat on his face while wooing Mistress Ford in the second act and was suspended from the oak tree in a net like a trapped fish in the final scene. Although critics were not enthralled with the production, *The New Yorker's* Winthrop Sargeant found no fault with her staging choices when the production came to the Brooklyn Academy of Music. In fact, he praised her emphatically: "Miss Caldwell's extraordinary gifts as an operatic director ... include nothing in the way of eccentricity and everything in the way of bringing to light all the musical and dramatic subtleties that a score contains. Opera issues from her hands as superb drama, but never at the expense of musical or vocal elements, and her taste appears to be infallible."[28]

The next offering was *Lulu*, Alban Berg's opera about a social climber turned prostitute who is murdered by Jack the Ripper. It generated significant interest, in part, because it was so new to American audiences, having premiered only four years earlier, but also because of the staging. Caldwell relinquished conducting duties to Osborne McConathy and worked closely with documentary filmmaker and professor at the Massachusetts Institute for Technology, Richard Leacock,[29] and scene designer Robin Wagner to incorporate film sequences into the production. They developed one for the Prologue showing the animal tamer introducing various reptiles (including Lulu depicted symbolically as a snake eating a small rodent). These images of the prologue and the first act were watched not only by the audience, but also by stagehands sitting on the stage, to create a metatheatrical context. A coincidental meeting between Leacock and Edie Sedgwick, an actress who had worked with Andy Warhol, led him to photograph her as the face of Lulu. The startling final image of the opera on the scenic backdrop was a deliberately overexposed one of Sedgwick as Lulu, with blood-soaked hair.[30]

The third offering, Puccini's *Tosca*, was staged by Caldwell and David Pressman, and conducted by Jonel Perlea. The directors chose to maintain the specific period setting of this political melodrama and the result was a

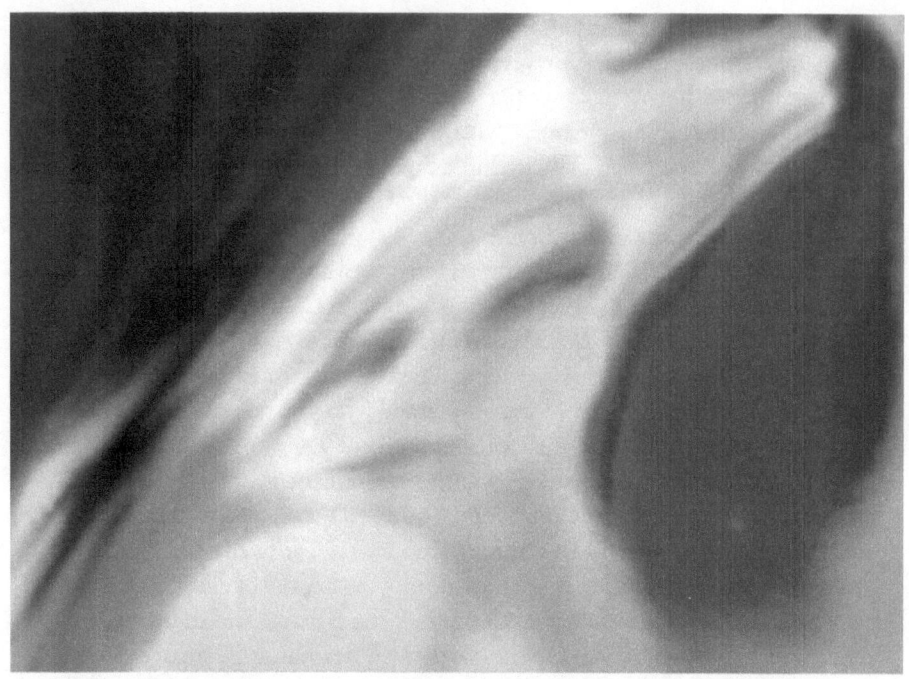

Edie Sedgwick as Lulu. A film still by Richard Leacock for Caldwell's 1967 production of Berg's *Lulu* (courtesy Victoria Leacock Hoffman).

success. The set was by Rudolf Heinrich, a designer at Felsenstein's Komische Oper. Rather than try to reconstruct in three-dimensional form the church of Sant'Andrea della Valle where Cavaradossi is working on his painting of Mary Magdalene or the Castel Sant'Angelo where he is held prisoner, Heinrich suggested locations by hanging large photographs around the stage. Those photographs were images of Rome that he had taken when he and Caldwell had visited that city to familiarize themselves with the locations in which the opera is set. He developed them into collages that became the setting. It was a workable solution for a touring production, but it proved problematic when performed at the Brooklyn Academy of Music. There were technical difficulties in setting up the photographs that caused a 40-minute delay at the beginning of the performance and again between the second and third acts.[31] Nevertheless, Arthur Darack thought the result "stunning," writing in *Musical America* that "the aspects of opera that are so often interpreted as residuals—staging, lighting, sets, costumes, acting—conspired to make this production as urgent as a headline."[32]

In a manner that seemed to echo the difficulties of touring companies of the past, the artistic merit of these productions could not offset the deficit created by undersold theaters. The first performance in Indianapolis sold 1800 seats in a 2200-seat house and brought in just $50,000—half of the potential earnings. Not surprisingly, perhaps, the audiences were the smallest for *Lulu*.[33] When the company performed *Falstaff* at the Brooklyn Academy of Music in October 1967, just days after Zefferelli's 1964 production made its return to the Metropolitan Opera, the audience was small. Excellent reviews for Caldwell's efforts were not enough. In May of 1968, after touring to 30 cities, the American National Opera Company filed for bankruptcy, citing over $800,000 in debts.

The American National Opera Company was a large-scale undertaking, and one that revealed the incompatibility of Caldwell's ambitions and her managerial abilities. Her bold experiment in offering cities their choice of opera was a significant economic risk, as was touring a contemporary work such as *Lulu*. Her decision to bring new or unfamiliar works to her audiences was an example of the enterprising spirit that was a hallmark of her repertoire with the Opera Company of Boston. To her credit, she believed that audiences were intelligent and discerning consumers of art and that given the chance, they would be interested in any opera as long as it was done well. However, her belief that she could sell the operatic equivalent of green toothpaste was misplaced.

The fiasco of the American National Opera Company did not dampen Caldwell's enthusiasm or ambition to tour, but her second attempt was much more limited. It stemmed from her interest in building new audiences for her company and her desire to give young people in the greater Boston area early exposure to opera experiences. One example of that work was the hosting of 200 disadvantaged middle school aged children from Worcester, Massachusetts, at each of the three Opera Company of Boston productions in the 1967 season: Stravinsky's *The Rake's Progress*, Puccini's *Tosca*, and Bartók's *The Miraculous Mandarin*. Her outreach efforts formalized in 1974 into Opera New England, an off-season wing of the OCB that included productions by the main company, as well as others specifically developed for children, to regional communities. The repertoire included Humperdinck's well-known *Hansel and Gretel* and others that were less familiar, such as *The Jumping Frog of Calaveras County* by Lukas Foss, based on a tale by Mark Twain; *The Fisherman and His Wife* by Gunther Schuller, based on a fairy tale collected by the *Grimm Brothers*; *The Second Hurricane* by Aaron Copland about high school students who become stranded while trying to help a nearby town recover from a hurricane, which premiered in 1937 in New York City, directed by Orson Welles; *Il trionfo dell'Onore* or *The Triumph of Honor*, an *opera buffa* written in 1718 by Alessandro Scarlatti; Mozart's compact metatheatrical comic opera *The Impresario; Der Vampyr* (The Vampire), an early 19th-century gothic opera by Heinrich Marschner; *Die Prinzessin auf der Erbse*, by Ernst Toch, an opera based on the Hans Christian Andersen tale *The Princess and the Pea*; and Les Pêcheurs de Perles or *The Pearl Fishers* by Georges Bizet.

In contrast to the model of the American National Opera Company, which had brought operas to different communities (after being selected by those communities), Opera New England was designed as a partnership. Caldwell hoped to develop reciprocal artistic relationships in which community members could participate in the development of an opera production. That approach would enable her to promote opera to new audiences and to rely on the input of volunteers to make the production possible. Since an overall goal of ONE was to develop new audiences, education played a central role. Performances for children included study guides provided by ONE, with brief discussions of the structure of opera, its history, and other contextual information to prepare the audience. The singers were typically not the same as those who performed in Boston. Rather, Caldwell developed training programs for aspiring singers who could audition for an opportunity to perform with ONE. She later expanded the program to include conductors, stage directors, designers, and technicians.

The first communities to be part of the Opera New England tour were in Maine (Portland, Brunswick), Connecticut (South Woodstock), New Hampshire (Manchester), and Massachusetts (Worcester). Her goal at the time was to develop a network of 12 sites that would each support its own company.[34] ONE established a 10-day residency in each city where performers and musicians were billeted in local homes and, in turn, provided workshops and audition opportunities for local artists. As with other Caldwell's endeavors, the idea was new and exciting, but glitches developed in its execution. The production of Aaron Copland's *The Second Hurricane* was an example of how difficult it was to carry out her plan. One battle-scarred director of that opera detailed a list of logistical problems not new to anyone who has worked in amateur theater: New England winter weather affects participation levels; family and school commitments affect participation levels; friends don't necessarily make good performers; few small cities have the facilities adequately equipped for opera productions; preparation and skill levels of singers and musicians varied widely; and girls far outnumber boys in choruses.[35] The fact that each production had to be tailored to the community members and the resources at hand was reminiscent of the unsuccessful strategy Caldwell had developed for the American National Opera Company. Although she claimed that she had learned a great deal from that earlier experience, she still clung to that goal. Not surprisingly, the result was similar, a high degree of chaos that was very familiar to those accustomed to working with her. Each of the difficulties mentioned above were repeated in each city because there were new singers, new musicians, and new crew members in every location. To make matters worse, despite her professed interest in the mission of Opera New England, Caldwell seemed to take only a modest interest in it, at times not showing up for either rehearsals or performances.

Opera New England was another idea of Caldwell's that not only required a larger budget to succeed, but also the organizational skill that she could not provide. Even with inexhaustible resources, the practical impediments may have been too great for anyone to succeed, given the logistical difficulties mentioned above. As with many of her ideas, the idea itself was laudable: build new audiences through partnerships with communities in order to educate and democratize the process by involving community members. But it was unable to be realized.

The trajectory of Caldwell's career and that of the Opera Company of Boston reached its zenith in the 1970s. During that decade, she reached the pinnacle of her creative powers, tackling the most challenging repertoire including large-scale works that solidified her reputation as a leading stage director in American opera. Moreover, she did so despite the fact that she did not have an opera house in which to work. She created each production in whatever space she was able to rent for the performances. Without adequate storage space, set pieces were often destroyed after the production closed (usually after only a handful of performances), making it difficult to revive productions or to rent sets to other companies. After years of producing operas in former vaudeville houses and movie palaces, she longed for a space that would enable her to realize her vision: "What can one do to place our own special, individual stamp on the great operatic tradition if we don't have money, or the time, or a place?"[36] The necessity of building an opera house continued unabated, but despite her best efforts at lobbying private and public supporters, it was not in the foreseeable future. Therefore, she did the next best thing. She bought a decrepit theater and made an opera house of it.

In 1978, Caldwell purchased the B.F. Keith Memorial Theatre (also known as the Sack Savoy), which she renamed the Opera House. It should have afforded her the luxury of stability, the opportunity to strengthen her company, and to serve as a focal point for adventurous opera in Boston. Instead, it added to the burden of her already heavy load of responsibilities. When she purchased the Opera House, it was a movie theater that had fallen into almost total ruin during a period of neglect in an area of the city that desperately needed revitalization. As a result, it required significant investment of the company's resources just to remain usable. For years, Caldwell struggled to make the Opera House a home and did so for 48 productions, from 1978 until 1990. However, the permanent venue she had dreamed of quickly became an albatross, a burden to manage, and a drain on the company's already scarce financial resources.

Over more than 30 seasons, the Opera Company of Boston had numerous artistic successes and regularly sold out its performances, but even from its beginning, it faced fiscal challenges that stemmed from Caldwell's inability to manage the funds that she raised. When the company was formed in 1958, it had only $5,000 as a start-up fund,[37] but she paid $12,000 for the costumes of its first production, Offenbach's *Voyage to the Moon*.[38] A year later, she decided to take it on a three-month tour and promptly lost another $20,000.[39] Subscriptions to its first full season of three operas in 1959 sold for $10 each and over 8,000 were sold.[40] The total would have been a windfall, except for the fact that the company had rented a theater that accommodated only about 500 people. Not only did it have to return 300 subscription requests, it also had to perform *La Bohème* 16 times in order to honor the remainder— for which Caldwell had to pay the singers, orchestra, and crew each time and keep the house rented. As she remembered, "Our $90,000[41] disappeared very quickly and we were once again scrambling for money."[42] Many early signs of fiscal inexperience and uncertainty foreshadowed the greater difficulties to come. According to Beverly Sills, as early as 1963 the company's financial situation was so precarious that the prison scene in the production of Gounod's *Faust* that season was performed with lighting effects as the only scenery. That was not an inventive directorial choice. Rather, the company had simply run out of money and could not afford any additional scenery.[43] The Ford Foundation provided the company with a "stability grant" at the time, but even it insisted that the company needed to improve its financial situation before any further assistance could be considered.[44]

In the mid–1960s, the Opera Company of Boston received a second stabilization grant of $195,000 from the Ford Foundation to help pay off the company's debts.[45] That relief seemed only to encourage Caldwell to undertake one of her first large-scale works, Schönberg's *Moses and Aaron*. It was a bold undertaking of a relatively new work and an expensive one as well, reportedly costing about $300,000 (almost half the company's totally operating income at the time) to produce. Her 1972 production of Berlioz's *The Trojans* set the company back about $200,000, also a very costly production for a small company. Caldwell was a successful fundraiser, but constant cost over runs and a reputation for careless bookkeeping discouraged private donations and made the major Foundations wary. In the 1980s, with the added strain of the Opera House, the financial situation of the company grew more urgent. When she attempted to curb costs and find new funding sources of funding, she became embroiled in a bitter union dispute and a political controversy at the same time.

On January 19, 1982, the *New York Times* reported that the opening performance of the Opera Company of Boston's American premiere of Zimmermann's *Die Soldaten*, scheduled for later that month, had been canceled because musicians were challenging their wage scale at the OCB.[46] In fact, financial difficulties (as well as rumors of managerial and artistic chaos) had delayed it from an initial scheduled opening in November to mid-December, then to late January.[47] The American Federation of Musicians was seeking a new contract that would increase members' pay, guarantee job security, and improve working conditions at the company. The dispute had originated the previous autumn after the Boston branch of the union accepted a new pay scale. Caldwell refused to honor it, angry at what she called its "militant" leadership. Her response was to hire out of state musicians for a tour of Rossini's *The Barber of Seville* in October and to pay the previous wage scale for the production of Humperdinck's *Hansel and Gretel* in December. She wanted union musicians to agree to the previous year's scale due to the company's "substantial cumulative deficits," a request that was met by the filing of an unfair labor practice complaint by the *Local 9* of the AFM. After a lengthy and very public dispute, both parties finally agreed to a compromise on wages.[48]

At the same time Caldwell was directing and conducting, managing a labor dispute, and running a regional touring company, she announced the creation of the (New) Opera Company of the Philippines in Manilla that would serve as a sister company for the Opera Company of Boston. The Philippine company would provide interns to the OCB and Caldwell would take production personnel and artists from Boston to Manila to perform and help develop its opera program. On the surface, it was a promising arrangement, rumored to have been worth about $100,000 over five years to the OCB— not a large sum, but desperately needed. However, the proposal soon came under fire from local musicians and human rights activists who opposed the repressive regime of President Ferdinand E. Marcos. Caldwell attempted to quell her detractors by insisting that the association was not political: "Our agreement is not with the government; it is with the Opera Guild of the Philippines, which is raising the money in the private sector. Many of the donors are highly respectable people with extensive business interests and activities in Boston. They are proud of what they are doing for their country."[49] She dismissed the criticism and went on to present Mozart's *The Magic Flute* in June 1983, a production that included musicians from the Philippines and members of the Opera Company of Boston.

The articulation between the two opera organizations drew additional criticism as political turmoil erupted in the Philippines. In August of that year, Benigno S. Aquino, Jr., a former senator and rival to Marcos, was assassinated as he was escorted off an airplane at Manila International Airport, although he was supposed to be under the protection of soldiers of the Aviation Security Command. The assassination led to widespread protests and the eventual overthrow of the Marcos government. In October, the Opera Company of Boston announced that it was severing its ties with the Philippines. Company President Laszlo J. Bonis denied that the protests influenced the decision, but it is likely that public pressure played a part. Members of the Boston Committee for Human Rights in the Arts attended the opening night of the new season and handed out "Thank you, Sarah" buttons.[50] Ironically, their gesture was at the presentation of Puccini's *Turandot*, the same one that Caldwell had created the year before in the People's Republic of China, without evoking any protest.

Caldwell had turned to the Philippines to generate a promising new revenue source for a faltering company. When that option closed, its debts increased. That same year she found another international opportunity for herself: she agreed to take an ongoing position as Artistic Director of the New Opera Company of Israel, a company formed after the former Israel National Opera had ceased operations the previous year.[51] The multiyear agreement, funded by the Tel Aviv Foundation and Arts Council, was to bring the Opera Company of Boston to Tel Aviv to work with the Israel Philharmonic, then under the direction of Zubin Mehta. For the first season, Caldwell intended to bring Puccini's *Madama Butterfly* and Mozart's *Don Giovanni*. She worked six days a week for eight weeks with artistic and production personnel to rejuvenate the company. However, as she said in *Challenges*, after making a significant number of plans she was confronted by the Board of Trustees and told that the budget, which she had thought was for one production, was actually the budget for the entire season and included publicity, administration, and educational expenses. Whether there was a misunderstanding or wishful thinking on Caldwell's part, it became evident that she could not realize her plans with the New Opera Company of Israel, so she disassociated herself from it and returned home.

Despite her political missteps and miscalculations, Caldwell retained loyal supporters in Boston, but even they could not rescue the company from its financial quagmire. She readily admitted that she was not a business person, and although she had staff members who worked with her for years at a time, there was significant turn over, personnel problems, and her own disregard for the advice of her Board of Directors. Numerous times the company was on the brink of collapse, but Caldwell always seemed to rebound. Her resilience earned her the reputation of a phoenix, resurrecting her company repeatedly, and producing operas on sheer determination. Eventually, however, determination was not enough.

After two difficult years that included the union strike, the Philippine controversy, and growing financial struggles, Caldwell, at age 61, succumbed to the strain. In early January 1985, she fell ill with double pneumonia and was admitted to Massachusetts General Hospital in serious condition. Her health worsened to the point that she was placed in intensive care and was on a respirator for a time. She remained in the hospital for three months.[52] It was the first time that she had been seriously ill and it left the company in a crisis of leadership. In February of that year, with Caldwell still incapacitated, the Board of Directors, led by Laszlo Bonis, decided that the season could not continue without the company's artistic leader at the helm. Publicly he reported that the decision was in deference to Caldwell, given that she had poured so much of her energies into the research for the operas that she had chosen for that season,[53] but it was clear that there was simply no one ready to step in for her. If she or her Board had ever anticipated the possibility of such a void they had clearly not planned for it. The result was the loss of the entire season and over $800,000.

Once discharged from the hospital, Caldwell continued her recovery for several months. She rested, exercised, lost weight, and slowly regained her strength. She spoke excitedly to the press about her plans for a production of *St. Francis of Assisi* by Messiaen, Bernstein's *Candide* or possibly *A Quiet Place*, and a return to additional Rameau operas.[54] She rebounded late that year to conduct and direct Humperdinck's *Hansel and Gretel* and followed that up with four additional operas in 1986. Nevertheless, the cancellation of the previous season had been a turning point. Despite her new vigor and plans for future productions, the company never regained even the slender financial foothold it had before her illness. In an effort to recoup its losses, the Board renewed its efforts for fundraising, hoping to lower the company's debt to about half a million by year's end and to erase it altogether the following year. It asked the subscribers to the canceled season not to request refunds, but rather to donate their payments and buy a new season subscription. The request was not well received. Subscribers lambasted the company in the press, sent numerous angry letters, and threatened it with lawsuits. If any subscribers did make the suggested donation, it was not enough. The company never erased its debt.

In 1988, Massachusetts Governor Michael Dukakis, the legislature, and Boston Mayor Raymond Flynn attempted to assist the ailing company. The plan was to issue a bond so that the city could buy the Opera House and complete the restoration of it. The sale price of $20,000,000 would erase the Opera Company of Boston's debt of about $6 million and enable it to launch an endowment program to secure its future. It would be able to use the theater for six months out of the year for 50 years. Unluckily, the bond issue was delayed and then, given economic difficulties faced by the Commonwealth at the time, subsequently withdrawn.[55] The Opera Company of Boston was poised on the brink of ruin. Distrust and negativity surrounded Caldwell stemming from the union dispute, the Philippine fiasco, and from the Board asking subscribers to forego the cost of their subscriptions for a season that was cancelled because of her illness. Yet, none of that deterred Caldwell from producing operas. Moreover, she decided the time was ripe to organize a mammoth music festival that brought together hundreds of artists from the Soviet Union and the United States.

Caldwell had long wanted to establish a partnership with a Soviet opera company and had travelled to the U.S.S.R. several times the previous decade with the prospect of producing an opera with one of them. However, in an era of political uncertainty and tensions exacerbated by the Soviet invasion of Afghanistan late in 1979, nothing came of her prospects. Only after the election of Mikhail Gorbachev, as General Secretary of the Communist Party in 1985 and the last head of state of the Soviet Union, did partnerships become possible. Shortly after Gorbachev took office, the American Secretary of State, George Schultz, and the Soviet Foreign Minister, Eduard Schevardnadze, signed a General Exchanges Agreement that permitted cross-cultural reciprocity. That agreement became part of a series of economic and political reforms that included *glasnost* (liberalizing of speech) and *perestroika* (restructuring of the economy), words that soon became familiar to many Americans.

Caldwell seized upon the opening up of the Soviet Union to meet with Russian composer Rodion Shchedrin. Initially, they discussed producing his opera *Dead Souls*, but soon their talks led to the idea of bringing together Soviet and American artists in a groundbreaking festival that mushroomed into an excessive and costly cultural enterprise. Ultimately, she did not direct *Dead Souls*, as she had originally intended, because she became absorbed with the largest logistical undertaking of her career. It is worth describing the festival in some detail, since it illustrates many of the characteristics of her stage directing process.

In September of 1987, the festival was announced to the public, with Shchedrin, his wife the ballerina Maya Plisetskaya, and Caldwell named as co-directors. Although it was called "Making Music Together" there was a rich array of poetry, drama, dance, workshops, theatrical presentations, and visual arts, in addition to music that was presented over a three-week period. At the Tremont Temple for instance, the Soviet poet Bella Akhmadulina read from her works, which were then read in translation by Phyllis Curtin, a frequent performer with the Opera Company of Boston. There was a retrospective of "Contemporary Moscow Theatre Design" at the Museum of Fine Arts, which featured scenes for Checkhov plays by eight different designers from the previous 20 years. There were composers' forums at Boston University, performances by the Pokrovsky Folk Ensemble (a performance group that travelled throughout the Soviet Union to experience folk life in order to perform folk music authentically, much in the way that so-called Method actors research their roles by actually living them first), original theater pieces, and works specifically for children. A performance of Prokofiev's perennial favorite *Peter and the Wolf* by the New England Conservatory Youth Philharmonic Orchestra in Jordan Hall, with narration by the Soviet actress Natalia Sats, a friend of the late composer, and the original narrator at the work's Moscow premiere in 1936.

In part because of the involvement of Plisetskaya, dance featured prominently in the festival. Eighty members of the Bolshoi Ballet performed mostly new works at the Wang Center for the Performing Arts, and Plisetskaya herself performed her own choreography in *The Lady with the Small Dog*. Perhaps the most poignant event of the festival was the *Homage à Plisetskaya* in which the 63-year-old ballerina performed *The Dying Swan*, choreographed by Mikhail Fokine to Camille Saint-Saëns' *Le Cygne*. The interpretation had been originated by Anna Pavlova and earned Plisetskaya acclaim in her youth. The event in her honor included principal dancers with the American Ballet Theatre, and a performance by one of the most famous Soviet defectors, Mikhail Baryshnikov.

Above all, music was the highlight of the festival. The Boston Symphony Orchestra in a concert led by Gennady Rozhdestvensky, played works by composers familiar to western audiences such as Rimsky-Korsakov, Prokofiev, and Stravinsky. But the real focus of the festival was on lesser known Soviet composers through the Composers Profile Concerts. These included performances of works by Andrei Petrov, a prolific composer of music for ballet, theater and more than 50 films, performed by students from the New England Conservatory and Moscow Conservatories. The three lesser-known Soviet composers featured by the Festival were Sofia Gubaidulina, Alfred Schnittke, and its co-director, Rodion Shchedrin.

American audiences were able to hear the work of Sofia Gubaidulina, whose output included string quartets, concertos, and choral works, as well as compositions that featured uncommon instrumental combinations, such as *Five Etudes for harp, double-bass and percussion* (1965); *Descensio* for three trombones, three percussionists, harp, harpsichord/celesta and celesta/piano (1981); and film music. The Boston Symphony Orchestra, led by guest conductor, Charles Dutoit, performed her most widely known work at the time, the violin concerto *Offertorium*, written in 1980.

Alfred Schnittke was a composer of classical forms: symphonies, concertos, chamber music, and choral music. He had scored over 60 films, and in the 1990s, near the end of his career, he wrote three operas. His first trip to America was for Making Music Together where his *Symphony no. 1* received its American premiere by the Boston Symphony Orchestra in Symphony Hall under the direction of Soviet conductor Gennady Rozhdestvensky.

The most prominent composer of the festival was its co-director Rodion Shchedrin. His *Self-Portrait* was one of the offerings on the opening night, performed by the Making Music Together Festival Orchestra, led by Seiji Ozawa. A performance and discussion of his *Frescoes of Dionysus* and *Geometry of Sound* took place at Harvard University and several other works were performed at the Opera House. The climax of the festival, however, was his opera, *Dead Souls*. Its libretto was based on Nikolai Gogol's satire about 19th-century Russian culture and economics that unfolds a money-making scheme by the main character in which he purchases "dead souls," deceased serfs that remain on the tax records of landowners and on which they continued to pay taxes. The visiting Russian designer, Valery Levanthal, known for his work at the Bolshoi Ballet, created a bi-level set that depicted interiors on the lower level, and exteriors including an elevated country road on the upper. Alexei Maslennikov, from the Bolshoi Theatre, who recreated much of the 1977 premiere production at the Mariinsky Theatre in St. Petersburg, directed. It was conducted by Dzhansug Kakhidze and starred mostly Soviet singers in a Russian language production with English supertitles. The performances received mixed reviews. *Time Magazine*'s reviewer Michael Walsh and the *New York Times* critic Bernard Holland found the music rather conventional, illustrating the action well, but not memorable in and of itself.[56] Richard Dyer of the *Boston Globe*, on the other hand, considered it a triumph of the festival, as did the audience, which reportedly applauded vigorously for the performers and especially for Shchedrin.[57]

The festival, though co-directed with Shchedrin and Plisetskaya, had the Caldwellian characteristics of scattered energy and recklessness that were typical in her rehearsal process. She over-packed the schedule and venues with as many events as possible and allowed the festival to grow beyond control both logistically and financially. Throughout the festival there were complaints about poor organization, misinformation, late starts, and low attendance. The official brochure was confusing, events announced for one venue ended up in another, and schedules were revised multiple times. The lower level of the two-level set for *Dead Souls*, which had been designed in Moscow and built in Indiana, had to be rebuilt in Boston, because it did not fit under the upper level of the set, which had been built in Israel.[58] Bostonian musicians who had not been asked to participate, or had been asked too late to enable them to participate expressed frustration.[59] Another kind of criticism, familiar given Caldwell's previous international initiatives, was that she had liaised with another country led by a repressive regime. The editor of *The New Criterion*, a monthly publication on the arts and cultural life, wrote: "It reminds us of what short political memories American artists and cultural bureaucrats have. They can so easily put aside the history of suffering that artists and ordinary citizens have endured and continue to endure in the Soviet Union."[60] Audience members on their way to the opening night performance at the Tremont Temple encountered protesters demonstrating against the Soviet oppression of the Baltic States.

Finally, financial difficulties affected the festival as they did in so many of Caldwell's productions. At first, the festival was to be financed by the City of Boston, the Commonwealth of Massachusetts, corporate and private donations, and the Soviet Union (which was to contribute $1.25 million) for a total budget of between $3.4 and $4 million.[61] Ultimately, however, corporate fundraisers in Boston had difficulty making their target of $900,000; ticket sales were weak, generating less than half of the almost $1 million expected, and private donations fell short of the goal. The Commonwealth of Massachusetts had originally agreed to donate $450,000, with the hope that ticket sales would make up the remainder. A year after the Governor of Massachusetts failed to secure a bond issue to save the Opera Company of Boston from financial ruin, he had to work with the Secretary of State, George P. Shultz and Harold Hestnes, a private businessman, to raise $200,000 and loan the festival another $200,000.[62] Their actions saved Boston the international embarrassment of having to cancel at the last minute, but sealed Caldwell's reputation as fiscal liability.

If it had it been better organized, Making Music Together may have made Boston the home of an ongoing international festival. It did not. Nevertheless, it did pave the way for important cultural exchanges that soon followed. The New York Philharmonic, under the direction of Zubin Mehta, went to the Soviet Union in May of 1988 to give three performances and master classes, as well as a joint concert with the State Symphony Orchestra of the Soviet Ministry of Culture.[63] The Metropolitan Museum, in conjunction with the Art Institute of Chicago, agreed to an exchange of four shows with the Hermitage and Pushkin Museum of Fine Arts, Moscow, between 1988 and 1990. The Dance Theatre of Harlem became the first American dance troupe to perform in the Soviet Union. It performed in Tbilisi, the capital city of Georgia, and in Leningrad at the Kirov State Theatre of Opera and Ballet, and as part of the cultural exchange, held open classes and rehearsals for Soviet artists. Theodor Mann, Artistic Director of New York City's Circle in the Square Theatre, directed Tennessee Williams' play *The Night of the Iguana* at the Leningrad Maly Drama Theatre in 1989. These examples of the early and important exchanges cannot be said to have taken place because of Making Music Together, but the festival's scope was such that it led the way as the largest endeavor of its kind, introducing American artists to Soviet artists to a degree not possible before and not imagined but for Caldwell.

The distraction of the Making Music Together festival was short-lived. At the Opera Company of Boston, internal tensions threatened to derail all efforts to keep the company viable. A rift developed between Caldwell and Robert Canon, who had recently been appointed as the company's President. Canon had previously held positions at the National Endowment for the Arts and the Joffrey Ballet School. Bruce Rossley, Boston Arts Commissioner, had brought Canon to the OCB in 1987, with the support of Caldwell, to assist in making the company and the Opera House central features in the revitalization of the Cultural District.[64] Canon made it clear, however, that he considered her the major obstacle to that plan.[65] His proposal was to close down the company for a three-year period, sell the Opera House to pay off the debt, and restructure a new company to be headed by Peter Sellars.[66]

Sellars, a flamboyant *wunderkind* stage director who had created dozens of off-the-wall productions as an undergraduate at Harvard University, was barely 30 years old at the time. He had an exhaustive imagination and enthusiastic supporters, but his administrative experience was limited to a short period when he was Artistic Director of the Boston Shakespeare Company. His reputation for revisionist interpretations became the subject of articles in major newspapers and in *America Theater, Opera News, The New Yorker, and Opera Journal.* Sellars was among a new generation of theater directors, lured to opera by the chance to extend their imaginations and budgets well beyond what was possible at the time in spoken theater. Julius Novick in *American Theatre* called him and contemporaries including Andrei Serban and Frank Corsaro "interlopers in the opera house"[67] but they were popular and companies looking to build audiences took notice of them.

Some members of the Opera Company of Boston Board who thought it was the only way to keep the company viable supported Canon's reorganization proposal. However, Caldwell loyalists on the Board considered the move a betrayal of the person who was the heart and soul of the Opera Company of Boston. A public feud erupted. The President of the Board, Arnett Waters, presented a letter to the *Boston Globe* that documented the suspension of Canon for "failure to implement a full scale development plan since [his] arrival here in November 1987, a very substantial example of poor administration."[68] Waters' reaction brought to light the behind-the-scenes drama, but complicated it as well, since he had been present at discussions about the restructuring. The following day, the *Boston Globe* reported that Canon had been reinstated after a late-night meeting of the Board, at which it decided that he had not actually breached his contract. The problem did not end there. Canon demanded back pay and a public apology from Waters for defamation of character.[69] The dispute fractured the Board and six of its members promptly resigned.[70] They were not the only ones to abandon what seemed to be a hopeless situation. The legal firm of Hale and Dorr, which had provided pro bono legal services to the company, withdrew its services because Caldwell wanted to borrow additional money to stay afloat, ignoring its advice to file for bankruptcy.[71]

In the midst of the controversy, Canon resigned his position, but remained in Boston to execute his plan for a new company, which he wanted led by shared leadership. "We do not," he said to the *Boston Globe* in July, referring to Caldwell's reputation for autocratic rule, "want the company identified with one person or with two people."[72] The following March, a press conference was planned to announce the formation of the Boston Opera Theater, with Peter Sellars in the role of "artistic advisor" and Craig Smith and Robert Canon as the executive directors. The new company was to begin presenting operas the following year with revivals of the Mozart-Da Ponte operas that Sellars and Smith had produced for the Pepsico Summerfare. It would then offer a mix of conventional fare with more avant-garde productions.

The company opened on a promising note with five sold-out performances of *The Marriage of Figaro* in January of 1991 at the Colonial Theatre (a turn of the century venue built for live theater and musicals that seated 1600 spectators), but the production ran over budget, reportedly because of costs necessitated by the theater's union contract. None of the other operas even made it to the stage.[73] The Boston Opera Theater immediately incurred a debilitating debt and no further projects were planned. Apparently, it was not without some satisfaction that Caldwell watched Canon fail. "The problem," she observed years later, "was that he didn't know enough about producing opera to succeed. He didn't know how to handle the unions; he didn't know how to handle people."[74] In addition, unlike Caldwell, neither Canon nor Sellars was willing to endure the hardships of producing opera in Boston. Canon's deal with Sellars was that he would be associated with the Boston Opera Theater, but remain open to accept other offers. After the presentations of his *Figaro*, that is exactly what Sellars did.

The Opera Company of Boston did survive, but for only one more season, and that under a cloud of a debt reported at over $6 million and amid ongoing negotiations about the future of the Opera House. The season was reflective both of the desperate situation of the company and its grit. It began with Puccini's *Madama Butterfly*, an opera that Caldwell had presented more than any other in her career. The *New York Times* no longer bothered to mention it and Richard Dyer lamented in the *Boston Globe* that "it's sad to see Caldwell reduced to pushing 'Butterflys' through a revolving door."[75] She did her best to make the three iterations of this opera (January, February and March) relevant by presenting first the final version, then the Brescia version and lastly, the La Scala version. In earlier years, that decision might have been accepted as a clever Caldwellian "gimmick," but that year, it was clear that the decision was made because of severely limited resources. The second opera that year was Mozart's *The Magic Flute*, the same production she had brought to the Philippines and which had elicited such ire from the Boston community. The timing of that revival may not have helped garner support for the company. Caldwell's third and final offering was an uncompromising choice that underscored her unfailing courage to present the kind of operas that she thought needed to be introduced. It was Robert Di Domenica's opera *The Balcony*, a contemporary piece of savage satire based on Jean Genet's 1956 play of the same name.

Di Domenica was a long-time teacher at the New England Conservatory of Music in Boston and composer who was respected as such, though not widely known. *The Balcony* was his first opera, a serial composition that he had completed in 1972. It is relatively short, just over 90 minutes long, and divided into nine scenes within two acts. Based closely on the play, it explores the nature of theater and self-referentiality in an irrational world. Genet's plays are examples of a "theater of the absurd," a post-war dramatic form in which characters and plots are not necessarily governed by logic or purpose. Both the play and the libretto include archetypal male characters (a Police Chief, a Bishop, and a Judge) who frequent a brothel in order to escape the reality of their actual powerlessness to contain a revolution that has erupted in the city and which they can hear from within the brothel. There they engage in sexual and social exploration of defined roles and expectations. The setting could have led to a highly sexualized staging by another director, but Caldwell was more cerebral than sensual in her interpretations and the result was a rather sparse and antiseptic staging that followed the indications in the score very closely.

The Balcony received mixed reactions from the audience and critics. James R. Oestreich described it in the *New York Times* as "a wonderfully intelligent construct," but not without musical shortcomings.[76] The *Boston Globe's* Richard Dyer liked most of the vocal performances, but had reservations about the music.[77] Di Domenica was pleased with the production and impressed with Caldwell: "She is determined to treat the opera with elegance and not turn it into something merely titillating. She is living with all these [sic], yet she is also remembering that the quarter note equals ninety-six on the metronome and treating the music with the greatest respect."[78] This thoughtful, but unremarkable world premiere was the final production of the Opera Company of Boston.

The accomplishments, defeats, and struggles of Caldwell the director played out almost exclusively within the context of her own opera company. In addition to directing and conducting, she determined the company's repertoire each season, managed administrative aspects of the company, and engaged in fundraising. All these aspects of running an opera company, not to mention her other initiatives over the years, were responsibilities far in excess of what most opera directors need to concern themselves with or would want to. Still, she needed her own company for the artistic freedom and opportunities it provided to her. The reality was that given her approach and rehearsal style, it was probably the only place she would have been able to direct operas at all.

Chapter 3

The Repertoire

The diversity of operas that Caldwell directed over the course of her career illustrates her eclectic tastes and the range of her directorial abilities. Moreover, it exemplifies a philosophical approach to producing opera, a belief in challenging and stimulating audiences with works that deserve to be considered or reconsidered, rather than merely presenting familiar fare. Despite her multiple creative and administrative responsibilities, and the perpetual financial struggles of the company, she adamantly refused to stage only "chestnuts" in order for her company to remain viable. Well-known operas were part of her repertoire, certainly, but they were not what interested her most and they were not what defined her as a stage director or impresario. As she once said, "One of the best reasons for doing an opera is that no one else is interested in doing it."[1] So she forged ahead with a risky repertoire that expanded the canon, continually tested the creative and financial limits of her company, provoked her critics, and delighted her audiences.

Over the course of three decades as a stage director with the Opera Company of Boston Caldwell realized over 130 productions (almost all both staged and conducted by her) that reveal the breadth of her interests and capabilities. They included 79 different operas ranging from the 17th to the late 20th century. The works of Italian, German, and Austrian composers formed the core of the OCB seasons, but her output included works from French (Bizet, Charpentier, Massenet, Offenbach, Rameau), Hungarian (Bartók), Russian (Glinka, Mussorgsky, Prokofiev, Stravinsky), Czech (Smetana, Janáček), Spanish (de Falla), British (Davies, Gay, Tippet), and American (Bernstein, Di Domenica, Kurka, Middleton, Sessions, Schuller) composers. The operas ranged from intimate chamber operas, such as Middleton's *Command Performance* to large-scale works (such as Schönberg's *Moses and Aaron*, Prokofiev's *War and Peace*, and Sessions' *Montezuma*).

Among her productions with the OCB were three world premieres. The first was Robert Middleton's *Command Performance*, commissioned by the Centennial Committee of Vassar College, which she staged in 1961. The following year, she brought it to the Kresge Auditorium on the campus of the Massachusetts Institute of Technology (MIT) in Cambridge, conducted by the composer at the piano, leading a small orchestra. In 1970, she produced the world premiere of *The Fisherman and His Wife*, by Gunther Schuller, who was then serving as the President of the New England Conservatory of Music. The hour-long opera for children, the second of only two by the composer, subsequently entered into the repertoire of Opera New England. The final production of the Opera Company of Boston was the world premiere of Robert Di Domenica's *The Balcony* in 1990. Caldwell also directed two other world premieres beyond the OCB. The first was *Be Glad Then, America*, an opera by John La Montaine, commissioned by the Institute for the Arts and Humanistic Studies at the Pennsylvania State University to celebrate the American bicentennial in 1976. It was performed in the Eisenhower Auditorium on the campus of the Pennsylvania State University. At the end of her directing career she presented the world premiere of *The Black Swan*, the first opera of Thomas Whitman, performed at Swarthmore College in Pennsylvania, 1998. In addition, she presented 13 American premieres with the OCB. Most had been written in the 20th century, but others, such as the 18th-century *Hippolyte et Aricie* by Rameau, were ones that were rarely produced by other companies anywhere.

Although most of the operas she directed outside her own company were repetitions of ones she had premiered with the Opera Company of Boston,[2] and many were operas on which she had worked with Goldovsky at Tanglewood, there were exceptions. In addition to those she premiered with Opera New England (see Chapter 2), she staged Henze's *The Young Lord*, Strauss' *Ariadne auf Naxos*, Rossini's *The Barber of Seville*, and Verdi's *Falstaff* for the New York City Opera. One spoken drama, Shakespeare's *Macbeth*, was her only production at the Vivian Beaumont Theater in New York City.

The selection of individual operas in any given season rested entirely with Caldwell. And since she was not just the stage director of the Opera Company of Boston, but also its impresario and conductor, her directorial preferences alone were not the sole reason for her choices. At times she wanted to feature specific star singers in particular roles and often they were the highlights of the season in which they appeared. For instance, *I Puritani* and *Semiramide* were tailored for Joan Sutherland, *Macbeth* and *Otello* were vehicles for Shirley Verrett, *Fidelio* and *Benvenuto Cellini* were selected for Jon Vickers. Her long association with Beverly Sills led to Donizetti's *Lucia di Lammermoor*, *La Traviata*, *The Daughter of the Regiment*, and others. There were other choices that were made because of powerful combinations of singers, including Joan Sutherland and Marilyn Horne in *Semiramide*, Plácido Domingo and Renata Tebaldi in *La Bohème*, Beverly Sills and Tatiana Troyanos in *I Capuleti e i Montecchi*, At the core of the OCB were singers like Donald Gramm, who was a company favorite featured in many of her productions from 1958 to 1983.

Seasons as a whole were assembled not only with a view to underscoring the bold artistic mission of the company, but also for commentary, and naturally, for economic reasons as well. For example, the 1959 season began with two frequently produced Italian operas, Puccini's *La Bohème* and Rossini's *The Barber of Seville*. Then she offered John Gay's *The Beggar's Opera*, a ballad opera that satirizes Italian opera. In 1977, she produced Gluck's *Orfeo ed Euridice* and followed it with *Orpheus in the Underworld*, Offenbach's satirical send up of the same myth, and staged it using the same set and costume designs. In 1990, she staged Puccini's *Madama Butterfly* in three versions: the 1907 most frequently performed version, followed by the earlier 1904 Brescia version, and lastly, the original 1904 La Scala version. In typical Caldwell style, she presented them in reverse order, with each iteration taking audiences further back to Puccini's original intentions and inviting immediate comparisons among the versions. Given the financial and managerial problems at that time, however, presenting *Madama Butterfly* multiple times during one season was also a financial expediency, a sign that the company was nearing its end.

Caldwell's selection of operas over the years confirms that she was drawn to new and lesser-known operas, but also that she was interested in revisiting works that were at the heart of the canon. She had an affinity for Verdi and staged more of his operas than any other composer, including *La Traviata*, *Otello*, *Falstaff*, *Rigoletto*, *Il Trovatore*, and *Aida*. She also presented *Don Carlos* (1973) in a newly restored five-act version that had premiered at La Scala only three years before. She followed that up in 1978 with the composer's rarely performed *Stiffelio*, and earned the praise of *New York Times* critic Harold C. Schonberg for going "wildly outside of the standard repertory."[3] Well-known operas by Mozart were regularly in her seasons, including *The Magic Flute*, *Don Giovanni*, *The Abduction from the Seraglio*, *The Marriage of Figaro* and *Cosí fan tutte* as well as *La Finta Giardiniera*, the opera she staged at Tanglewood and with Goldovsky's New England Opera Theater. The works of Donizetti entered her repertoire in the mid–1960s with *I Puritani* starring Joan Sutherland, and continued with *The Daughter of the Regiment*, *Don Pasquale*, and *Lucia di Lammermoor*, all starring Beverly Sills. Puccini was a staple, with *Turandot*, *Girl of the Golden West*, *Tosca*, *La Bohème*, and *Madama Butterfly* (which she staged multiple times between 1962 and 1990).

A consideration of Caldwell's selection of operas sheds light on her tastes, but also on the restrictions imposed by financial considerations. Arts organizations, especially in America, must take audiences and donors into consideration when making such choices since they rely on them for a greater share of their income than do many European houses. The Metropolitan Opera, for one, has long had a reputation for a conservative repertoire, which Rudolf Bing addressed very pragmatically during his tenure there: "My colleague in Hamburg does contemporary opera after contemporary opera and the press loves him, he plays to empty houses, and the state pays. But in America the state does not pay.... I am always told that opera will dies unless the new works are performed; it seems to me that these days a better case can be made for the proposition that opera will never die unless the new works are performed."[4] Regional companies have tended to be more adventurous, but not without risk. Since neither large companies nor small have the ability to raise income significantly through ticket sales (given limited seating and a limit on prices that audiences are willing to pay), they rely for about half their revenue on unearned income, such as donations from private individuals or corporations, and grants from government agencies. At the national level, direct federal support in America lags far behind other countries, including Canada and those in western Europe.[5] As a result, revenue must be raised through more indirect means, such as tax incentives for giving to the arts. And while the American approach gives individual citizens more influence over the kind of art that is produced, it has the effect of limiting risk taking and suppressing the introduction of new or potentially controversial works that could anger donors or scare away audiences.

Opera companies, regardless of size, incur the highest production costs of any arts organization, not because they recklessly spend money on lavish *mise en scènes* (although there is a certain expectation for opulence), but because most operas require a large number of specialized individuals including orchestral musicians, chorus members, dancers, soloists, designers, and other key artistic personnel. The salaries paid by professional companies, whether large or small, account for about half of their overall operating budget. In addition, operas require sets, lighting, costumes, rehearsal space, performance space, storage space, rehearsal time and artistic and production staff—each on a larger scale than most spoken theater plays or dance pieces. It is possible, of course, to mount a small-scale *Aida*, for instance—and Caldwell did just that, to popular and critical acclaim—but that is not the *Aida* of Verdi's score, nor that of his librettist, Antonio Ghislanzoni. If a director adhered strictly to the libretto for the triumphal scene, for instance, she would need a set design for Act II, scene 2 that included the "Entrance gate to the city of

Thebes. In front a clump of palms. R.H. a temple dedicated to Ammon—L.H. a throne with a purple canopy; at back a triumphal arch." And a host of people including "the King, followed by State Officers, Priests, Captains, Fan-bearers, Standard-bearers. Afterwards Amneris, with Aida and Slaves."[6] Such a setting would require a stage that could highlight the visual splendor worthy of ancient Egypt's royal inhabitants and satisfy contemporary expectations of operatic opulence. All that leads to an expensive production, and no matter how many tickets a company sells, the number of paid seats in even a large house cannot pay for the production in its entirety. Ticket revenues still tend to cover only about half of the cost.

Critics frequently praised Caldwell for her inclusion of little known or rarely performed works, such as Rameau's *Hippolyte et Aricie* or Zimmermann's *Die Soldaten*. Yet, such choices were costly (regardless of the visual presentation) given their more limited audience appeal. For example, when she gave audiences a choice of seeing Verdi's *Falstaff*, Puccini's *Tosca*, or Berg's *Lulu* during a tour of the American National Opera Company, *Lulu* was the least requested. Producers must make difficult decisions about what is feasible and what is not in the selection of repertoire. In order to remain viable they must strike a balance between providing expected operas in familiar ways and pushing artistic boundaries and audience tastes with less familiar works that may lead to additional production costs, not to mention the possibility of lower ticket sales. The Boston Lyric Opera, a company founded in 1976 that competed with the OCB, faced these same challenges. Janice Del Sesto, General Manager of the Lyric at the time, said, "We would like to do more unusual things, more new America work, but we can't risk it."[7] In contrast, Caldwell did take that risk, repeatedly. As a result, she was appreciated as an impresario who expanded the opera canon in America, and through her staging revealed the integrity of both the drama and the music of for her audiences. Yet, she also gained a reputation as an impresario who made choices that contributed to the debts of her company and put it in jeopardy multiple times.

When it came to repertoire, Caldwell had never been one to shy away from controversy or risk. That was evident early in the company's history when she opted to present the American premiere of Luigi Nono's *Intolleranza 1960* early in 1965, on the heels of her triumph with *Semiramide*. The opera may have appealed to her for several reasons, one possibility being the composer's resistance to calling the work an opera, and his insistence on the unity of music and dramatic action without hierarchy. Its world premiere in Venice four years earlier had been a controversial one, during which conservative attendees who objected to its *avant-garde* music were joined by Neo-fascists, who opposed 12-tone music in principle. They booed and whistled throughout the performance, at one point forcing a stoppage for several minutes. Eventually, the police had to be called in to maintain order.[8] Boston was a different cultural setting, but given the subject matter and the composer's politics, it was still a risky choice for the young company.

Intolleranza 1960 is a two-part political manifesto that rages against cruelty and inhumanity. Nono wrote the work in a 12-tone musical idiom with an aggressive orchestration in order to underscore the pain of human suffering depicted in the work. He did not describe it as an opera, but rather as a "scenic action" or "theatrical composition" that resembles a Brechtian episodic drama. The main character is a Refugee on a journey back to his homeland after a long absence, accompanied by a female Companion (a role sung by Beverly Sills). On his journey, the Refugee is arrested, tortured, and finally released. He resolves to fight for justice, but perishes in a catastrophic flood just before arriving home.

Caldwell brought Czech set designer Josef Svoboda to Boston to design the production. It was the first time she had worked with Svoboda, but it was not the first time that Svoboda had worked on this opera. He had designed the set for the 1961 premiere, but it had not gone according to his plans. Italian authorities censored the film material that he had selected, so that abstract paintings had to be substituted.[9] In Boston, the production was filmed and broadcast by WGBH, a local public broadcasting station. That film provides an important historical record of the production and Svoboda's scenic intentions.[10] Svoboda left the stage of Back Bay Theater almost empty of scenery, relying more on multi-media techniques in his design to establish location and mood. For instance, he projected images on to multiple screens so that audiences could see the singers engaged in live action both on the stage and on the screens simultaneously. The production merged live action, delayed action, and negative images of the live action. One of the most innovative choices was to project a live image of the audience on to one of the screens. For example, the audience was shown a reflection of itself behind barbed wires in a concentration camp and in another scene, a negative image was used to make the mostly white audience appear black.[11] These techniques for engaging the audience were quite new in opera performance at the time. They were intended to provoke the spectators, unmask their voyeuristic position, and force them to see themselves as part of the stage action, rather than just passive observers. By removing the safety of aesthetic distance audience members were pushed to confront their own culpability in intolerance. Many times throughout her career Caldwell worked with her designers on sets that reduced the physical distance between stage and audience, but never again to make such a cogent political statement.

In this multi-media production, technology took center-stage as a means to convey off-stage actions and viewpoints and to substitute for realistic scenery. In the torture scene, the Refugee sat in a chair on the stage, while images of barbed wire and graves being dug by prisoners were shown on the screens, along with the words "Concentration Camp." The most striking stage image was at the end of Part Two when the Refugee and his Companion reach the river. In order to depict the cataclysmic flood, theatrical lighting strips were placed on the sides of the stage and harsh beams from the rows of white light were slowly raised, drowning the singers on stage.

Caldwell had invited Nono to Boston for consultation on the production. In the era of the Cold War, however, the composer (a political activist and member of the Italian Communist Party) was initially denied a visa for entry to the United States. Once the Boston press learned of the denial, they wrote editorials against the ban, and leading musicians and composers protesting the ban submitted a petition to the American Consul General of Trieste. As a result of the pressure, Nono was admitted, but by the time he arrived Caldwell had almost completed the staging. Regardless, he interpolated his notions of how to proceed, especially with the film sequences. Beverly Sills recalled in her autobiography, *Bubbles: A Self-Portrait*, that he had wanted images depicting the history of intolerance in America, particularly with respect to slavery, while ignoring examples in other countries. Tension mounted as the singers protested and eventually their demand for a more balanced slide show of examples of intolerance prevailed.[12] For her part, Caldwell willingly deferred to the composer. She thought that the production was "critical of America like it was critical of every country in the world. It was simply to lament intolerance wherever it was found."[13]

There were no riots accompanying the Boston premiere as there had been in Venice, despite the controversial images. The critics praised Caldwell's courage in premiering such a visceral and politically charged modern opera, but were divided on the merits of the composition itself. Harold C. Schonberg declared the production "a feather in the cap of the Boston Opera."[14] Others voiced strong reservations about the quality of Nono's score. For his part, the composer was unhappy with the production and later denounced it in a letter to an Italian magazine (reprinted in the *Boston Globe*). In it, he blamed its lack of greater success on the orchestra (the Boston Symphony Orchestra, led by Bruno Maderna, who critics had praised for his conducting of the BBC Symphony Orchestra at the riotous Venice premiere) for not being able to play his music.[15]

In the repertoire of the Opera Company of Boston and Caldwell's career, *Intolleranza 1960* represented a milestone. It was the most controversial opera she ever staged. Further, it incorporated a blend of film and live performance, a combination she continued to explore throughout her career. Her deference to Nono's vision underscores the fact that her directorial ego was not as strong as her belief that the composer's vision is what needed to be realized on stage. Finally, her collaboration with Josef Svoboda was a highlight in the company's history and in opera staging in America. The Boston premiere was the first time the opera had been staged using his original scenic conception. Even though not all the equipment necessary to realize Svoboda's vision completely had arrived in time to be used, he was able to incorporate his *Laterna Magika* technique, pioneered only a few years earlier, in which projected images and live actors merge into a fully integrated performance. When interviewed almost 30 years later about the experience, Svoboda remained ecstatic about the experience and recalled it as "the biggest, most complicated and best production I have ever done. It has not been surpassed since."[16]

Caldwell's determination to present a challenging selection of operas was evident in other choices she made. One of her early triumphs was her staging of the America premiere of Schönberg's *Moses and Aaron* in 1966, starring Donald Gramm and Richard Lewis. Osbourne McConathy, who worked with Caldwell on several productions at the Opera Company of Boston, conducted. This opera, which the composer had labored over for years, but never quite finished, had its first staging in Zurich in 1957, six years after his death. *Moses and Aaron* is challenging to produce effectively from both a musical and theatrical viewpoint, but Caldwell took up the task. The large-scale production, which included a chorus of 200 singers and live animals on stage, cost the company about $300,000, almost half its total operating budget at the time. The libretto (by the composer) begins with Moses being called upon by God to become a prophet. He agonizes over his shortcomings (mostly in *Sprechstimme*). Although he is able to understand the concept of God, he has difficulty communicating his understanding to the Jewish people. He must, therefore, rely on his brother Aaron, whose gift of speech (he sings throughout) enables him to communicate God's word as emotional truth, but who lacks the profound understanding of God possessed by his brother. Caldwell introduced the audience to the differences between the siblings with a powerful visual representation. She had them stand back to back, like two sides of the same coin, succinctly capturing the opposition in their natures. Much of the staging of the opera was static, and what could have been spectacular in the scenic design (by Oliver Smith) was absent. Both Robert Jacobson in *Life*[17] and Winthrop Sargeant[18] in *The New Yorker* noted unhappily that the audience was left to imagine the miracles, such as the staff of Moses turning into a snake, the slaughter of the animals, and the pillar of fire. Moreover, the orgy scene which included live animals, was staged as a rather tame pantomime. Nevertheless, *Moses and Aaron* was a bold addition to the repertoire of the company and brought the work of an important composer to America. Harold C. Schonberg had a mixed reaction to the opera itself, but he recognized the significance of its premiere: "At last," he wrote in the *New York Times*, "we have had the chance to see and hear what all Europe has been talking about for the past ten years."[19]

It was not until 1974 that Caldwell staged another large-scale work, the American premiere of Prokofiev's operatic rendering of Tolstoy's masterwork *War and Peace*. Despite the small stage of the Aquarius Theater, she and designers Helen Pond and Herbert Senn guided the spectator quickly and easily across the expanse of the action in its 13 scenes. Peter G. Davis marveled at the fact that the battle scenes, which could have slowed the action down, especially given the size of the performance area, instead "strengthened and gave sharper focus to the sweep and impact of events."[20] Critics praised her achievement in bringing the vast panorama of *War and Peace* to the Aquarius. That summer when she took the production to the large stage at the Wolf Trap National Park for the Performing Arts in Virginia, they were equally impressed. Paul Hume, writing in the *Saturday Review* pronounced it "one of the greatest demonstrations in many years of the art of directing and conducting a difficult, complex, uneven opera."[21] The highlight was a memorable "Retreat from Moscow" in the final scene. Charles Jahani wrote in *Opera* that it was "played against seemingly limitless sheets of ice and snow, [and] was the most brilliant stroke of all."[22] According to Jahani, the production "brought the noisiest ovations of the summer."[23] The success of Caldwell's staging such a demanding work in a small theater and capably translating it to a large space was surpassed only by her boldness in attempting it in the first place.

Bostonians were treated to an even rarer work in 1975 when Caldwell staged Bellini's *I Capuleti e i Montecchi*, starring Beverly Sills as Giulietta and Tatiana Troyanos as Romeo. The casting marked a return to Bellini's original conception of Romeo for a mezzo-soprano, much to the delight of Donal Henahan, in the *New York Times*, who praised the production and hailed Caldwell as "one of Boston's and the nation's prime artistic assets."[24] Andrew Porter joined in, stating in *The New Yorker* that the dramatic power of the soprano and mezzo-soprano singing in unison during the first act finale confirmed the wisdom of the choice on the part of the composer and led him to declare that Caldwell, along with Troyanos and Sills, "have now rewritten the 'Capuleti' chapter of Bellini criticism."[25] In her staging choices as well as in her casting of the vocal roles, Caldwell opted for authentic elements. For instance, she staged Bellini's version of the tomb scene, rather than the frequently substituted scene by Nicola Vaccai from his opera on the same theme. However, despite the fact that Bellini based the opera more on *Giulietta e Romeo* by Vaccai, than on *Romeo and Juliet* by Shakespeare, she added Shakespearean touches as a way of making the opera seem more familiar to audiences. For instance, Lorenzo the physician, who is a character in the libretto, became Friar Lorenzo (a.k.a. Friar Laurence from the play), a character not in the libretto. Moreover, she placed Giulietta in one of the theater boxes to sing "Oh! quante volte, Oh! quante" in order to evoke the familiar balcony scene from the play.

Clearly, Caldwell frequently strove to bring new or rarely performed operas to her audiences, but when she couldn't do that, she attempted to enliven well-known works with what some critics saw as one of her gimmicks—the infusion of traditionally excised musical passages as a way to market a "new" version of an opera. Her production of Rossini's *The Barber of Seville* in Boston starring Beverly Sills as Rosina, Alan Titus as Figaro, Bruce Brewer as Almaviva, and Donald Gramm as Dr. Bartolo, is an example of a production marred by her insistence on inserting music, even to the detriment of the dramatic effect.

The Barber of Seville is one of the few productions both conducted and directed by Caldwell that is preserved on professional quality video and is still commercially available.[26] It is not the Boston production, but rather the one at New York City Opera in 1976, with the same staging as in Boston and with Sills, Titus, and Gramm repeating their roles. The set designers, Helen Pond and Herbert Senn, created a sepia colored period inspired setting that served as a neutral backdrop to the costumes and action and gave it a fairy tale quality. Rosina's room on the upper level of the revolving unit set was enclosed not by walls, but with grille work to suggest that she was a caged bird. A swing and a costume (all costumes were by Jan Skalicky) accented with feathers completed the image. Even though the stage space in the New York State Theater at Lincoln Center was larger than the stage of the Aquarius where she had conceived it, she used familiar techniques for involving the audience. For instance, Figaro, dressed in a red and white striped jacket, made his first entrance from the back of the theater, distributing his business cards to audience members as he sang his first aria, "Largo al factotum."

As for the music of Rosina, Caldwell made two key choices. First, although the role of Rosina had been written for a mezzo-soprano she opted for soprano Beverly Sills, following a tradition of altering that vocal part to feature sopranos. Then, she made the lesson scene a showpiece for her. In the 1974 production in Boston, Caldwell included "Ah, se è ver che in tal momento" not only during the lesson, but also just before the storm scene later in the act. The scene in Boston and New York City was further extended by the inclusion of the Adolphe Adam's variations on "Ah! vous dirai-je maman." Those additions, among others, lengthened the performance time and drove Arthur Jacobs to complain in *Opera* that the result was merely a "stylistic hodgepodge that seemed to go on forever."[27] Robert Jacobson agreed in *Opera News*: "The whole proved to be a relentless soprano ego trip that made this delightful work sense-numbing in its Wagnerian length, musically diminishing in its returns."[28] Neither the fine bits of stage business that Caldwell sprinkled throughout (such as hats flying off during the stormy instrumental interlude of the second act) nor Sills' sparkling Rosina were able to win over critics.

One work that she had wanted to stage for many years finally came to fruition in 1976: *Montezuma* by Roger Sessions. She had first heard the opera in 1964 when it received its world premiere in Berlin. Afterwards, she had met the composer to discuss the possibility of a production in Boston, but it was another decade before that came to pass. At the world premiere, a major criticism of the work was that the historical figures were no deeper than pageant figures. When she presented its American premiere, she, too, had difficulty in bringing a depth of character to the work. Sessions was present for the Opera Company of Boston rehearsals and praised her preparation in the press, but the production proved disappointing. Robert Jacobson wrote in *Opera News*, "Sarah Caldwell for the first time in her long career, grappled with something she could not quite control in actuality as she undoubtedly had seen it in her head."[29] Andrew Porter was appreciative of her herculean efforts to bring the work to the stage, but acknowledged that he could not write, as he had hoped, that "at last the glory of the work was revealed."[30] Although it was not a success, it was an important addition to the repertoire of the OCB, a contemporary work, a serial composition, and a large-scale work, presented—despite the poverty of space and resources—in its entirety. No other American company produced the work until 1982 when it was given by the Juilliard American Opera Center in 1982 as an homage to Sessions, who was not only the opera's composer, but also a long time Juilliard faculty member.[31]

In a discussion of Caldwell's directorial repertoire, one production stands out, not because it is her best work or even her worst. Rather, because it was unique in being the only spoken play she ever attempted. At the height of her career, she agreed to stage Shakespeare's *Macbeth*. It was an unusual choice, to say the least, and prior to its opening the media characterized it as a great reputational risk. Nevertheless, it is one that supports a view of her creative interests as broad and challenging. The play was staged as part of a revival of the Vivian Beaumont Theater, a situation that was itself, replete with drama.

When the Vivian Beaumont Theater opened in the mid–1960s as part of the Lincoln Center for the Performing Arts in New York City, it was to be a focal point of American theater, functioning as a true repertory house for classics and new American plays. Conceived by scenic designer Jo Mielziner and architect Eero Saarinen, it was a challenging physical space in which to direct plays, given the large size of its thrust stage. Moreover, the organization itself was plagued by artistic disagreements and financial difficulties. Its first directors, Elia Kazan and Robert Whitehead, stayed only for the first year, replaced by Herbert Blau and Jules Irving. Blau resigned after one year, leaving Irving in charge until 1973, when he turned over sole leadership to Joseph Papp, the founder of the free theater in Central Park, and original producer of the enormously successful musicals *Hair* and *A Chorus Line*. Rather than follow the theater's original mission, Papp steered the audiences towards new plays, but after four years he, too, resigned, complaining that even with a financially successful production the operation of the 1,100-seat theater was so expensive that a deficit was inevitable.[32]

Immediately after Papp's departure in June 1977, the theater went dark and Richard Crinkley, formerly of the American National Theater and Academy, stepped in to develop a new plan for the theater. Crinkley's experience with the ANTA made him well aware of the difficulty in defining "American theater" and of having a single artistic director to represent it. "The richness of the classics has to be diverse one," he said. "We're working through a directorate because that's what the literature of theater demands. The world of theater should be reflected in microcosm in the directorate. Our offerings should reflect the diversity and richness of the theater itself."[33] So, instead of a one-person artistic leadership model, five prominent theater artists assumed that responsibility: Liviu Ciulei, a Romanian born theater and film director, Robin Phillips, Artistic Director of the Stratford Festival in Canada, Ellis Rabb, founder of the Association of Producing Artists, Woody Allen, actor, writer, and film director, and Sarah Caldwell. This diverse group prepared to confront the formidable task of reestablishing the Vivian Beaumont Theater as a leading theater in New York City.

Caldwell's interest in directing a play would not come as a surprise to anyone familiar with her career. Like many of her choices, it stemmed from a sense of adventure and a desire for artistic growth beyond opera staging. It also was in keeping with her tendency towards taking risks, so evident in her choice of repertoire for her company: "[I]t seemed like a really fun thing do, a really interesting thing to do, a way to sharpen myself as a director and to develop a new experience."[34] Since the early 1950s when Margaret Webster had staged Verdi's *Don Carlos* at the Metropolitan Opera, theater directors had been recruited to direct operas. Caldwell may have wanted to set a precedent and reverse the trend-from the opera house to the legitimate stage. Finally, participating in the directorate may also have been a very refreshing change from having the sole responsibility of an entire company.

It is unlikely that Caldwell and her colleagues anticipated the robust reaction to the announcement of the directorate, which ranged from enthusiastic to truculent. Papp was very vocal in his disdain, saying: "There has never been a theater run by a directorate. This proposition is unrealistic and will lead to a dead end."[35] John S. Samuel, 3rd, Chair of the Board of Directors, retorted by characterizing that position as "theatrical chauvinism."[36] Other artists came to the defense of the idea as well. Albert K. Webster, managing director of the New York Philharmonic, professed his faith in the committee, noting that "it works in the grant-making process,"[37] and Beverly Sills, newly appointed as the general director of the New York City Opera, weighed in by stating that "the diversity of people chosen makes it very stimulating. Who says it has to be one person?"[38] Regardless of the skepticism expressed, the directorate proceeded to organize its first season. The Vivian Beaumont Theater reopened after almost three years with Philip Barry's *The Philadelphia Story*, directed by Ellis Rabb, and *The Floating Light Bulb*, a new play by Woody Allen, directed by Ulu Grosbard. The unusual inclusion was the second play, Shakespeare's popular tragedy *Macbeth*, directed by Caldwell in January 1981.

Caldwell was no stranger to the drama of *Macbeth*. She had staged and conducted Verdi's *Macbeth* with the Opera Company of Boston in 1969 and again in 1976. The libretto follows Shakespeare's narrative about the Scottish noble who seizes the throne after being misled by three witches and goaded by his wife to murder the King. However, as is necessary in opera, Verdi's librettists reduced Shakespeare's shortest play from about 2,000 lines to about 600, compressing over 20 characters to 12, and five acts to four. Other changes included the elimination of the speaking lines of King Duncan and the elimination of the heart-wrenching scene in which Macbeth's hired thugs brutally murder Lady Macduff, wife of his rival, and her children. Finally, the three witches became a chorus of women.

In light of the similarities between opera and play, one might expect an imaginative and experienced director like Caldwell to make an easy transition, but that was not the case. A video recording made of one performance[39] documents one of her most flawed efforts. There are several causes for the failure of the production to achieve the emotional power and psychological depth of the play. One of the most significant was her use of the performance space. It is ironic that she was so successful in producing monumental operas on cramped stages, and yet was confounded by staging a play—originally performed on a platform that may have measured as little as no more than 20 feet wide and 15 feet deep—on a large stage. The set design, created by her longtime colleagues Helen Pond and Herbert Senn, was a serviceable constructivist structure consisting of a large open area in front of an extensive raised horizontal walkway. It created an acting area on an upper level that evoked parapets and castle walls, but the enormity of the structure was more suited to opera than to a compact psychological drama that needs physical proximity to heighten the tension for the audience.

The second difficulty appears to have been matching the style of acting to the needs of the space. Caldwell added incidental music to cover entrances across the large stage, but that just made the movement of characters seem prolonged and laborious. She added a pantomimed scene of the crowning of Macbeth, but that only made the play longer and more languid. In particular, the acting of Philip Anglim in the title role seemed at cross-purposes with the intensity of the drama. He had satisfied critics with his portrayal of John Merrick in *The Elephant Man*, in a highly acclaimed 1979 Broadway production, directed by Jack Hofsiss and produced by Richard Crinkley. He and Lady Macbeth, played by Maureen Anderman, were a youthful duo, in contract to the more seasoned actors that often portray the couple. The casting choice had the potential to connect political power with sexual power and use youth as the explanation for their rash behavior. However, a sense of urgency and sexual excitement did not translate. Frank Rich complained in his *New York Times* review that Anglim was "a strolling vacuum that swallows up the rest of the production.... [Caldwell] at times betrays her operatic roots as an iconoclastic opera impresario. Much of the staging is too stately and there are sequences that sacrifice the text for pointless visual conceits."[40]

The staging of Shakespeare's *Macbeth* had been an opportunity for Caldwell to establish herself in New York City as a legitimate stage director. Evidently, she had wanted to tackle the spoken theater repertoire, but had gotten herself into an impossible situation: directing a play wholly unsuited to a large stage in just such a space, and filling it with an operatic *gravitas* that manifested as listlessness. The result was the perception that while theater directors added viability to opera productions, an opera director in the legitimate theater had nothing to offer it. Her staging seemed only to remind critics of what they disliked about opera. The lack of critical success of *Macbeth* also underscored the problems of Vivian Beaumont Theater. It closed in July 1981, after only one season. Caldwell never directed another play.

The 1980s became more and more turbulent for Caldwell and the Opera Company of Boston, but she remained undeterred in her goal of presenting unconventional operas in unconventional ways. One of those she selected was the American premiere in 1982 of *Die Soldaten*, the only opera by Bernd Alois Zimmermann, a German composer who had committed suicide 12 years earlier. Although the work had been completed and performed for radio broadcast in the early 1960s, its first staging did not take place until 1965 at the Cologne Opera. The four-act, pantemporal drama follows the life of Marie, a young woman who becomes the victim of her own naivety, sexually abused by soldiers, and a symbol of the brutalism of society caught up in war. Zimmermann had initially envisioned the realization of this protest opera on 12 separate stages that would engulf the audience with music, action, pre-recorded sounds, and film. Although, he eventually curtailed his stage vision somewhat in order to enable it to be produced, the work remains complex and challenging. Zimmermann's 12-tone score requires 17 singers, several non-singing roles, and 18 chorus members portraying "officers and cadets whose functions are as follows: rhythmical speech and control of the 'percussion arsenal' which consist of tableware, tables and chairs."[41] It also calls for over 100 orchestral instruments and eight to nine percussionists to manage the dozens of different percussion instruments required. Caldwell's orchestra fell short by 20 musicians and some of those had to play from the proscenium boxes. It was a mammoth undertaking for a company with the OCB's resources.

Although Caldwell had succeeded with large-scale works before, this one fell short of the mark. John Rockwell expressed dismay in the *New York Times* review: "The staging, with functional scenery by David Sharir, was ambitious, busy but ineffectual. It lacked gripping tableaux and sometimes descended into muddled silliness. The lighting was inept. The multimedia scenes were either fudged or clumsy."[42] Thor Eckert, Jr., writing in the *Christian Science Monitor* agreed and advised readers to stay at home rather than be subjected to "a multimedia extravaganza that was betrayed at every point."[43] It was not a triumph as a production, but it was another example of Caldwell's determination to expand the canon and introduce American audiences to operas that other companies did not dare produce. *Die Soldaten* was not seen in America again until 1991, when the New York City Opera produced it.

At the end of the decade, despite the escalating turmoil over the artistic leadership of the OCB, Caldwell delivered one of her most powerful productions, Leonard Bernstein's *Mass*. She had known Bernstein since he had been a faculty member and she a student at Tanglewood in the 1940s. *Mass* had been commissioned for the 1971 inauguration of the John F. Kennedy Center for the Performing Arts. Although its reception by the audience had been enthusiastic, Harold C. Schonberg was one of the prominent critics who had found the work "a pseudo-serious effort ... cheap and vulgar ... a show-biz Mass."[44] The challenge for Caldwell was to overcome its reputation. She deployed all her creative resources to illuminate this eclectic work about a crisis of faith.

Caldwell's *Mass* was a production that honored the large-scale resources required by Bernstein. It included not only an orchestra, but also onstage musicians and three choirs. Pond and Senn were the designers, dividing the stage of the Opera House into three playing levels, each defined by gothic arches. Stairs led from the center of the auditorium to the main playing area, then to the second level and finally to a third where a huge crucifix hung over an altar. Caldwell staged it as the parable it was intended to be, with recognizable and representative characters. The action began with children playing together on the main stage. Suddenly, they stopped, startled by the sound of singing coming from a portable cassette tape machine that was located just out of their reach. As they listened to the "Kyrie," they displayed curiosity followed by fear, then abruptly dismissed the sound and resumed their play. At that point, the Celebrant entered, guitar in hand. He was almost tentative, yet friendly, the symbol of belief that is pure and accessible. His appeal was immediate. Suddenly dozens of people filled the auditorium and cascaded through the audience towards the stage. The Street Chorus became a town parade, replete with a band, dancers, flag twirlers and representatives of all walks of contemporary life—soldier, police officer, housewife, business man, etc.—all ready to join the Celebrant. First, they followed the Celebrant's teaching. Then they doubted him, challenged his teachings, and tested his faith.

The production included humor and timely references. One example came in the form of the Preacher in the Gospel sermon scene for "God Said." He was costumed in a tailored suit, and followed closely by a carefully coifed wife—an allusion to the charismatic televangelist of the 1980s, Jim Bakker, and his wife, Tammy Faye. The most powerful scene of *Mass* comes during the "Agnus Dei" when the Celebrant is accosted by the Crowd demanding peace, "Donna nobis pacem! Pacem! Pacem!" (Give us peace! Peace! Peace!). In Caldwell's staging, as the music intensified, the crowd pressed upon him, demanding his attention. He tried to celebrate the mass, clutching the challis of wine and bread for communion as if trying to draw strength from them.

After the subdued music of the middle section, the crowd grew more hysterical. Beginning with the tenor solo "We're not down on our knees," the rhythm of the music acted as a driving force, pushing the Celebrant up the stairs towards the crucifix on the upper level, merging the image of the Celebrant with Jesus. In a desperate attempt to continue with the Holy Communion he almost shouted "Panem!" (Bread!). Finally, he could tolerate their demands no more. He violently threw down the sacrament, destroyed the altar, and tore off his priestly robes. Under the sacred garments, he wore a plain black robe, signifying the death of the Celebrant as a celebrity. In the next section (Fraction: "Things Get Broken"), as he sang of his profound despair, he slowly removed his black robe, and revealed his true self dressed in a simple shirt and jeans—the clothing of the man he had been. Exhausted, he lay face down on the stage, until revived by a boy singing "Lauda, Laude" (Praise, Praise) as the Celebrant had done in his innocence at the beginning of the opera. The scene and the theater piece ended with the revival of the Celebrant in body and in spirit.[45]

If the reaction of the composer is any indication, then Caldwell's interpretation of Bernstein's *Mass* was a success. One of the few archival video records of her productions that has survived in reasonably good condition is the performance of *Mass* on January 29, 1989. That evening, Leonard Bernstein was present in the audience and afterwards came up to the stage during the lengthy ovation. First, he knelt before Caldwell, then hugged her warmly. Evidently, he approved of the production and so, too, did critics. Leighton Kerner of *The Village Voice* marveled that "Sarah Caldwell is at her unpredictable best when faced with the hardest challenges." His review expressed his exaltation: "A major American music-drama came into the hands of an inspired theatrical artist."[46] Richard Dyer, writing in *Opera*, was more reserved in a review that began, "Bernstein's *Mass* is a mess..." Yet he, too, acknowledged that Caldwell's concept strengthened the work by balancing the work's entertainment value with its humanistic values.[47]

Caldwell's directing repertoire extended across multiple opera periods and styles. Still, there were operas that she wanted to do, but could not bring to fruition. For example, she had staged Wagner's *Die Meistersinger von Nürnburg* (1962), and *The Flying Dutchman* (1970), but plans to present *Tristan and Isolde* with Shirley Verrett never materialized. She had staged Charpentier's *Louise* in 1971, but after having contacted the composer's nephew to discuss new sources, she wanted to revive it. That never came to pass. She was always interested in presenting new operas and even as the Opera Company of Boston was in its final days, talked of staging Kurt Weill's *Die Bürgschaft (1932)*, Virgil Thomson's *Lord Byron* (1972), and Leon Kirchner's *Lily* (1977). Despite her penchant for realism in design and character detail, she never staged the two most popular *verismo* operas, Pietro Mascagni's *Cavalleria Rusticana* or Ruggero Leoncavallo's *I Pagliacci*, although these had been planned for the American National Opera Company and for the 1991 season of the OCB.[48] She was enthusiastic about Tippet's *The Ice Break* and had wanted to initiate a Tippet Festival to premiere his other operas, but that never took root. Had she been a director who worked in different opera houses, rather than one who ran her own company, she may have been able to stage additional operas that she found interesting, but that situation may also have limited her choices.

Over the years even when financial difficulties were at their worst, Caldwell presented a repertoire that was not just varied, but also risky, even though the consequences of taking risks in Boston was evident. One case in point was the Boston Lyric Opera, which had remained conservative in its repertoire and production budget until it took a chance on Wagner's Ring Cycle in the 1982–83 season. Although the public and critics received the Cycle enthusiastically, the company incurred a substantial debt. It lost about $500,000, which took several years of more restrained programming to erase. In 1988, the Boston Concert Opera tried an operetta called *Desert Song*, composed by Sigmund Romberg with lyrics by Oscar Hammerstein II and Otto Harbach. It had been extremely popular when it opened in 1926, and the New York City Opera had revived it just the year before. Not so in Boston. Critics were unimpressed, audiences stayed away, and because of the financial loss from that one production, the company folded.[49]

Season after season Caldwell risked the survival of her company and her own career by producing a bold and unusual selections of operas. "I know I do strange and unprecedented operas," she said before the premiere of *The Balcony*, "but that's the enchantment. I like being different. I like taking the different approach."[50] Neither personal risk nor financial risk deterred her from the vision she had her for company when she founded it. Her aim had been to develop an American company, one that was not merely a derivative of European houses "but a company that is truly American."[51] If the definition of an "American opera company" is understood to mean simply a company that features American operas and artists, then she did not succeed. However, if it encompasses the qualities of individualism, audacity, and risk that are part of the American pioneering spirit, then she succeeded entirely.

Chapter 4

Preparation and Rehearsal

The total musical and theatrical experience that Caldwell sought to create for her audiences was, for her, embodied on stage in the singer. She deeply admired the complex art of the singing actor, whose vocal and physical portrayal within the context of a dramatic scene was, to her, "a very, very remarkable human achievement."[1] As a director, she was able to develop impressive conceptions and memorable visual images on stage. Yet, one of her greatest strengths was her ability to work with singers on developing compelling characters. It is that characteristic, more than her visual sensibility that links her to both Boris Goldovsky and Walter Felsenstein. Like Goldovsky, she was a coach, a mentor, and teacher. Like Felsenstein, she was a perfectionist who insisted on complex characterizations grounded in psychological realism. However, in contrast to Felsenstein and Goldovsky, she left little evidence about the thoughts and inspirations behind her choices. She never wrote detailed production notes, never sketched out her ideas or concepts for particular productions, nor did she write manuals or books to explain her directorial process for posterity. Consequently, the evidence of her process is available only through archival evidence on video and audio, occasional references in scores or in personal letters, recollections of singers and others with whom she worked, and the descriptions found in performance reviews by leading critics of the time.

As an impresario, Caldwell looked for particular assets in the singers that she hired. She preferred ones who would be open to her intense approach, who not only possessed musical gifts, but also were willing and able to contribute to the dramatic integrity of her work. She actively worked with her publicist, Edgar Vincent, to contract with singers who would do much more than simply "stand and deliver." She wanted active collaborators and, over the years, she found an impressive group of world-class artists who also wanted to work with her towards that aim. The Opera Company of Boston alumni list includes Victoria de los Angeles, Régine Crespin, Plácido Domingo, Maria Ewing, Tito Gobbi, Marilyn Horne, James McCracken, Louis Quilico, Anja Silja, Joan Sutherland, Renata Tebaldi, Tatiana Troyanos, Shirley Verrett and Jon Vickers. Many other singers—Eunice Alberts, James Billings, Edith Evans, Sarah Reese among them—returned to work with her so often that they formed a kind of repertory company.

One of the most familiar members of Opera Company of Boston casts was the bass-baritone Donald Gramm. His first appearance was in the company's premiere performance in 1958 of Offenbach's *Voyage to the Moon*, his final one was in Bellini's *Norma*, less than a month before his sudden death in 1983 at age 56. In between were more than a dozen roles including Colline in *La Bohème*, Dr. Schön in Lulu, Sancho Panza in *Don Quichotte*, Falstaff in *Falstaff*, Dr. Bartolo in *The Barber of Seville*, Don Pasquale in *Don Pasquale* and Méphistophélès in Berlioz's and Gounod's *Faust* operas. Gramm was modest about his own talent, especially as an actor, but Caldwell recognized his gifts. She told the *New York Times* in 1975 that "Donald's high level of musicianship and intelligence and his beautiful voice are attributes which make him the logical choice of a conductor.... His remarkable ability for physical characterization and his deep interest in its development make him the logical choice of a stage director. This fusion of musical and dramatic abilities sets him apart as one of the most extraordinary singing actors of our time."[2]

The singer who became associated most closely with the Opera Company of Boston was Beverly Sills. Sills was not just a local celebrity and favorite of Boston audiences; she was Caldwell's close friend as well. They began their professional association in 1962 when Sills debuted in Massenet's *Manon*. Subsequently, she sang 17 roles with the company, until her last appearance in Strauss' *Die Fledermaus*, in March 1980, the year she retired from the operatic stage and became General Director of the New York City Opera. In addition to her many live performances under the direction of Caldwell, Sills also recorded Donizetti's *Don Pasquale* and Bellini's *I Capuleti e i Montecchi* with her. She was instrumental in bringing Caldwell to the Metropolitan Opera as its first female conductor for Verdi's *La Traviata*, in which Sills sang the role of Violetta. Their collaboration on Rossini's *The Barber of Seville* at the New York City Opera the same year, remains the only commercially available video of a production directed by Caldwell. Finally, her two autobiographies *Bubbles: A Self-Portrait* (1976) and *Beverly: An Autobiography* (1987) include descriptions of their work together and attest to the satisfaction that Sills felt when working with Caldwell. It was that satisfaction, beyond any other reasons, that led Sills to declare: "Sarah always came first."[3]

In preparing her productions, Caldwell was not only interested in finding the right individual singer, but also in finding the right combination of singers for musical and dramatic reasons. Her casting choices resulted in powerful combinations, such as Joan Sutherland as *Semiramide* with Marilyn Horne as her young lover, Arsace, in a highly acclaimed production of the first performance in America of Rossini's tragedy in over a half century. In another example, Beverly Sills and Tatiana Troyanos won critical praise for their portrayal of Giulietta and Romeo in Bellini's *I Capuleti e i Montecchi*. Plácido Domingo, who sang two roles with the company during the 1966 season (Hippolyte with Sills in Rameau's *Hippolyte et Aricie* and Rodolfo with Renata Tebaldi as Mimi in Puccini's *La Bohème*) noted in his autobiography, *My First Forty Years*, that for *La Bohème* Caldwell searched diligently to bring together the perfect ensemble of singers. "Perhaps she went a little too far," he writes, hinting at the perfectionism that she was known for, "but I must admit that in the end she got what she wanted and the results were outstanding."[4]

Beverly Sills as Bellini's *Norma* in 1971. It was one of many roles that she sang with the Opera Company of Boston (photograph by Albie Walton).

Caldwell was also thoughtful and forward thinking in her casting of singers of color long before authentic and non-traditional casting were widely adopted elsewhere. In contrast to the hiring of actors in the spoken theater, where appearance is a major consideration, the selection of singers in opera has always, necessarily, prioritized the voice. A singer's range (tenor or baritone, soprano or mezzo-soprano, etc.) is the primary criteria for selection, followed by other important vocal qualities (dramatic or lyric, etc.) necessary to execute the musical and dramatic interpretation. Consequently, opera audiences have generally accepted singers whose physical characteristics do not necessarily reflect their roles, because their vocal attributes were valued more highly. They accepted the illusion even when it required the use of skin darkening make-up or prosthetic modifications of a singer's facial features to portray a character of a different race or ethnicity. Significantly, it was not until 2015 that the Metropolitan Opera broke with tradition for a production of Verdi's *Otello*. The Latvian tenor, Aleksandrs Antonenko, appeared without wearing skin darkening make-up, leaving audiences to imagine the physical contrast.[5] It is noteworthy, therefore, that decades before, Caldwell had made non-traditional casting choices for a number of lead roles.

Caldwell was particularly attentive to the role Cio-Cio San in the multiple iterations of Puccini's *Madama Butterfly* that she staged over the course of her career, opting most frequently to cast women of color. The first production in 1962 featured Asian singers as Cio-Cio San (Taeko Tsukamoto) and Suzuki (Umeko Shindo). And while some directors have typecast Asian women opera singers in these roles, Caldwell had a broader vision of their accessibility. Two years later, she selected Camilla Williams, an African American soprano, for the role, which further highlighted Pinkerton's racial abuse of Cio-Cio San and her family for an American audience. While that choice may not seem remarkable in the 21st century, it should be noted that it was less than a decade after Marion Anderson had made history as the first African American opera singer to appear at the Metropolitan Opera and only three years after Grace Bumbry's controversial appearance at Bayreuth.[6] In the 1979 revival, Sung Sook Lee sang the lead role, followed in 1990 by Yoko Wantanabe. In the 1987 revival, Caldwell cast Sarah Reese, an African American soprano, in the role, once again making a forceful social critique of Pinkerton, even though Reese did wear skin-lightening make-up for those performances. Over several years, Reese sang multiple and varied roles with the company, including Fevronia in *The Legend of the Invisible City of Kitezh* (1983), Liu in *Turandot* (1983, 1986), Donna Anna in *Don Giovanni* (1984), Agathe in *Der Freischütz* (1984), Antonia in *Tales of Hoffmann* (1984) Jenny in *Three Penny Opera* (1988), and Musetta in *La Bohème* (1989). In 1982, she sang Mimi opposite Noel Velasco, a Philippine born tenor, as Rodolfo. The *New York Times* critic, Anthony Tommasini, reminiscing in 2012, remembered that production as landmark: "For me—and surely Caldwell intended this—the racial identities of these two artists lent touching richness and humanity to the opera. Theirs was exactly the kind of impulsive love affair that would have occurred on the left bank of Paris in the world of *La Bohème*."[7]

One of Caldwell's favorite singers was Shirley Verrett who worked with her on six different productions between 1976 and 1989. She began her association with the Opera Company of Boston in Verdi's *Macbeth* (1976), then Gluck's *Orfeo ed Euridice* (1977), Verdi's *Otello* (1981), Bellini's *Norma*

(1983), Puccini's *Tosca* (1986), and Verdi's *Aida* (for all three of the company's productions: 1980, 1982, 1989). Caldwell's boldest non-traditional casting choice put Verrett on stage as Desdemona against James McCracken's Otello. The reversed racial roles presented a more psychologically complex consideration of the relationship between Desdemona and Otello than traditional casting. Another forceful and deliberate casting choice was that of Simon Estes as Figaro in *The Marriage of Figaro* in 1969 with Carole Bogard, a white soprano, in the role of Susanna. That pairing added a racial dimension to the social tensions aroused by the impending marriage and gave a stronger voice to Figaro's sense of injustice.

In rehearsal, Caldwell's process was closely tied to and anchored in the score. Often she worked from the podium, conducting the rehearsal pianist or orchestra as the case may be, while at the same time, directing the singers on the stage. She was not a physically restless director like Felsenstein, ready to pounce into a scene at any moment and demonstrate her ideas, although at times she did direct while standing or moving about the stage. Her weight limited her mobility, but that never seemed to curtail her energy or enthusiasm during rehearsals. She was a tireless worker consumed by ideas who needed to get a scene exactly right. Similar to Felsenstein, she could work for hours on a particular dramatic moment. One lighting engineer recalled working for 16 hours on a 10-minute lighting sequence between the second and third acts of *Madama Butterfly*.[8]

Caldwell's communication style was most often patient and encouraging, not at all brusque or autocratic. She was polite, even formal, referring her singers, musicians, and crew as "ladies" and "gentlemen."[9] When there were questions that she wanted to discuss or when she sensed that a singer was struggling, she would call that individual down from the stage and chat with them about their role. She could be funny, generous, and supportive. During rehearsals, she embraced a collective approach. She was more apt to say, "Shouldn't we all look at this point?" or "I think it would be better if you stood over there"[10] rather than give specific directions. Her light touch may also have been the result of her almost unique role as an opera stage director at a time when that was exceedingly rare for a woman. Women could not carry out their tasks with the same direct, authoritarian bravado that was tolerated (even expected) in their male counterparts. To do so would have appeared unseemly and unfeminine and risk ridicule or rejection. It is no accident that all the *enfants terribles* of stage directing have been men. Caldwell's way of working with singers may have been shaped by her understanding that there were certain expectations of woman director—and indirectness was among them.

Still, Caldwell could be direct when she decided to be. She told one world-class singer quite bluntly and publically during a rehearsal that she was singing flat. In another rehearsal, she chastised a singer for complaining that the character of Gilda in Verdi's *Rigoletto* was boring. That singer was Beverly Sills who wrote about the exchange in her autobiography: "actually she screamed at me—and said, 'There are no boring roles. There are only boring *singers*.'" This retort was an echo of a saying attributed to Stanislavski: "There are no small roles, only small actors." Caldwell's response jolted Sills, but the outcome was positive. Together they delved into the history and temperament of the character and Sills ultimately admitted that Caldwell "made Gilda come alive for me."[11]

Above all, Caldwell's rehearsal style was highly collaborative. She placed great importance on the process of collective creative discovery. As she explains: "In my office, we have a big blackboard. As we approach some specific opera, we start by writing questions on that board: who is such-and-such a character; why has he come to a certain place at the certain time; what is there in his background that makes him react the way he does. I make it my business NOT to know these answers when rehearsal starts. Then I get together with singers, and we try to figure out the answers together. That way, when we finally raise the curtain, everybody gets a piece of the action."[12] Caldwell was not the kind of director who came to rehearsals with a *Regiebuch* under her arm, ready to impart her instructions to the cast. She had definite ideas that she wanted to try out, but she did not cling to them because they were hers. Instead of coming to rehearsals with stage movements pre-determined or characterizations already developed, she came to rehearsals to ask questions, to suggest ideas, to try out possibilities. Her creative partnership with the singers was evident even at the beginning of her career. Lois Marshall, who sang the roles of Mimi and Tosca in the 1959 productions of *La Bohème* and *Tosca*, appreciated being part of the decision-making process. "Caldwell was wonderful. We would rehearse together and she would come up on stage and walk through every single movement she had planned for me *with* me, and we would decide whether it would work or not."[13]

Caldwell seemed to enjoy the relentless exploration of possibilities with her singers during their time together. Adelaide Bishop, who worked with Caldwell at the beginning of her career on Offenbach's *Voyage to the Moon* (1958) and Gay's *The Beggar's Opera* (1959), recalled that her questions and indirect entreaties forced singers to make choices about what to do, leaving the director to edit them into the final product.[14] In a 1981 interview, Donald Gramm spoke about how he would experiment in rehearsal, not always meeting Caldwell's approval: "Sarah ... being a close friend after all these years, is not above saying, 'Donald, what was that?'" After trying to explain his intentions, she might tell him, "Well, you didn't do anything, so do something else. So then you try that."[15] Shirley Verrett, too, wrote about how Caldwell probed her constantly with questions. She would ask, "'What are you thinking about when you sing this aria? What are you about?' I respected her musicality and, what is more important, her sense and knowledge of the theater."[16] This Socratic approach to discovering a character was a slow, plodding process that frustrated some singers who preferred to be given definite directions that they could simply execute. Yet, others found it intriguing and even inspiring. Freda Herseth, who sang the role of Rosalie in *The Black Swan*, recalls rehearsals in which she felt "free to explore" her character with Caldwell in a way that was not always possible with other directors.[17] Indeed, Caldwell wanted to do more than give singers "blocking," that is, telling them where to move and stand, or even how to think and feel as the character. She wanted to have an artistic dialogue with them as equals, and she engaged in that dialogue from her earliest production to her last.

A defining characteristic of Caldwell's productions was their psychological realism. It is a theatrical style that emerged in the late 19th century. It reveals the inner life of the character through motivated stage action. Realism was the hallmark of the Constantin Stanislavski, the founder and director of the Moscow Art Theatre. Stanislavski expected his actors to conduct field research on their characters in order to understand their history and inner life. He maintained that their knowledge of their characters could not come from merely reading or thinking about them. They needed to have personal experiences that mirrored those of their characters in order to portray them realistically on stage. One example comes from his rehearsals for a production of Gorky's *The Lower Depths*, a play about the day to day struggles of misfits in the Russian social underclass. Stanislavski sent his actors to the Khitrov Market (at that time a sordid area of Moscow) so that they could not only observe, but also interact with the kinds of people they were to play on stage.[18]

Stanislavski's techniques were intended for, and are most applicable to, realistic plays, where characters have been written as fully developed human beings with rich inner lives. Yet, he was also well versed in music and formed his Opera Studio in order to explore the application of his acting System to opera. Caldwell utilized his teachings to assist singers in developing the inner lives of their characters. For instance, when she directed the New York City Opera's production of Henze's *The Young Lord* in 1973, she sent tenor Kenneth Riegel to Central Park Zoo to observe the apes that were kept there at the time, since he was to sing the role of an ape who passes for a human being (Lord Barrat). Henze's score makes allowances for a dancer rather than the tenor to appear as the ape in the circus scene of Act I, since singing is not required at that point. Her intention, however, was to have the tenor serve in both roles, in order for him to understand each and portray each realistically. It was a directorial choice aimed at helping Riegel discover the inner truth of the role. She decided that it was not enough to be dressed as an ape in dinner clothes. She wanted him to be able to embody the physicality of the ape, not as ape, but as an ape-human. At the end of the opera, when Lord Barrat is exposed, the attention is typically on the greedy small-town residents who had accepted his eccentricities because they thought he was a rich aristocrat. However, Riegel's ability to depict an ape that had learned to be human and then was reduced to an ape again, redirected the empathy of the audience back to the ape, as if seeing Frankenstein's monster confronting his limitations.

Caldwell's insistence on psychological realism was not limited to soloists. She also attended to details for every member the chorus. One such example was in her American premiere of Berlioz's *Benvenuto Cellini* in 1975. A nine-minute film about the Opera Company of Boston entitled *What Time Is the Next Swan*, which includes clips from the rehearsals for that opera, affords a glimpse into her practice. At the end of the first act, the chorus is on stage when canon shots indicate the end of Carnival and the beginning of Lent. In the staging, all the lights were extinguished except candles carried by a few people. In the chaos of the sudden darkness, there was a frantic scramble on stage as others sought to light their candles. While the chorus rehearsed, Caldwell sat at the conductor's podium and coached them to move in a way that was genuine rather than stylized: "I don't want you to look like dancers-look like people," she said. And a moment later, "Everything you do must be logical."[19] Whether singers or dancers, the actions of the chorus were as much her concern as the actions of the principal singers and both needed to be motivated.

When Goldovsky wrote *Bringing Opera to Life*, a kind of instruction book for directors and singers, he described a meeting with a composer who told him, "I put the inner life of my characters into my music. You are the stage director. It is your business, not mine, to exteriorize this inner life, to make it visible."[20] That succinct description of the art of directing had a profound effect on Goldovsky who thereafter saw himself as a guide, leading singers deeper and deeper into the score to extricate the composer's intentions with regard to the inner lives of the characters. His approach, adopted by Caldwell, was in contrast to that of directors who view singers as puppets and expect them to follow the *director's* instructions in order to execute the *director's* concept.

Caldwell, like Goldovsky, always maintained that she guided her singers in service of the composer, even when that composer was still a novice. One illustration of that occurred during a rehearsal for the premiere of *The Black Swan*, Thomas Whitman's first opera, in 1998. The story is about a mature German woman who falls in love with the American tutor she hired to teach her daughter English. At one point in the rehearsal, it became apparent that the natural word stress on the line "There is nothing like that where I come from," sung by the tutor, did not match the rhythmic stress in the musical line. Caldwell coached the singer to counteract the mismatch, emphasizing the word "I" and tapering off in the word "come" where the young composer had inadvertently place the downbeat. While this example shows the benefit of a director who also understood the music, it is also noteworthy for the way she served as a guide to the singer. She recognized the problem and simply worked through it with him. Whitman, who was just beginning to learn how to write for the voice, was present as she addressed this difficulty. He remembered the example as a learning experience. Caldwell never criticized him, but through her coaching, demonstrated how important it was for a composer to shape the vocal line for the singer.[21]

In a Caldwell production, all action on stage needed to be justified, motivated by psychological truth. When preparing Bellini's *Norma* in 1971, starring Beverly Sills, she struggled to dramatize the reason the Druids would be mesmerized by Norma as the High Priestess: what special quality did Norma have that would have such an effect, and how could she make it obvious to the audience. She decided that Sills should be made up to look like an albino, with white hair and skin, an anomaly that could be both frightening and significant to ancient peoples and serve as a justification for their reverence of her.[22] Interestingly, when she staged it again in 1983, she cast Shirley Verrett as Norma, and achieved the dramatic justification she was seeking in the racial contrasts. Another example of her pursuit of psychological truth and realism comes from Puccini's *La Bohème*. Caldwell insisted that the artists' garret be devoid of chairs because, she maintained, that Rodolfo, being a true artist, would certainly have burned all the chairs first (contrary to the libretto) before burning the manuscript of his play, as he does in the first scene.

One of the most detailed applications of realism was in her production of *Madama Butterfly* in 1990 (captured on archival video). The stage curtain was already raised as the audience arrived and settled into their seats in the Opera House. As they did so, Markella Hatziano, in the role of Suzuki, scrubbed the floor of the house in preparation for Pinkerton's arrival. It was not a stylized scrubbing, but a thorough and systematic scrubbing of each board, from the exterior to the interior, and it was timed to be completed just as the music began. That physical preparation for the arrival of Pinkerton conveyed the depth of Cio-Cio San's commitment to the marriage and the esteem she felt for him—all before the entrance of either character.

Shirley Verrett in her autobiography, *I Never Walked Alone*, describes her work with Caldwell on Verdi's *Macbeth* in 1976 and her insistence that all stage action be justified. For instance, it struck Caldwell as implausible that King Duncan's guards would sleep through his murder. In Shakespeare's play, Lady Macbeth adds a sleeping potion to their drinks ("I have drugg'd their possets") which explains why they did not awaken. Yet, no such reference is in Boito's libretto. Caldwell's idea for Verrett was to borrow that action from her spoken theater counterpart. It not only made their oblivion to the murder taking place so near to where they slept more plausible, but also made Verdi's Lady Macbeth more culpable. Later in the opera, she heightened that culpability even further, when Lady Macbeth appeared in the third act as Hecate. In Shakespeare's play, the character appears only once, in Act III, to chastise the three witches for daring "to trade and traffic with Macbeth" and not include her. However, it is a role not mentioned at all in the libretto. Caldwell created the association as a means to underscore the absolute evil nature of Lady Macbeth.

Verrett sang *Macbeth* in Boston only a year after her triumph at La Scala in a production directed by Giorgio Strehler that she described as "highly stylized and cerebral" in contrast to Caldwell's more visceral approach.[23] As an example, she referenced the sleepwalking scene in which, as in the Shakespeare's play, Lady Macbeth struggles to rid her hands of the blood that she imagines to be on them. In Strehler's production, Lady Macbeth walked across the stage wearing a long gown with a long train dragging across the stage. The silhouette was visually striking. The weight of the fabric pulled at her like her sense of guilt. Caldwell took a more literal and literary-based approach. She coached Verrett in the pantomime of Lady Macbeth washing her hands, trying desperately to scrub away the blood she sees there, as she sings.[24] In her interpretation of *Macbeth*, Caldwell did not highlight visual images but, rather, the inner life of one of Shakespeare's most compelling female characters.

Caldwell respected and replicated Felsenstein's deep character research, his thoroughness in rehearsal, his attention to details of motivation, his uncompromising pursuit of the right action, his work with actors in exploring the off-stage life of their characters. He insisted that opera, or in his words, "music theater," must "turn music-making and singing on the stage into a communication that is convincing, truthful, and utterly essential.... Music theater exists when a musical action with singing human beings becomes a theatrical reality that is unreservedly believable."[25] He insisted that all actions on the stage be motivated, not empty or puppet like, but that they stem from a need so strong that the character cannot express him/herself in any other way but through singing. His was psychological realism blended with an equal and detailed attention to the interplay of music and drama.

Although Caldwell was certainly serious and driven in rehearsal, she also found great joy in directing. In large part, it stemmed from re-creating a world "with real people who really lived, who really sat in particular type of chair and wore particular kinds of clothes and had a particular set of problems.... It's like being in another world for a little while and that is interesting, that's fun."[26] She immersed herself in learning about the cultures and historical periods of the operas she staged. For instance, in order to prepare for Puccini's *Madama Butterfly*, she studied Japanese culture. Every detail was important to her, not just to create a visually complete world, but also to create a realistic one where everything and every action related and made sense. That reason caused her to alter the staging of the preparations that Cio-Cio San and Suzuki make for Pinkerton's return during "Tutti i fior?" In the libretto, Cio-Cio San orders Suzuki to bring in all the flowers from the garden to decorate the house. Yet, instead of strewing them about the house as the libretto describes, Caldwell directed them to engage in *ikebana*, the Japanese art of flower arranging, and captured the formal elegance expressed by the harmonies of the duet. This simple choice revealed Cio-Cio San's joyful anticipation at her husband's return, but also underscored her adherence to formality and ceremony. It was a character revelation. At the conclusion of the opera, when Cio-Cio San decides to take her own life, the audience can understand her choice more clearly. Her suicide was not an emotional response to rejection, or a selfless act, but a formal and culturally anchored response to the shame she felt.

Caldwell's focus on detail heightened the normal level of intensity of the rehearsal period and sometimes caused a great amount of friction and anxiety. When she presented *Fidelio*, she delayed the beginning of the performance by a half hour because she would not stop giving stage directions. No detail was too small for her attention. In her autobiography, Beverly Sills described an errand to an antique music box shop in New York City to pick up a mechanical bird for the Opera Company of Boston's production of *The Barber of Seville*. Caldwell's idea for Rosina was that she was a caged bird herself, who in turn had a caged bird as a pet. She wanted to have the bird sing during the production so that Rosina could imitate it. While at the shop, Sills dutifully telephoned Caldwell and played the bird calls into the phone then sang into the phone until Caldwell decided on the one that had the exact sound she was looking for.[27]

There were singers who were exasperated by Caldwell's perfectionism, but others who appreciated the extent to which she attended to details overlooked by other directors. They understood her desire to "get it right" and to rehearse for hours, or change her mind multiple times—even when an audience was waiting—in order to realize her vision. Phyllis Curtin, who sang several roles with the Opera Company of Boston, said, "She stimulated and enlivened the thinking of those of us who worked with and were pushed by her. Often relentlessly and maddeningly!"[28] Joan Sutherland, who was not known as a strong singing actor, nor a singer who tolerated long rehearsals, once stayed for 12 hours while she and Caldwell worked on the mad scene in *I Puritani*.[29] It is significant, therefore, that Sutherland felt a high degree of satisfaction when working with Caldwell: "I know how rare real consideration for a production is. As a matter of fact, the only place I have ever found it was with the Boston Opera Group when I worked with Sarah Caldwell on a production of *I Puritani*. I have never duplicated the feeling that experience gave me. There was very little money and all of us had to think—I mean really think—about everything we did."[30]

When Andrew Porter observed Caldwell in rehearsal, he was reminded of Peter Brook, the British director who has a reputation for collaboration and stylistic simplicity. Porter wrote: "[T]here is the same fiercely accelerating intensity of concentration toward the first performance, which can be tough on a cast, and yet lift it to fresh achievement; the same gift for disconcerting last-minute improvisations that suddenly refine the expression of a long-held, long-pondered idea. In the work of both directors, preliminary research to the deepest foundations of a piece does not preclude spontaneity in its execution."[31] The norm was (and continues to be, especially in opera) for the director to have most of the planned in advance of working with the singers. Ostensibly, it is to save precious rehearsal time, but it suggests a view of stage rehearsals and the singers' role in the creative process as almost tangential to directing. Brook was known for rejecting the manufactured approach to directing in favor of a more collaborative one in the spoken theater. Caldwell practiced it in opera.

At the Opera Company of Boston, Caldwell's long rehearsals spent exploring characters or in working out technical details often resulted in productions that were highly effective. Yet, the process was often marred by her weaknesses. There were times when she exhibited an almost crippling inability to make a decision. Her tendency to ask questions could serve as a way of deepening the exploration of character. Yet, it could also appear contrived, used as a way to buy time because she did not know what she wanted. Creative paralysis could surface even in the face of an apparently simple directorial decision. On one occasion, assistants moved two topiaries that were part of the set decoration in *Der Rosencavalier* from one location on the stage to another, and *another*, and *another*, until she finally settled on exactly where they were to remain. Such an obsession with a decorative detail that most directors would not have seen as central to the action contributed to slowing down the rehearsal process and frustrating those involved.

The difficulty Caldwell had in making up her mind was compounded by her tendency to constantly change her mind. One designer admitted to designing a unit set for a touring production specifically as a way to prevent her from changing her mind about how the set was to look. Even when time was of the essence, she vacillated, disregarding all other considerations, until she was satisfied. With so many changes, it is not surprising to find critics complaining, as Robert Baxter did in 1975 about her *Falstaff*, that some scenes look *under* rehearsed.[32] Even Beverly Sills was shell-shocked after a rehearsal for *Norma* that lasted until four o'clock in the morning. Yet, she admitted that the experience with Caldwell helped her learn the role deeply[33] and she returned the work with her many times over her career. Shirley Verrett, too, was another singer who seemed immune to the aspects of Caldwell's process that frustrated others. In her autobiography Verrett alluded to the director's tendency to waiver, but wrote kindly, "She could always put an entirely different spin on various opera roles and productions. She is gifted individual and a fabulous musician. This was the reason I happily returned to Boston each time I was invited."[34]

Caldwell frequently complained that she did not have enough rehearsal time to work on her productions, but former colleagues have pointed out that most of her difficulties stemmed from how she used the time allotted. She was chronically disorganized, but obsessively determined to do what she wanted to do regardless of the time required—as in the example of *Fidelio* described above. Over the years, various stage managers tried in vain to develop rehearsal schedules with carefully restricted blocks of time to keep her on task. Yet, schedules were quickly discarded because she directed according to her own clock, focusing her energy on whatever she thought needed attention at any given time. There were even times when—for no known reason—she did not come to rehearsal at all. It happened frequently enough that company members began a game of putting quarters in a cup as their bets on whether she would show up or not. The only rehearsal schedules to which she adhered closely were those with full orchestras, because those were so costly. The remainder of the rehearsal period was unpredictable. Caldwell did not just have difficulty adhering to time limits, however, she also had difficulty adhering to budgets. The Opera Company of Boston Board had once attempted to implement a "control budget" whereby it would need to approve all production spending,[35] but that plan did not succeed. Caldwell simply did not seek their approval prior to spending on productions. As Houston Grand Opera General Director, David Gockley, observed after she had conducted Donzietti's *Don Pasquale* there, "No one controls Sarah, but Sarah."[36]

Opera Company of Boston rehearsals could be inspiring, but just as frequently, they could dissolve into endless hours of disorganization that led to frustration and tension. To give one example, when Caldwell staged Kurka's *The Good Soldier Schweik* in the Rockwell Cage athletic facility on the Boston College campus (see Chapter 5), there were about 40 students involved in the performance and another 25 who participated through publicity, sales, stage crew, etc. Afterwards, the students were asked to reflect on their involvement in writing. They wrote about the profound and humanizing experience of working on an opera for the first time, but also complained bitterly about the pandemonium that they witnessed. Among their complaints was the fact that they were required to be on call 12 hours a day, yet only spent a small portion of that time rehearsing. Another was that when the time came for the set pieces to be moved from the MIT campus to the Boston College arena, that work did not begin until 10 p.m. Finally, they complained of a duplication of effort and pervasive miscommunication.[37]

Whether an Opera Company of Boston rehearsal was in an unconventional venue such as a hockey rink, or at the Opera House, disorder reigned. And while Caldwell's personal style was responsible for much of it, there were other reasons as well. For example, since the Opera House was non-union she employed less-experienced production assistants. She viewed them as apprentices who could learn her philosophy and methods. Moreover, their wages could be lower compared to unionized personnel or even artists who were more experienced. To these young artists she was a mentor who provided the kind of training they could not receive elsewhere, and many took that experience forward to establish successful careers elsewhere. Still, inexperienced crew members and unregulated working conditions most certainly contributed to some of the disorganization and even to some dangerous situations. In 1981, a company report described 12 major accidents that season. These included a 32-foot A-frame extension ladder falling into the orchestra pit, a fire igniting in a power box, a portion of a lighting instrument falling and striking a supernumerary, a carpenter falling 12 feet into a concrete pit during the load-in, and the collapse of the entire set of *Don Pasquale* during the striking of the set. The report pointed out that "opening night performances could be much better if the crew were able to have a full night's sleep prior to the performance" but that "technicians often found themselves in a state of such fatigue that they were unable to remember what they were to do on the next shift, in spite of the fact that they had rehearsed the shift five or six times in the previous three days."[38] Almost all of the accidents described, the writer of the report concluded, could be attributed to fatigue, an inexperienced crew, and/or a lack of proper supervision.

While much of the chaos associated with Opera Company of Boston rehearsals can be explained by Caldwell's personality and work habits, it does bear remembering that she wore multiple hats within the organizations. As a result, there were often business matters and administrative tasks that she needed to address before, during, or after rehearsals. Rarely could she simply focus on rehearsing in a way that a freelance director could. In later years, she admitted that she had carried too much of the responsibility for the organization, done too many things. Whether by choice or necessity, she rarely agreed to sharing or delegating responsibilities that would have enabled her to focus more on her stage directing and alleviated some of the disarray of rehearsals.

Caldwell in rehearsal could be collaborative, intense, imaginative, and supportive. She could also be disorganized, obsessive about details, and careless about time. She seemed to thrive on chaos, which at times created an exhilarating experience for some, but a frustrating and even dangerous environment for others. She was a polarizing figure in rehearsal who inspired and, not infrequently, exasperated her artistic team. Most, however, agreed that "the only thing worse than working for Sarah was not working for Sarah."[39] Although she was collegial, she served the opera above all. Everything else—time, money, a private life, and even personal well-being—she sacrificed for opera. She surrounded herself with ambitious young people and world-class artists who genuinely admired her and wanted to collaborate with her again and again. Both groups recognized her gifts and shortcomings and also the uniqueness of what she offered. Each wanted to tackle the challenging repertoire she chose and to engage with her in the deep character exploration and musical analysis that was not the practice in other opera companies or typical of other opera directors. In this way, Caldwell advanced and vindicated the vision of Felsenstein and Goldovsky, and elevated dramatic values in American opera.

Chapter 5

Spaces

From the late 1950s until the early 1990s—the entire tenure of the Opera Company of Boston—the city was without an appropriate performance space for an opera company. As noted in an earlier chapter, that had not always been the case. The original Boston Opera Company occupied a fine opera house that had been built especially for it, but the structure had met an ignominious end. After the failure of the company in 1917, the building was sold to the Schubert Corporation, a continuation of the entity formed by the Schubert brothers, producers and owners of many theaters across the United States in the early part of the century. It served touring companies, and later Goldovsky's New England Opera Theater. In September 1957, the Boston Building Department determined that the 48-year-old Opera House needed significant structural repairs. Whether it actually was in dire condition has been the source of some speculation, since its demise came about so quickly. Nevertheless, the Schubert Corporation wanted the city of Boston to purchase the property and take on the burden of its repair, but the city declined the request. Consequently, the Corporation sold it to a local construction company for the sum of $135,000, which then sold it to Northeastern University for $160,000.[1] With the shortsightedness that characterized many urban renewal projects of the time, the president of the university announced his plan to raze the building and build dormitories: "[T]his same site will continue to serve our community constructively, especially the young people of this area both present and future."[2] In the summer of 1958 (when the newly formed Opera Group made its debut), the original Opera House was marked for demolition. By late autumn, it was gone.

Since the demolition of Boston's Opera House had occurred soon after the founding of The Opera Group, Caldwell was forced to seek out alternative performance spaces, a predicament that was repeated multiple times during the first two decades of the company's existence. Most frequently, she rented former vaudeville houses and movie theaters, but she also produced operas in such unconventional venues as a gymnasium, a hockey rink, and the Boston Cyclorama. Opera performances in these kinds of spaces with all their attendant complications were almost unprecedented for a professional opera company and unthinkable for most professional stage directors. Repeatedly Caldwell faced the prospect of producing operas on small stages with limited backstage areas, non-existent orchestra pits, unsophisticated or unavailable technology, and a myriad of other challenges. Yet, she refused to concede to these difficulties. Her response was to create productions that transcended their spaces, and to build bridges (literal and figurative) between the performers and the spectators. She recalled in her memoir, "We were by necessity creative in selecting and adapting our productions to spaces that were available to us. That forced us to do some of the most innovative staging of our experiences."[3] Indeed, she demonstrated that creating memorable and important opera productions could include new technologies, but they did not depend upon technically advanced theaters, or for that matter, on theaters at all.

Initially, The Opera Group used the Fine Arts Theater, located on the upper level of the Loew's State Theater building complex on Massachusetts Avenue. The complex, built in 1922, also housed the Donnelly Theater, a ballroom, and a bowling alley. The Fine Arts Theater had a small stage at one end and may have been used as a rehearsal space for the larger theater, but it was eventually developed into an intimate art film house with 656 seats. Although Caldwell dubbed it the "Little Opera House" with some affection, it was too small for that use. The company's first performance there on January 29, 1959, was of Puccini's *La Bohème*. In order to enlarge the performance area, Caldwell and set designer David Hay extended the footprint of the stage, building out into the house, causing the orchestra to be split, with musicians sitting on either side. Reconfiguring the stage area to acquire more performance space was characteristic of many of Caldwell's productions. Its application in this early production shows that it was an idea she had independent of the input of later stage designers. In this instance, her attempt at overcoming the limitations of the tiny space was scoffed at by one reviewer who thought that the artists' garret looked more like a tool shed.[4] Evidently, a "Little Opera House" was not going to be viable for an opera company driven by Sarah Caldwell's expansive vision.

The company's next two operas, Rossini's *The Barber of Seville* and John Gay's *The Beggar's Opera*, were presented in the Boston University Theatre on Huntington Avenue. It had opened in 1925 as the home of a repertory theater company, but subsequently functioned as a movie house for two decades after the Great Depression until it was purchased by the university. Since it had been built for spoken plays, it lacked an orchestra pit and the necessary stage depth and breadth for opera performances. It was not a long-term solution.

The following season, the company moved to the Donnelly/Back Bay Theater, the downstairs portion of the Loews State Theater complex that also housed the Fine Arts Theater/Little Opera House. The Donnelly/Back Bay, which had been designed in 1922 by Thomas W. Lamb, was originally an opulently furnished movie house that could accommodate 4,000 spectators. By 1959, however, the era of the giant movie "palaces" was over. It was closed, acquired by the Archdiocese of Boston and subsequently renamed the Donnelly Memorial until 1963. Then the Archdiocese of Boston sold it to the Church of Christ, Scientist and it became the Back Bay Theater. At that time, the city of Boston had a number of former vaudeville theaters and movie palaces that were used for live performances. The main drawback of using these venues for opera, however, is that they cannot accommodate two fundamental needs: an orchestra and a chorus. The orchestra pit in a vaudeville house needed only to hold a handful of musicians and the side wings needed only to accommodate the next act, not dozens of chorus members awaiting their entrance. In addition, the depth of the stage in a movie house tends to be very shallow. Even in a vaudeville house, there was no need for any substantial depth because scenery was often limited: a simple backdrop or even nothing at all.

Since the Opera Company of Boston had no opera house and there was no plan on the horizon to build one, Caldwell produced operas where and how she could. It is noteworthy that the lack of a proper opera house did not lead to a compromised repertoire. In fact, she staged the most challenging operas of her career prior to purchasing the Opera House. A variety of unlikely and even inhospitable performance spaces were transformed through Caldwell's imagination and the skill of distinguished designers who she brought to Boston. Among them was Wolfgang Roth, a designer who began his career under the German directors Erwin Piscator and Bertolt Brecht. He designed the lights and sets for Verdi's *La Traviata* and *Otello* during the 1960 season. Another was Ming Cho Lee, the American designer who created the scenery and lighting for Puccini's *Madama Butterfly* in 1962, a production Caldwell presented seven times, all using the same unit set by Lee. Her admiration for the work of the Komische Oper led her to invite Rudolf Heinrich to design Berg's *Lulu* in 1964 (shortly after he had designed it for the Santa Fe Opera and a year before he first worked at the Metropolitan Opera). He returned a number of times to the OCB to collaborate with Caldwell, adding Offenbach's *The Tales of Hoffmann* (1965), Mussorgsky's *Boris Godunov*

(1965), Puccini's *La Bohème* (1966), *Tosca* (1967), Verdi's *Macbeth* (1969), and Mozart's *The Marriage of Figaro* (1969) to their list of collaborations prior to his premature death in 1975. Finally, the acclaimed Czech designer, Josef Svoboda, designed Nono's *Intolleranza 1960* (1965), giving American audiences the opportunity to see his innovative integration of film and live action onstage for the first time.

Caldwell the director was always eager to embrace anything that was new, whether that was a new opera, a new discovery about an existing opera, or a new stage technology. One of her enduring interests was in the way video images could complement three-dimensional scenery and heighten the drama. The incorporation of multi-media effects became a frequent element in her work, beginning with Nono's *Intolleranza 1960* (1965) and continuing until Whitman's *The Black Swan* (1998). Her use of film in several productions was possible because of her association with Richard Leacock, who she had met when she was developing a conception for Berg's *Lulu* for the American National Opera Company. She had examined Berg's notes and found that he had sketched outlines for brief films that he had wanted as part of the scenic design of the opera. The idea intrigued her, so she called on Leacock to assist her in developing those sequences. At first he was reluctant, given that he made documentaries, not films for opera productions. However, he agreed to meet her in New Hampshire where she was working, in order to discuss the project. Caldwell's unconventional interpersonal style and collaborative spirit appealed to Leacock immediately. His description of that initial meeting is worth quoting at length for its insight into her personality and process:

> A vacated boarding school. A stream of people arriving; important people, singers, conductors, designers ... public relations people, journalists ... all waiting to talk to Sarah Caldwell. I ran into a friend from Harvard; we had worked together on a theater piece as undergraduates; he too was waiting for Sarah; we chatted. We chatted a lot. It seemed hopeless. Chaos. I looked at my watch and decided that I had better things to do in life, and asked about a flight to Boston. Miss Caldwell suddenly introduced herself and asked if I could wait till late that night so we could meet and talk ... midnight! I waited and we met on the school stage. Sarah Caldwell and I talked for three hours with no interruptions. I have, since then, worked on many projects with her. I have never known her to dismiss an idea out of hand. She never says, "Oh that's corny...." You take every idea and you try it out ... and you go on to another, until something begins to build. Curiously, I have very rarely encountered people with this open, playful and productive bent of mind. We had a wonderful time.[5]

Leacock's description of their meeting speaks eloquently to why he and other designers wanted to collaborate with her. Her enthusiasm for new ideas, her support for their creativity, and her trust in them outweighed whatever frustrations and chaos they encountered as part of her process. In addition to his work with Caldwell on *Lulu*, Leacock collaborated with her on *The Flying Dutchman* (1970), *The Good Soldier Schweik* (1970), *The Ice Break* (1979), and *Die Soldaten* (1982). He also filmed Caldwell in rehearsal with the Ural Philharmonic Orchestra in 1996 for a documentary entitled *A Musical Adventure in Siberia*.

Many of Caldwell's productions bear the creative stamp of two designers, Helen Pond and Herbert Senn, who collaborated with her on almost 50 productions that spanned every period and every style of opera. Pond and Senn had met while attending Columbia University and formed a personal and professional relationship that lasted more than 60 years. Together, they designed hundreds of plays, musicals, and operas. Their work overlapped in many respects, but Pond specialized in painting, Senn in building architectural elements. They were closely affiliated with the Cape Playhouse, a long-standing professional summer theater on Cape Cod, from 1956 until 1994, designing productions there in the summer and for the Opera Company of Boston during its winter season. They accepted their first commission to design Mozart's *The Abduction from Seraglio* at the Back Bay Theater for Caldwell in 1965. Their experience designing together for the Cape Playhouse with its quick turnaround time for a packed short season may have stood them in good stead to work in Caldwell's company, where time was a luxury they did not have. Their strength and greatest contribution to the company was in finding creative solutions to overcome the challenges of the inadequate spaces in which Caldwell staged operas.

In 1966, Pond and Senn designed baroque sets for Caldwell's American premiere production of Rameau's *Hippolyte et Aricie* at the Back Bay Theater. The libretto (by Abbé Simon-Joseph Pellegrin) is based on Racine's *Phèdre*, which explores the theme of illicit love (in this case a woman in love with her stepson), first treated in *Hippolytus* by Euripides and later in *Phaedra* by Seneca. The score calls for a ballet and a number of supernatural elements, but the area of the Back Bay Theater stage was very small. Therefore, Caldwell and her designers adopted the space maximizing strategy they used many times afterwards: "We built a ramp out around the orchestra pit. We built stairs from the stage to the ramp, providing massive areas for activity. We used boxes that were quite high on either side of the stage for part of the set, creating places to which the cast could go that they could not have reached on a conventional stage."[6] Together, they created the space they needed for the production. Their set design, drawing heavily upon baroque spectacle, included a cloud machine to create Olympus for Diana and Jupiter, a wave machine inspired by drawings in Diderot's Encyclopédie, and a sea monster, sent by Neptune at the request of Thésée to devour Hippolyte as a punishment for what he believed was the attempted rape of his wife. The production was performed before sold out houses and was very well received by critics. Despite all its spatial shortcomings, the Donnelly/Back Bay Theater was the Opera Company of Boston's home for almost 10 years and over 40 productions.

The loss of the original Opera House in Boston may not have been significant before the Opera Company of Boston was established in the late 1950s. However, by the mid–1960s, Caldwell had put Boston on the international opera map with world-class productions, starring world-class singers, making the absence of an appropriate venue widely known. In 1967, Massachusetts State Representative Charles Iannello sponsored *Bill 1130*, which would fund a $15 million state opera house—a so-called "baby Lincoln" to rival the newly completed Lincoln Center for the Performing Arts in New York City.[7] Michael Steinberg, music critic for the *Boston Globe*, argued passionately that the amount of opera activity around Boston (Boston University, the New England Conservatory, the Boston Conservatory, the Metropolitan touring shows, and the Opera Company of Boston) justified a proper space.[8] Despite evident need, neither Caldwell's persuasive abilities, legislative initiatives, media attention, nor the challenge of civic one-upmanship was enough to spur the building of an opera house in Boston. *Bill 1130* was defeated and the possibility of a new opera house in the city remained as remote as ever.

The lack of support for a new opera house left the Opera Company of Boston in a precarious predicament. In 1969, the Back Bay Theater was scheduled to be torn down in order to make way for an apartment complex, so the company had to look for other available venues. For one season, it moved to the 1500-seat Schubert Theater on Tremont Street. The Schubert had been built in 1910 primarily for Shakespearean productions, and although it did accommodate musicals, the OCB did not remain for long. Caldwell staged only four productions (a Bartók trilogy, *Lucia di Lammermoor*, *Macbeth*, and *The Marriage of Figaro*) there before looking for another performance space.

In order to secure a venue in which to perform the following season, Caldwell applied to recently established National Foundation on the Arts and Humanities for a $100,000 grant to form the Eastern Opera Consortium. The proposal was to establish an alliance between the Opera Company of Boston and seven area colleges (Boston College, Boston University, The College of the Holy Cross, Northeastern University, Tufts University, the University of Massachusetts Boston, and the University of Rhode Island).

The intent was to "bring about closer cooperative ties between a professional artistic organization and the faculty and students of the participating schools."[9] The benefits to the institutions were that they had a professional company in residence and opportunities for students not only to observe, but also to participate in productions. The benefits to the company were that it had students who could assist with the productions and access to the performance spaces on the different campuses. Those spaces, however, were no better than the movie palaces and vaudeville theaters it had previously used. They included a concert hall, a gymnasium, and a hockey rink. Caldwell later referred to this period with some nostalgia as her "gypsy years" or her "magic wandering years."[10]

The plan for the consortium in its initial phase was to rehearse and perform *The Flying Dutchman*, *The Daughter of the Regiment*, and *The Good Soldier Schweik* during the winter of 1970. The Kresge Auditorium was the venue for Wagner's *The Flying Dutchman*, which included members of choral groups from Boston College and the University of Massachusetts Boston. Finnish architect Eero Saarinen had designed the auditorium 15 years earlier as a multifunctional space. It included a concert hall seating about 1200 spectators, a small theater that held about 200, a rehearsal space, and dressing rooms. In the stark, modern interior of the concert hall, with its low stage, lack of an orchestra pit, and ocean like waves of green and blue seats, Caldwell brought to life the romantic myth of the man condemned to sail around the world until redeemed by the true love of a woman.

Since no scenery could be attached to the walls of the concert hall, Pond and Senn designed a suggestive, multi-level set, with a projected image of the Dutchman looming over the background (the contribution of Richard Leacock and the MIT film department). Every time that Senta looked at the portrait, it increased in size as if growing in importance in her psyche. Caldwell and her designers did not conceive of the audiences as passive observers, but rather as part of the opera, intimately involved in the action by their presence in the performance space itself. Robert Baxter was enthralled with Caldwell's ability to engage the audience, which he described in his *Opera* review: "The Dutchman made his entrance on the left side of the auditorium from a choir loft made to represent a ship that opened into and engulfed the audience. This bold stroke intensified the sense of immediacy and intimacy that had been created when the ship's crew walked into the audience to mime its docking and then sat down in the aisles for the remainder of the act. As a result, the Dutchman's monologue, always musically effective, became at this performance a terrifying emotional experience. This was opera at its most exciting."[11] At the end of the opera, the sinking of the Dutchman's ship was

Interior of the Kresge Auditorium on the campus of the Massachusetts Institute of Technology in Cambridge. Caldwell staged Wagner's *The Flying Dutchman* there in 1970. A concert hall was no substitute for an opera house, but she made it work (photograph by Albie Walton).

captured in a video image projected onto the side walls of the theater, a practical solution to performing in a space that could not easily hold a chorus, an orchestra, or large set pieces. Most importantly, however, is the insistence from Caldwell that she did not agree to the design for its own sake: "[I]t was legitimate because I feel we were trying, aesthetically and intellectually, not to do something that would create an impression just for its own sake, but rather to find a way to express this work in this theater. In a different theater, in different circumstances, the ideas would come in a different way."[12]

The next production of the consortium, *The Daughter of the Regiment*, took place on the basketball court of the Cousens Gymnasium at Tufts University in Medford, Massachusetts. The Tufts University Navy Drill Team supplemented the chorus of soldiers and performed a drill routine as part of the production. There could be no denying the fact that the performance was taking place on a basketball court. Yet, it had features such as a wooden railing and a staircase to an upper balcony that suggested the architecture of an early 19th-century village in the Tyrol region. Therefore, Caldwell worked together with Pond and Senn to make the most of those elements, rather than trying to hide them. Permanent features such as the door to the men's locker room became the entrance to Marie's house with the addition of a façade. The railing and staircase remained exposed because they suggested elements of a country cottage. The physical space was able to be adapted to a certain extent for the opera, but not everything in the space could be incorporated or changed. Beverly Sills, who sang the role of Marie, recalled that on the day of the dress rehearsal there was a track and field meet in the same athletics complex with all its accompanying noise, including the occasional sound of the starting pistol going off, followed by the sound of pounding feet![13]

One of the most memorable conclusions of a Caldwell production came at the end of the opera. Marie and her fiancé Tonio left in a small cart pulled by a donkey, the chorus danced its way down the aisles, and members of the audience on the gymnasium bleachers created a giant French flag by holding up the red, white, or blue placards that had been given to them prior to the start performance. This production of *The Daughter of the Regiment* confirmed that an artistically sound production with broad audience appeal could be achieved outside of the traditional opera house. Beverly Sills remembered it in her autobiography as "the most spectacular production of that opera I've ever seen."[14]

Both *The Flying Dutchman* and *The Daughter of the Regiment* were examples of Caldwell's ability to master unlikely performances spaces. They were also characteristic of her practice of reaching out to audiences both literally and aesthetically. She and her designers intentionally extended the area of the stage to the side boxes, into the auditorium, and built platforms and ramps to connect the stage and the auditorium. Certainly, these were deliberate attempts to overcome the limitations of stages that were simply too small. Yet, they were decisions of historical importance in opera stage directing. They diminished (and sometimes erased completely) the physical gulf of the orchestra pit that separates performers and spectators in a traditional opera house. That degree of intimacy at an opera performance was highly unusual with works in the standard repertoire.

The consortium brought together the students, the company, and resources in multiple ways. For instance, the production of *The Good Soldier Schweik* was realized at the Rockwell Cage, an athletic facility on the MIT campus. The permanent hardwood floor that is now in place was, at that time, removable and underneath was a dirt track. Students in the Arts Management program at Boston College worked on the production. And

A publicity pamphlet for the production of Kurka's *The Good Soldier Schweik* at the Rockwell Cage, one of the most unusual spaces in which Caldwell produced opera (photographs by Albie Walton).

since it included multi-media elements in the design, Richard Leacock was part of the design team and students were part of the crew. Caldwell divided the seating area into six sections separated by aisles for performers and golf carts (disguised as army vehicles) to move around freely. At the center of the arena, she placed a low stage, measuring about 16 by 30 feet that she divided into three separate playing areas. Each of those areas was then bifurcated by a screen that could be raised or lowered during the performance. At any given time a particular section of the audience might be watching live action, or a shadow play of the action, a projection of the action on film, or a separate film completely.

Pond and Senn were masters in designing for spaces that were awkward or small, and in ones that lacked the technical capabilities of most modern opera houses. One such example was their work in Boston's historic Cyclorama. The Cyclorama was a circular structure opened in 1884 as an entertainment venue. The entertainment was "The Battle of Gettysburg," a massive painting on a canvas measuring 50 by 400 feet that surrounded visitors with an epic depiction of that turning point in the American Civil War. After a few years, public interest waned and the building was used for boxing matches, a roller-skating rink, a manufacturing space, and the Boston Flower Exchange from 1923 until the late 1960s when the Boston Redevelopment Authority reclaimed it for an arts center.

The Opera Company of Boston performed Charpentier's *Louise* in 1971 in the Cyclorama. As she often did for her productions, Caldwell researched atmospheric elements for the design with the same degree of fervor she applied to musical and dramatic research. She, along with Pond and Senn, traveled to Montmartre (a district in the northern part of Paris) to immerse themselves in the Paris of the composer's time and to watch the sunrise they subsequently recreated for the prelude to Act II.[15] The partnership between Caldwell and Pond and Senn was close and productive. Ideas emerged after long conversations in seclusion and were brought to fruition (sometimes to the amazement of members of the company) despite the chaos of the rehearsal period and limited funds. What Pond and Senn particularly enjoyed about their work with the OCB was the freedom of working in a non-union house where they were in control of executing their designs and changing them at will. One of their practices was to create models of the set they were working on. Caldwell liked to see the set in three dimensions as she planned her staging. She spent hours with their models, considering her staging options. That period of contemplation did not solidify her ideas, but rather generated multiple options that she then explored during the rehearsal process.

The next home for the Opera Company of Boston was another former vaudeville house, the Aquarius Theater. There the company mounted 26 productions, including seven American premieres. The Aquarius had opened in 1852 as the Boston Music Hall, seating about 2500 patrons who came to hear the Boston Symphony Orchestra until Symphony Hall was built in 1900. In 1906, it was renamed the Orpheum and later, redesigned by Thomas W. Lamb, converted to a movie house. The auditorium was expanded to accommodate 3300 seats, eliminating the orchestra pit and diminishing the stage depth to only 25 feet.[16] In 1971, the theater re-opened as the Aquarius. Once again, the theater proved a challenging space for opera production. Yet, there she staged one of her most imaginative and important ones—Berlioz's *The Trojans*, in 1972.

In 1955, Boris Goldovsky's presentation of *The Trojans* in Boston with the New England Opera Theater, did not receive much acclaim beyond its importance as an American premiere. Seventeen years later, Caldwell's interpretation of the work solidified her reputation as one of the most important opera directors in America. Almost from the beginning, however, there were obstacles in her way—some of her own making. For instance, when she tried to secure the performing rights for the 1969 Barenreiter edition of the opera it was unavailable because it had already been contracted for a concert version to be performed at the same time elsewhere. Her only alternative was to have the original manuscript in the Bibliothèque Nationale microfilmed and to create her own performance edition. Then, rather than follow the precedent established by Goldovsky in editing the score in order to try to improve the original work, she staged and conducted the American premiere of the opera in its entirety.

Caldwell understood that many of the members of her audience would be unfamiliar with Virgil's *Aeneid*, Berlioz's inspiration for *The Trojans*. Nevertheless, the Opera Company of Boston performed it in its original language, French. This was a departure from Goldovsky's choice to present *The Trojans* in an English translation. She had long ago broken with her mentor's position that operas for an English-speaking audience should be presented in English, but with this one she seemed less certain, even apologetic in the program notes: "As a producer faced with the task of putting on stage this remarkable work, we have been concerned that the audience understand as many of the incredible happenings as possible. The obvious question to some—why not perform it in English?—can only be answered—'it should be, it must be in English in the very near future.' However, the temptation and, perhaps, responsibility to hear and see *The Trojans* as Berlioz conceived it and in his language is shared, I am sure, by many in our audience."[17] She used the French libretto, but tried to overcome the language barrier by projecting verses from the *Aeneid* that explained the action first in Latin, then in English (a choice that may have been inspired by Berlioz's writing of an exploratory prologue, or by a similar technique employed by Bertolt Brecht) to video screens prior to each scene. They functioned as a kind of early form of supertitles, helping the audience understand the action on the stage while at the same time reminding them of the origins of the story.[18]

The realization of this epic work would be a daunting task for any stage director, but it was made even more so on the stage of a former movie theater with a depth of only 25 feet. George Movshon described her plight: "As usual Miss Caldwell had to contend with a wholly inadequate space. Without an orchestra pit, front stalls were removed in order to accommodate fifty-six musicians, a number still smaller than optimal. Removing stalls in the Aquarius was necessary to accommodate the orchestra, but it also cut down on the number of tickets available to sell. The theater had so few dressing rooms that the space next door (a beauty school at the time) served as one for the large chorus, which had to cross between buildings to make costume changes."[19] The singers of *The Trojans* battled inhospitable February chills as they went back and forth. They experienced the same cold winter conditions as the chorus members had in the December 1966 production of *Moses and Aaron*. Since there was no room for them in the wings at the Back Bay Theater, they shivered on the sidewalk in their scant costumes of Egyptian slaves as they waited for their next entrance cue.

Despite the poverty of the physical space, Caldwell with her designers, Pond and Senn, managed to expand it and develop a lavish production with characteristically realistic touches. They created a horseshoe shaped performance area that enlarged the stage and extended over the first few boxes on either side. Into that space they managed to incorporate waterfalls, trees, and a real boat for Dido and Aeneas. There was even a large statue of Athena placed in the balcony. The transformation of the theater was expensive, however, reportedly driving up the cost of the production to $200,000, but it succeeded in overcoming the shortcomings of the performance space, making it appear larger and serving the needs of the opera.

The *coup de théâtre* in *The Trojans* production was the illusion of Greek soldiers spilling out of the Trojan horse. In the first act of the opera, as in the legend, the Greeks pretend to abandon their camp, leaving only a large wooden horse near the gates of the city of Troy, which the inhabitants mistake for a peace offering and bring inside the city walls. Pond and Senn built a realistic looking equine set piece that was 22 feet high, 11 feet long, and weighed 900 pounds.[20] Caldwell's "gimmick" in recreating the famous emergence of the Greeks was to position the horse behind a scrim, and to have children dressed as the Greek soldiers. Their diminutive size made the horse appear larger than it actually was and completed the illusion.

The Opera Company of Boston production of *The Trojans* was in many ways typical of what audiences had come to expect from Caldwell: an imaginative staging of an unfamiliar work, a costly production, and a logistical nightmare. Overall, however, the public and the press showered her with praise. The production brought increased critical attention to opera in Boston, and even prompted a challenge to other companies. Louis Snyder in *The Christian Science Monitor* wrote, "Aside from awakening the general consciousness to the beauties of the complete Berlioz score, Miss Caldwell has proved in three-dimensional form, the viability of *The Trojans* on the stage. It takes imagination, large forces, and unshakable conviction—all of which Miss Caldwell commands. In the whole U.S.A. are there others who will follow her lead?"[21]

Indeed, Caldwell had issued a significant challenge with *The Trojans*. It drew not only the attention of national critics, but also international observers. Colin Davis, who had conducted the 1969 Covent Garden production and the newly released recording, attended one performance. John Nelson, who had conducted the concert version heard in New York City in March of that year, and Göran Gentele, who had been named to succeed Rudolf Bing as General Manager of the Metropolitan Opera, also watched Caldwell's work. The Met's own production, directed by Nathaniel Merrill, opened the following year. It was a vastly different staging that made full use of the large revolving stage for scene changes, but presented the Trojan horse only as a film image.

The Opera Company of Boston continued to build its reputation as an exciting maverick company, and Caldwell had clearly emerged as one of America's leading opera stage directors. Yet, these achievements did not spark any civic movement towards the rebuilding of a suitable venue for opera performance. One might well wonder about the reasons for the reluctance of Boston's leaders to invest in building an opera house. After all, an opera house is not just another building in the civic landscape; it makes a clear assertion about the value of the arts in that community. A city that will take on the expense of building of an opera house is probably rich in other artistic traditions as well. As one writer put it, "No law says a civilized city must have an opera house, but even so, the term has become a euphemism for a city having reached a level of cultural maturity."[22]

Martin Green argued in *The Problem of Boston* that the city's reluctance to support opera stemmed from its Puritan view of that art form as decadent and even degenerate.[23] Certainly, Boston did appear to favor the visual and literary arts in its past: the American Academy of Arts and Sciences was founded in 1780, the Boston Library Society in 1784, the Massachusetts Historical Society in 1791, and the Antiquarian Society in 1812, all before its first musical society, the Handel and Haydn Society was formed in 1815. Yet, while history and cultural factors were certainly at play, economic realities were also present. In the late 20th century, the cost of building an opera house had become almost astronomical. It could financially strain any city and would have been an extraordinary burden for a relatively small city like Boston with a population of about 700,000 at the time the first opera house was demolished.

Building any significant cultural edifice typically involves many people from both the private and public sector who cautiously size up the enormous economic risks involved, want to have strong voice in every decision, and often complicate, politicize, and slow down the process. In the past, it had been a less complicated and a quicker process than in modern times because private funding, rather than multiple government entities or even a combination of public and private investment, could shoulder much of the expense. A small group of wealthy citizens could rally to bring an opera house project to fruition in a manner and within a time period that today would be almost impossible. One such example is the story of the response of Mrs. William K. Vanderbilt after she was reportedly turned down for a box at the New York Academy of Music. She and her friends decided to have an opera house of their own built where their boxes would be guaranteed. The resulting (Old) Metropolitan Opera House was completed in three and a half years, opening in 1883 with plenty of private boxes for Mrs. Vanderbilt and her large social circle. The world's most famous house, La Scala, was built in only two years, funded by wealthy box holders distraught over having lost their first opera house to fire in 1776. But the record may—somewhat ironically—belong to Eben Jordon, Jr., who in 1908 announced his intention to build an opera house with his own money. Only one year elapsed between the laying of the foundation stone and opening night at the Boston Opera House, in November 1909.

While such heroic individual efforts have had an enormous impact from time to time in opera, they are not entirely limited to the distant past. As recently as 2005, the cost of the new opera house in Copenhagen, Denmark (about $500 million) was financed entirely by its richest citizen, shipping magnate Maersk Mc-Kinney Møller. In most cases, however, the complexities of building an opera house have grown over the years and are not at all unique to Boston. A key example is the extraordinary coordination and political will that was required to replace the "Old Met" with the new house that opened in 1966 in the Lincoln Center for the Performing Arts in New York City.

The planning phase to build a new opera house started in the early 20th century when Otto Kahn, President of the Metropolitan Opera Company, began to spearhead efforts for a new building, including commissioning a design from Joseph Urban in 1926 that was derailed by the stock market crash three years later. After Rudolf Bing became the General Manager of the Metropolitan Opera in 1950, he added urgency to the construction of a new theater by arguing that it was needed in order to incorporate new production values. The combination of the forceful will of Bing with the almost unlimited political power of New York City's master builder Robert Moses were key factors in the realization of the Lincoln Center plan. Moses targeted the Lincoln Square neighborhood on the Upper West Side of the city as part of his urban renewal agenda and approved the demolition of several blocks of housing to clear the way for the envisioned multi-building arts complex. In 1962, Philharmonic Hall (renamed Avery Fisher Hall in 1973 and David Geffen Hall in 2015) opened its doors, followed by the New York State Theater (renamed the David H. Koch Theater in 2008), and the Vivian Beaumont Theater in 1965. Finally, in 1966, after years of fund-raising efforts, led by John D. Rockefeller III, and a contentious and lengthy design process (carried out by group of architects that produced no fewer than 44 designs for the opera house to meet artistic and budgetary requirements) the new Metropolitan Opera House opened to the public.

Meanwhile in Boston, Caldwell grew ever more frustrated. In 1972, she complained that "our audience is tired of traipsing all over the area … and we're thoroughly tired of performing in any kind of facility. We accept it, we have fun and we do our best-but we have to build a theater and stage an opera every time. We need a permanent facility."[24] In fact, she wanted three separate facilities: one seating 600 to 700 patrons for Baroque operas, one seating about 1700 for 19th-century grand operas, and one seating 3,000 for 20th-century works.[25] The enormity of that project was not possible for most cities, let alone Boston, but Caldwell was ambitious. In the 1970s, she and her company were very successful, at least artistically. She was at the peak of her powers, but despite her accomplishments, despite the international reputation the company had achieved, and despite the cultural and economic growth potential that an opera house could provide, civic leaders were not able to bring any plans to fruition. In Boston, politics and cost were simply insurmountable.

Although Caldwell had produced a number of operas in unusual and sometimes wholly inadequate venues, it would be an error to assume that these spaces always worked against her or that a few were not of her own choosing. After all, she once admitted to wanting to present Bellini's *Norma* in a remote area in the woods, but gave it up when she realized the logistical complications, including the fact that the audience would have be led to and from the spot by a forest ranger if they were ever to find it.[26] Most venues that she was forced to use, however, had no particular charm; they were merely ill suited to the needs of opera production and poor substitutes for the demolished Boston Opera House. What is abundantly clear is that Caldwell was equal to the challenges they presented.

In 1978, Caldwell made what turned out to be a fatal error, one that drained her energies, and pointed her company towards financial ruin. She purchased a theater. The company moved into its new—and finally permanent—home, the B.F. Keith Memorial Theatre, which she had purchased for about $900,000 and renamed the Opera House. Thomas W. Lamb had designed the building in honor of B.F. Keith, the creator of the American vaudeville circuit, and completed in 1928 for about $5 million.[27] Its interior décor was intended to suggest the Palais Garnier, built in the late 19th century for the Paris Opera. The focal point of the lobby was a statue of Keith, surrounded by marble pillars at the staircase landing under a domed ceiling. Wood paneling lined the downstairs public area that included a fireplace, a smoking room for the men, and a large women's lounge. The auditorium, which seated about 2900 patrons, was wide rather than deep, the ceiling there was also domed and decorated with murals. The stage was large for vaudeville (35 feet deep by 55 feet wide), but it lacked side wing space and the orchestra pit was small. Below the stage was a handball court, billiard room, nursery, kitchen, barbershop, library, laundry, and a room to house the trained seals that were to perform there.[28]

Ironically, although the B.F. Keith Memorial Theatre was a memorial to vaudeville's founder, on its opening night, the entertainment was a feature length film and it was not long before it became strictly a movie house. Sack Cinemas, a chain in the Boston area, acquired the theater in 1965 and renamed it the Sack Savoy. The company closed it temporarily for refurbishing and reopened it later that year with significant changes. It had converted the stage area to a second theater, the "Savoy 2," walling it off from the auditorium with concrete blocks and lowering the ceiling. By the time Caldwell purchased the theater, it had deteriorated significantly and was covered with graffiti, dirt, and "tons of gum."[29] The pit, which had been designed to hold a few vaudeville musicians, was too small for an opera orchestra. The dressing rooms had been converted to apartments and there was no longer any way to get from the downstage area to the performance area without going out on to the street. To make matters even more complicated, the loading dock was eight feet up the back wall of the stage. The list of construction upgrades needed in the theater was long, but she approached it like an optimistic new homeowner with the hope of building "sweat equity."

Within 10 days of officially moving in, Caldwell inaugurated the new theater with Puccini's *Tosca*, starring Magda Olivero, a performance that had been postponed from the previous year when Shirley Verrett was to take the role. It was the fourth opera in a season that had begun with Verdi's *Stiffelio*, followed by Berlioz's *The Damnation of Faust*, and Donizetti's *Don Pasquale*. That year Caldwell celebrated 20 years at the helm of her own company in her own theater. The conversion of a run-down theater into an opera house presented her with an enormous challenge, but it also seemed to energize her. In interviews, she talked excitedly about the theater and its potential for use by other performing groups, and of developing an expanded opera season. And as always, she was eager to present new works.

The B.F. Keith Memorial Theatre interior in its original condition. Note the small orchestra pit—fine for vaudeville, but not for opera orchestras (Historic American Buildings Survey, Library of Congress).

The new theater gave Caldwell a permanent space in which to work, but it did not alleviate the challenges that she had always faced when staging operas in houses designed for films or vaudeville acts: no orchestra pit, limited offstage space, cramped performance areas. Once again, she and her scenic designers were forced to reconfigure the space with scenery that spilled

The B.F. Keith Memorial Theatre, after it was renamed the Sack Savoy in 1965 and prior to its purchase by Caldwell in 1978. She renamed it The Opera House (photograph by Albie Walton).

out into the side boxes, the balcony, and even into the auditorium. These choices had positive effects: they blurred the division of audience and performance space, brought singers physically closer to the spectators, and broke down aesthetic barriers. Most importantly, they created a sense of intimacy, a unique kind of experience not possible in a traditional opera house. Yet, at times, they gave the impression that the setting was crammed into the space, rather than developed as an organic part of it. It was as if a traditional opera house shaped Caldwell's vision for her realizations and she tried to make them fit into the spaces she had.

Andrew Porter had described her rehearsal style as one similar to that of the British director Peter Brook: grounded, intense, able to be spontaneous. Yet, the scenic designs that they employed could not have been different. Brooks has been admired for his ability to convey great depth of ideas and characters through simple scenic elements that work with the performance spaces rather than against them. One such example was his production of *A Magic Flute*. Brook's alternation of the title was indicative of his approach to the work as a variation on a theme, not intended to represent Mozart's *The Magic Flute*, but certainly an evocation of its ideas. It received its American premiere as part of the Lincoln Center Festival in 2011 on the small, bare stage of Gerald W. Lynch Theater at John Jay College with a piano accompaniment. The only set pieces were tall bamboo stalks mounted vertically on small wooden stands that the singers moved as needed. They easily transformed the stage to accommodate the many different settings, gracefully incorporating the changes as part of their stage movements. Brook's technique was exceedingly effective, and argued for realizations of operas in ways that complement their spaces rather than refusing to conform.

Throughout her career with the Opera Company of Boston Caldwell was able to stage captivating performances in venues not intended for opera. She and her designers frequently overcame a lack of adequate performance space by extending it into the auditorium with ramps and using the aisles or boxes as secondary stages. These choices created a sense of immediacy between performer and audiences that is impossible to attain in a large theater and an experience that could not be had from any other opera company. Yet, they also became arguments against the need for a proper opera house, since she showed herself capable of producing exciting and high-quality experiences without one. Ultimately, her ability to turn any space into an opera house simply underscored her conclusion that the best opera productions were not space dependent. At their core, they had two key ingredients: "exciting theater, wonderful music."[30]

Chapter 6

Experiments

Caldwell was committed to rediscovering the composer's original intentions and developing productions from them. As a rule, her preparation began with an examination of the original manuscript and other sources (notes, letters, etc.) left by the composer. Her research often included extensive time in libraries, archives, and museums around the world. At times, she travelled to relevant locations so that she and her artistic team could absorb, then translate, elements of the historical and cultural context to the stage to the singers and to the audience. Yet, on several occasions over the course of her career, she experimented with creative conceptions that obfuscated the composer's intentions and prioritized a dramatic conception over the musical evidence. These rare, but significant, forays into director's theater made her one of America's first *auteur* opera directors.

The extensive research that was a hallmark of Caldwell's process was evident early in her career. It was first noted in an article that appeared in the *Boston Herald* about the formation of The Opera Group, which stated that "her research in Paris was responsible last season for the production of Bizet's *Carmen* in its complete original version by the Boston University Department of Opera and Music Theatre." At the time, she was working on Stravinsky's *The Rake's Progress*, which the composer conducted for the first time in the United States. The article went on to cite Robert Craft, the assistant conductor, who said, "I have watched *The Rake's Progress* in preparation in Sarah Caldwell's remarkable Boston University Opera Workshop, and I can honestly say that it has not been more thoroughly prepared by any of the great opera houses of the world. Musically, it is the first performance I have heard which does full and faithful justice to the composer's intentions."[1] Of course, at that time she was able to consult directly with the composer. It happened rarely in her career, but when it did she relished the opportunity. Her discussions with Roger Sessions began after *Montezuma*'s premiere in 1964 and continued during the preparation for the Opera Company of

Boston production in 1976. Her deference to Luigi Nono on the production of *Intolleranza 1960* (noted earlier) is yet another example.

When it was not possible to have a direct conversation with the composer, Caldwell did the next best thing—she tried to find the autograph score or to get as close to the first version of the score as she could. Of course, there were times when there was no definitive version and she had to weigh which score or which parts of a score she thought represented the composer's intentions most accurately. That was the case when she was preparing to stage Mussorgsky's *Boris Godunov* in 1965. Rather than present the more often performed 1908 Rimsky-Korsakov version, she opted for an amalgam of two early versions (1869, 1872). Typical of Caldwell, however, she had not planned exactly how to acquire those editions. Consequently, she had to travel to Oxford, Wiesbaden, and Paris and finally to the Staatsoper in East Berlin in order to piece together the orchestral parts.[2] Another key example was her American premiere of Rameau's *Hippolyte et Aricie* at the Back Bay Theater, described earlier. At the time, there was no performance edition that contained all the orchestra parts, only the vocal lines and bass lines. Caldwell and a colleague went to the Paris Opera Library on a hunch that the orchestral parts used in the performance conducted by Rameau would be there (even though they were told they were not). After several days delay, they were given permission to search the stacks and after a week, found a score containing orchestral parts, presumably the ones used when the opera premiered in 1733.[3] Caldwell's persistence enabled American audiences to hear Rameau's score as it had not been heard for over 200 years. What she did was possible for anyone to do, but it was not the norm for a stage director to conduct that level of musical research.

As noted in the previous chapter Caldwell introduced additional music in the lesson scene of *The Barber of Seville* that critics thought added nothing to the drama or music. They viewed such choices as "gimmicks" to publicize her productions and herself. There were instances when that was a valid criticism. The number of such gimmicks, however, were outweighed by the number of times her research did lead to a legitimate restoration that provided new insight into a composer's dramatic vision. The American premiere of the complete version of Verdi's *Don Carlos* in 1973 is a prime example. The opera, based on *Don Carlos, Infant von Spanien* by Schiller, uses 16th-century Spain as a setting for the love story of Don Carlos and Elisabeth of Valois, which becomes complicated when a peace treaty requires that she marry his father, Philippe II. The opera is both theatrically and musically grand in scale, but its scale was something of an impediment from the very start. Even before it premiered at the Paris Opera in 1867, the composer cut significant portions

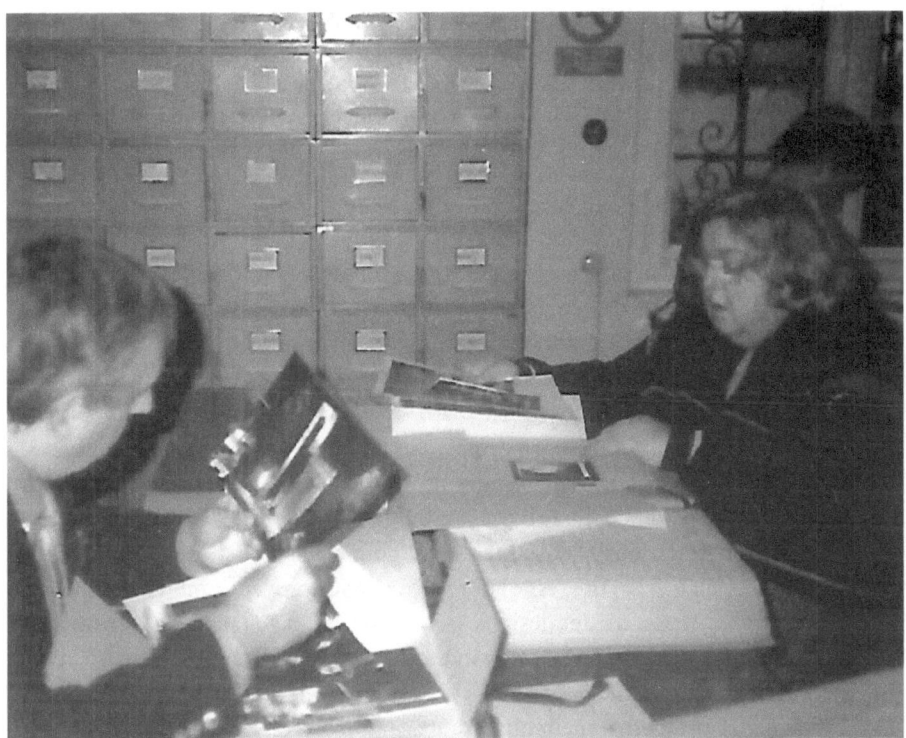

Caldwell and Herbert Senn conducting research in Prague in preparation for Janáček's *The Makropulos Case* (from the Helen Pond/Herbert Senn Collection, courtesy Deirdre Taylor Paster).

of the original five-act version. Later, Verdi alternated between arguing for the opera to be performed in its entirety and editing the work as he struggled to clarify his dramatic vision. Opera audiences came to expect either the four-act 1884 version, or the 1886 version, but not the original five-act version of 1867, with a French libretto. The five-act version was finally performed at La Scala in 1970, after the complex evolution and performance history of the opera had been pieced together by Verdi scholars David Rosen and Ursula Günther, and the musicologist and critic Andrew Porter. The second time that audiences heard the five-act version was in 1973 when Caldwell conducted and directed it at Boston's Aquarius Theater. Her excitement about the performance of the restored music was still evident over 20 years later, when she wrote to Laurence Picken about her experience seeing Verdi's score at the Paris Opera Library for the first time:

> A number of cuts had been marked in the parts by simply pasting over them with brown paper. All we had to do was unstuck [sic] the brown paper and copy.

After a time I managed to persuade the Paris Opera Library to let me have all the orchestra parts microfilmed. Our musicians played from those very parts, which had fingerings, bowings, sometimes breadth marks, pencil sketches of singers (as well as Verdi) and cautionary and irreverent comments about tempi and the conductor. One of the few times in my podium life I actually cried was when they started to sing the incredibly beautiful chorus Verdi originally composed for the death of Posa [Rodrigo], but was forced to cut.[4]

The restored opera (which lasted more than four and a half hours omitting only the ballet "La Pérégrina") garnered critical praise for Caldwell's efforts to bring Verdi's original version to light. Raymond Ericson wrote in the *New York Times* that the production was illuminating: "The expanded action of the original makes dramatically plain what often is not in the telescoped version."[5] The result of having a director-conductor who worked to integrate the music (as it was conceived originally) and the drama was that audiences were able to experience the full dramatic intensity and integrity of the opera.

Although the Paris score for the first time was a highlight of the production of *Don Carlos*, the rest of the performance proved somewhat uneven. According to critics, the set design by Donald Oenslager, borrowed from the San Antonio Opera, fit awkwardly in the Aquarius Theater, and that affected the quality of the lighting. Porter's review in *The New Yorker* pointed out several other problems: inadequate stage space, under rehearsed scenes, and a lack of gravitas. Still, he was struck not only with the power of the restored work, but also by Caldwell's handling of it. Moreover, he praised her inventiveness in finding a solution to the vaguely drawn final scene. In the Paris version, at the end of the farewell duet between Don Carlos and Elisabeth at the tomb of Charles V, King Philippe enters and calls for their deaths. One staging option is for Charles V to emerge from the tomb and drag Don Carlos back with him during the final, austere measures of the score. That would leave the audience to wonder if Charles V is a ghost dragging Don Carlos to his death, or the former monarch who retired to a monastery and is saving his son by giving him sanctuary. The ending is ambiguous, and arguably, awkward, so that directors have taken different and sometimes drastic approaches to make sense of it. In one production, Charles V, dressed as a monk, stepped forward to bring Don Carlos and Elisabeth together to sing their farewells then saved his grandson from the Inquisition. In another, less sentimental interpretation, a distraught Don Carlos stabbed himself to death.[6]

Caldwell took her inspiration from a note that Verdi had scrawled in a draft version of the libretto "L'enfant Carlos est mort! Priez pour lui" (The child Carlos is dead! Pray for him). That note led her to have the Inquisition soldiers execute Don Carlos, and to show definitely that his grieving grandfather had not died, but rather entered a monastery. It was an unexpected, but rational ending for the title character. In this interpretation, the final words of Charles V, "Mon fils, les douleurs de la terre Viennent expirer en ce lieu, La paix que votre coeur espère Ne se trouve qu'an près de Dieu" (My son, the sorrows of this world follow us even in this place, The peace for which your heart longs, can be found only through God)[7] over the stately music, became a condemnation of the injustices suffered by Don Carlos. Overall, Porter concluded, Caldwell had taken the lead in demonstrating the dramatic worthiness of an original score and in doing so "opened a new chapter in the stage history of the piece."[8] Indeed, Caldwell's production remains a significant and rare performance of this work.

Caldwell went even further into the origins of an opera in her presentation of Gounod's *Faust* in 1981. The opera was completed then revised prior to its premiere at the Théâtre Lyrique in Paris, 1859. A year later, Gounod added music to the spoken dialogue sections and a decade later, added a ballet. The program notes for the Opera Company of Boston production, reprinted here in part, attests to Caldwell's passion for researching the origins of operas and her commitment to authenticity:

> The version of *Faust* which we are performing is based upon the best knowledge now available on Gounod's original conception of the opera as well as the first performed version as it appeared at the Théâtre Lyrique in 1859. *Faust* was conceived as an opera with spoken dialogue and melodrama (spoken text synchronized with illustrative music), leading into short recitatives and formalized musical numbers (arias, several duets, three trios, and a single quarter). The dialogues which we are using were taken from the original libretto as it was submitted to the official Parisian censors. The musical materials supplied by the Bibliothèque Nationale de Paris, the libraries of the Paris Opera, the publishing firm of Choudens *et fils*, several excerpts belonging to private collectors and various early scores.
>
> These performances mark what may be the world premiere of three lovely musical numbers: a trio between Faust and his two students Wagner and Siebel, in the prologue ("A l'étude, o mon maître"); a farewell duet between Valentin and Marguerite in the second act ("Adieu, mon bon frère"); and a romance for Siebel following Marguerite's spinning song (itself rarely performed!). We have restored the original, logical order of the church scene so that it comes after the death of Valentin and serves, in fact, as his requiem. The format of the "Walpurgis Night" is based, as nearly as we can reconstruct, on Gounod's original scheme. This also contains some unfamiliar music—the witches "arithmetic" chorus which also acts as a musical frame for the entire scene, and the brilliant "Minuit" aria for Mephisto.[9]

Of course, it is true that composers have often had to sacrifice portions of their work against their will. Yet, to assume that some operas have not

Håken Hagegård (Valentin; back to camera) and Diana Soviero (Marguerite; in glasses) rehearsing the farewell duet "Adieu, mon bon frère" that Caldwell (at right) premiered in her 1981 production of Gounod's *Faust*. Pianist unidentified. Photograph by George Kufrin. Courtesy of Joan Kufrin.

benefited musically and dramatically from judicious editing is to give undo credit to composers who, like other artists, are not necessarily their own best critics. As the musicologist Joseph Kerman has pointed out in *Contemplating Music*, authenticity is no guarantee of a good performance.[10] The strength of a performance is a subjective judgment by critics and audiences, whose frame of reference and expectations are inevitably different today than they were when the composer conceived the opera. Consequently, modern directors have often tried to recreate the impact of the original performance on an audience, either by seeking to understand the composer's intentions as expressed in different elements of the opera, or—at the other extreme—by ignoring them entirely.

A stage director has three main sources from which to draw an understanding of the composer's intentions. If the director is a competent musician, s/he can seek guidance for the realization in the music itself (which may suggest location, character, mood and action through changes in instrumentation, motif, tempo, rhythm, repetition, etc.), but it is at best suggestive rather than prescriptive. For instance, Mozart chose the key of G minor for

Papageno's lament as he prepares to hang himself in the second act of *The Magic Flute*. Since the key is also associated with Pamina's music, the musical suggestion is that Papageno's feelings of despair are equally genuine and even noble. Accepting that connection would indicate to a stage director that Papageno's intention to commit suicide is sincere and that his preparations should be staged with solemnity rather than as a comic interlude.

The second source would be the libretto (though often not written by the composer, since it is most often created in collaboration with the composer, it can be assumed to be consistent with the composer's intentions) which often specifies scenery, as well specific action. For instance, the fight between Don Giovanni and the Commendatore in the opening scene of Mozart's *Don Giovanni* leads to the mortal wounding of the latter. He sings, "Ah, soccorso! son tradito! L'assassino m'ha ferito, E dal seno palpitante Sento l'anima partir" (Help! I am betrayed! The assassin has wounded me, and from my heaving breast I feel my soul escaping). The old man's collapse is evident not only from his own lines, but also from the confirmation that Don Giovanni sings immediately afterwards, "Ah, già cade il sciagurato!" (Ah, the wretch has fallen already!).[11] In short, the words guide the action, the music, the emotional context.

Thirdly, the paratextual information found in the libretto often includes valuable information such as the stage directions or descriptions of scenery or atmosphere that at the very least give clues as to how it was first staged. For example, *The Marriage of Figaro*, Act I, scene 1: "Camera non affatto ammobiliata, una sedia d'appoggio in mezzo. Figaro con una misura in mano e Susanna allo specchio che si sta mettendo un capellino ornato di fiori" (An incompletely furnished room with an armchair in the middle. Figaro with a ruler in his hand and Susanna at a mirror, trying on a small hat decorated with flowers)."[12] Since stage directions are often a record of the premiere performance, they may document, at least to some extent, the composer's original vision for the visualization of the action.

Composers may reveal their intentions in ways that are more indirect. Richard Wagner, for one, wrote extensively about how he wanted his works to appear on the stage. For instance, his "Remarks on Performing the Opera 'The Flying Dutchman'" details his expectation for the scenery: "Special attention is demanded by the lighting, with its manifold changes: to make the nuances of the storm in the First Act effective, a skillful use of painted gauzes, as far as quite the middle distance of the stage, is indispensable." It includes directives for characterization, such as his insistence that the Dutchman must retain "a certain terrible repose in his outward demeanor, even amid the most passionate expression of inward anguish and despair." Moreover, it details his dramatic interpretation of musical choices. One example occurs in the second act when the Dutchman first meets Senta. Wagner wrote: "Throughout the lengthy first 'fermata' [the Dutchman] stays motionless beside the door; at the commencement of the drum-solo he slowly strides towards the front; with the eighth bar of that solo he halts (the two bars 'accelerando' for the strings relate to the gestures of Daland, who still stands wondering in the doorway), awaiting Senta's welcome...."[13]

The director may also seek out inspiration from the novel or play that may have inspired the composer. Pierre Loti's book *Madam Chrysanthème*, which led to John Luther Long's short story *Madam Butterfly* and subsequently David Belasco's short play that inspired Puccini, is one example. Others include Shakespeare's *The Merry Wives of Windsor*, which became the foundation of Verdi's *Falstaff* and Beaumarchais' play *Le Mariage de Figaro*, which led to Mozart's *The Marriage of Figaro*. Of course, while these literary sources may provide ideas, directors who utilize them more than the score risk staging a musical version of a play, rather than the distinct artistic work that is the opera.

When the intentions of the composer are not evident, many directors consult additional materials for their conceptions such as related artistic works, paintings, or writings of the time. These may be helpful to enable them to achieve indirectly some degree of faithfulness to what were most likely the composer's intentions. However, unless they are trying to recreate the work as a historically accurate period piece, directors update the *mise en scène* to some degree in order to appeal to the different visual sensibilities of the modern audience (and sometimes out of practical necessity). Perspective scene painting, the marvel of previous ages, may be replaced with three-dimensional scenery, using colors enhanced by advanced lighting technology and moved easily by invisible stage machinery such as revolving stages. More radical is the approach of the "creative directors" or "*auteur* directors" who emerged in the latter part of the 20th century. They dismissed every historical source as a guide for staging and instead, developed concepts that might complement the libretto and score, serve as a juxtaposition, or even depart from them completely. Their approach assumed that in order for operas written in a previous era to remain viable for a modern audience, the entire realization needed to be re-conceptualized.

Wieland Wagner, grandson of the composer, was one of the pioneers of this "director's theater" or "Regietheater" movement. In post-war Europe, he introduced audiences at the Bayreuth Festival to highly stylized realizations that made full use of the stage as an artist's canvas. The younger Wagner revered his grandfather's works as eternal, but knew that "the actual staging—

and it alone—is subject to change. To avoid change is to transform the virtue of fidelity into the vice of rigidity. Ultimately, it spells death."[14] His scenic conceptions complemented or contradicted the music, but they did not simply illustrate it. He rejected the literal scenic depictions of Nordic mythology that Richard Wagner had painstakingly described and utilized on stage and, instead, promoted the universality of his grandfather's works through archetypal images that transcended historical periods and specific cultures.

In the post-modern period of literature and drama, theorists have argued that the text, which had previously be viewed as a definitive authorial statement to be interpreted in performance, is in fact a moving target of sorts, as subjective and ephemeral as performance itself because the context in which it is being read/viewed is ever-changing. Directors who adopted this view approached indications for staging as records merely of how the opera *had* been staged or *could* be staged, but not how it *should* be staged. They posited that in order for the visualization to be effective and even comprehensible for a modern audience far removed from the social and historical era in which the opera was first produced, it needed to be filtered through a modern lens. The result was often a complete "revisioning" of the opera that at times included forceful political statements. For example, in Ruth Berghaus' 1974 production of Rossini's *The Barber of Seville* at the Bavarian State Opera, a female torso on a bare stage was Rosina's house, her window, an opening in the left breast to underscore the heroine's enslavement in a patriarchal societal structure. In 1978, Harry Kupfer's staging of Wagner's *The Flying Dutchman* dismissed the romantic sentimentalism of the composer's vision and staged it as a series of hallucinations experienced by Senta. By the time the Dutchman departed, she was suicidal and threw herself out of the window of her father's house. In the 1980s, Peter Sellars updated the stratified 18th-century social structure depicted in Mozart's *The Marriage of Figaro* by moving the Almavivas to Trump Towers in New York City, with Figaro and Susanna serving as their butler and maid to underscore the power inequities. Clearly, neither Rossini nor Wagner nor Mozart envisioned their operas staged in these ways, but such imaginative interpretations were attempts to make opera relevant and attract new audiences and interest.

Since director's theater emerged in the mid–20th century, it has been practiced mainly in European opera houses. There, substantial government subsidies provide an atmosphere where contemporaries of Caldwell, directors such as Walter Felsenstein, Harry Kupfer, Herbert Wernicke, and Gerard Mortier, had more freedom to experiment, regardless of whether critics approved of their conceptions or whether audiences attended the performances. In the United States, however, where funding for the arts relies more heavily on popular support, experimentation is tempered by a watchful eye on fiscal sustainability. Opera companies may venture new works or radical interpretations at times, but tend to incorporate mainstream offerings in their seasons as a means to help balance the budget.

Although American directors working in America have struggled to be innovative in ways their European counterparts take for granted, there have been those who were able to be successful with revisionist interpretations. One of the early practitioners of experimental approaches was Frank Corsaro, a Yale School of Drama trained theater artist, whose early work as an actor and director was with the Actors Studio in New York City. After having directed successfully on Broadway, he became interested in directing opera and worked frequently at the New York City Opera. There he found audiences who welcomed his attention to the quality of acting in his operas and were most often accepting of his radical conceptions. But even they booed after his 1972 *Don Giovanni*, which eradicated all subtlety and refinement out of the title character, set much of the action around a brothel, and made prostitutes Don Giovanni's constant companions.[15] Like Caldwell, he emphasized theatrical values, relentlessly insisting that opera singers be singing actors, but he could not match her ability to blend music and drama without compromise.

Compared to many of her European and American contemporaries, Caldwell may seem a rather conservative director. She was generally uncomfortable with radical realizations of opera and described them as "the personifications of something that I find very disturbing these days: staging opera in a different way just to be different."[16] She insisted (as did her mentor, Boris Goldovsky, and her idol Walter Felsenstein) that new interpretations stem from close readings of the libretto and score, research, and a reconsideration of accepted performance practice rather than from a director's imagination alone. Although her body of work is largely exemplary of a directional approach that prioritized the composer's vision over the director's, it does include several forays into revisionist staging that challenged the composer's intentions.

Caldwell's first experiment with a radical revision came in 1967 with a flamboyant production of Igor Stravinsky's *The Rake's Progress*. She had already staged the work in the 1950s at Boston University (see above), but this time she rejected Hogarth's depictions of 18th-century England as a setting for the opera, and opted instead for the modern era. Theodore Strongin of the *New York Times* described an atmosphere with "mod clothes, black leather jackets ... and large photographs of Allen Ginsberg and Timothy Leary in the Act II bedroom." The scene in Mother Goose's brothel took place in a discotheque. Add to that Caldwell's choice to forego having Baba the Turk sung by a mezzo soprano, in favor of a hermaphroditically costumed counter tenor, and one can understand Strongin's bemused conclusion that "The Opera Company of Boston is anything but complacent."[17]

Another of Caldwell's revisionist experiments was her conception for Smetana's *The Bartered Bride*, which she staged in 1973. She was convinced that it was not merely a folk opera, but rather, an assertion of Czech nationalism in the guise of a folk opera. Therefore, she shaped the production into an allegorical tale of resistance to political oppression. In doing so, she promoted Smetana's identity not merely as a nationalist composer, but as an activist nationalist composer. She viewed *The Bartered Bride* as a subversive work of art, written under the watchful eye of its foreign rulers[18] with political messages woven subtly throughout a seemingly harmless comedy. It was an unusual choice for Caldwell who was consistently apolitical in her personal life.

Walter Felsenstein, who had also insisted that *The Bartered Bride* was more than a collection of "pretty tunes," likely influenced Caldwell's interpretation.[19] When he staged the work in 1951, he discovered a richer and even darker side to the character of Mařenka by closely examining a more literal translation of the Czech language libretto. To his surprise, he discovered that the entire libretto was more forceful than the German translation he had been using. He found her to be a much stronger character; more determined to control her own future and that affected his directing choices for her. For Caldwell, too, Mařenka's sweetness thinly masked her strength and desire for independence.

Caldwell staged and conducted *The Bartered Bride* at the Aquarius Theater. The set design, by Lester Polakov, depicted an idealized village largely through projections on multiple sepia drops, with specific locations created more realistically with three-dimensional set pieces. The proscenium arch augmented with soft cloud formations that suggested the production would provide a light evening of entertainment. Immediately after the buoyant overture, however, Caldwell subverted the audience's expectation. As an introduction to the entrance of the chorus in the first scene, she staged a pantomime depicting the invasion of Czechoslovakia by the Nazis and Russians, accentuated with graphic historical images projected onto the drops. Perhaps anticipating a negative reaction to the video sequence, she wrote in the program that she was "not trying to put something in that is not there." If the images contrasted the lighthearted music, they did echo the words of the opening chorus "Proč bychom se netěšili," in which the villagers sing of trying to be merry at a time of uncertainty. Her intention was to acknowledge the nationalist fervor in the work.[20] Indeed, she did not change the music or the text, but the pantomime gave the audience a political lens through which to view the remainder of the opera. Her interpretation rejected the cheerful music as indicative of the mood of the people and the period. Instead, it was shaped by the serious premise of the plot and Mařenka's emotional turmoil as she navigates the uncertainties of her love and her fate. As a result, Smetana's opera was not simply a superficial comic tale about two young lovers, but a drama of the Czech people faced with their own uncertain future.

A conceptualization of *The Bartered Bride* as a political allegory, depicting the resilience of the Czech people under the rule of the Austro-Hungarian Empire was a radical choice. It may not have been well grounded in the composer's intentions, but it did have historical merit. Whereas Czech language and culture had been subdued in towns and cities, it survived in the rural countryside. That was where the folk dance tunes of Smetana's opera, especially the polka, were symbols of cultural autonomy and solidarity at the time. Caldwell staged the opera in 1973, only five years after the Prague Spring, when the Soviet Union sent troops to Prague to crush a democratic reform movement and reestablish its dominance. One could argue, therefore, that the themes of political domination and cultural resistance in the 19th-century opera were quite vivid for a modern audience given the recent events in that region.

Although Caldwell's interpretation linked the present to the past through the music and staging, the resulting production did not impress the critics. Raymond Ericson described the pantomime in his *New York Times* review as "a terrible waste of time."[21] Speight Jenkins in *Opera News* balked at her attempt to inject political relevance into the opera. Still, he championed her work, even though it was not to his liking: "She is an amazing artist. With extraordinary zeal, she makes the company come out with something exciting and controversial every year, and no matter whether all her experiments work, her musical judgment is so good that the backbone of the performance leaves you elated."[22]

The following year Caldwell experimented with an even more radical reconception, this time turning her attention to Massenet's *Don Quichotte*. The composer was inspired by a 1904 play, *Le chevalier de la longue figure*, by Jacques Le Lorrain, which had been based on the early 17th-century novel *Don Quixote* by Miguel de Cervantes. The five-act libretto, by Henri Cain, situates the action in Spain, during the time of Cervantes. It begins with Don Quichotte and Sancho Panza arriving at Dulcinea's house, where the lanky knight serenades her with "Quand apparaissent les étoiles" (When the stars begin to shine). She feigns interest in him, then in jest, entices him to promise that he will retrieve a necklace stolen from her by the chief of the local bandits. Don Quichotte eagerly agrees because he believes that his success will win her favor. The bandits capture Don Quichotte and mock him mercilessly, but his composure impresses them and his simple, but eloquent prayer "Seigneur, reçois mon âme" (Lord, receive my soul), moves the chief bandit to restore the necklace to him. Don Quichotte returns to Dulcinea and solemnly asks for her hand in marriage as his reward, but she rebuffs him. His spirit is crushed. In the brief final act, in a lonely place in an ancient forest, he asks Sancho to say a prayer for him and dies dreaming of Dulcinea.

In a decision that clearly demonstrated her belief that the era of the composer was more relevant to the realization of an opera than the era of the literary source, Caldwell moved the setting from 17th-century Spain to early 20th-century Montmartre at the time of Massenet and Le Lorrain. It was an area that she and her set designers had explored for atmospheric elements to bring to their production of Charpentier's *Louise* three years earlier. She altered the drama further. The stage action began inside the Moulin de Rêve where a lanky, older man (perhaps the aging Massenet himself?) sat watching a theatrical performance. In a confusion of dream and reality, he interjects himself into the play and takes on the role of the lovelorn knight on his quest for the necklace. It is Don Quichotte/Massenet who fights the windmill, is tortured by bandits, and triumphantly returns to Dulcinea only to suffer mockery and rejection.

Caldwell's revision did not alter the music or the words of the libretto, but the *mise en scène* served her directorial conception and, in doing so, made her the *auteur* in a long line of *auteurs*, each of whom had made the original drama their own. Cervantes wrote about a man who stepped from his world into a role in another world, that of a Spanish knight in medieval times. The character created his own narrative. Le Lorrain added yet another layer to the drama—new interpretations of the characters, and action that did not appear in the book, such as the death of the would-be knight. As the original story's themes were retold, whether in drama or in music (Massenet was a French composer using French opera elements and style to tell a story set in Spain), they were necessarily, if not intentionally, reinterpreted for the new time and place. Caldwell's directorial conception added yet another layer for her era. In the modern era, her work demonstrated the post-modern observation that there is no definitive "text."

The most startling element of Caldwell's revision was to change the death of Don Quichotte from a surrender to an intentional act of suicide. In the libretto, the dispirited knight, attended by a grieving Sancho Panza, dies quietly. He hears Dulcinea's voice sing a tender, angelic invitation (evoked by the harp) and he succumbs. In Caldwell's production, however, Don Quichotte stabs himself, a blunt act that seemed unprovoked and contradicted the serenity of the music. She left no explanation that might shed light on her inspiration for this startling change. What is clear is that instead of surrendering quietly to his despair, Don Quichotte actively claims his fate in the ultimate act of free will. Through that gesture, Caldwell elevated him from a pathetic character to a tragic one. It was bold reinterpretation and one of her most startling directional choices.

The production received a mixed review from Harold C. Schonberg in the *New York Times*, who praised her staging, but took exception to her reconceptualization of the drama. Schonberg's argument was that the opera was overproduced. Although he praised the effect created when Don Quixote appeared to be swept up in the windmill (audience members reportedly gasped, not realizing that a dummy had been substituted for bass-baritone Noel Tyl), he contended that the moment diverted attention from the music. Another element of the production that he criticized was the use of realistic puppet horses ridden by Don Quichotte and Sancho. He found them distracting and an example of a Caldwellian "gimmick." In sum, he dismissed her as "one of those ego-trip directors, and she can give even Frank Corsaro lessons in reinterpreting opera librettos. It was the kind of performance in which everybody went out talking not about the music, but about the animals and the Don's encounter with the windmill."[23] Robert Baxter in *Opera* agreed that the reconception did not quite work, but found the production overall "a diverting entertainment in the best Caldwell tradition."[24] Caldwell's Don *Quichotte* took its ending from mid–20thcentury existentialism, its ambiance from the early 20th-century France of its composer, and its metatheatrical conception from the 17th-century novel. It was not the only time she had dabbled in metatheater. Her boldest experiment was in her 1978 production of Berlioz's *The Damnation of Faust* at the Aquarius Theater.

In the libretto for *The Damnation of Faust*, the aging scholar falls prey to Méphistophélès, who promises to cure him of his world-weariness, but instead tricks him into sacrificing his soul. Berlioz was inspired by Goethe's *Faust*, which, in turn, was derived from earlier dramatic sources and legends. The lineage of creation and recreation inspired Caldwell to examine the process of artistic creation itself. She conceived an environment in which the composition of the opera by Berlioz and the realization of it became as much a part of the drama as the legend itself. She set it backstage at the time of the composer, but contemporary references were interspersed. The composer became a character in his own opera (as Massenet had in *Don Quichotte*). Further, his real-life wife, Marie Recio, entered as a prima donna to sing for Berlioz and as she did, transformed into Marguerite. The opera chorus members were simultaneously 19th-century singers rehearsing their parts and characters in the drama proper. Finally, Caldwell included herself, choreographer Ben Stevenson, and dancers in the opening scene, which she staged as a rehearsal in progress.

Opera critics viewed the recasting of *The Damnation of Faust* into a postmodernist deconstruction of the creative and re-creative processes as audacious and egotistical. They were beside themselves with a combination of revulsion and fascination that is typical of responses to radical revisions. The production became something of a *succès de scandale* for the Opera Company of Boston. Richard Dyer wrote in the *Boston Globe*, "Nearly everything about it is appalling and absurd and irrelevant, and therefore it is essential for you to go see it. People are going to be arguing and laughing at this production for years to come, and you might as well be able to say that you were there."[25] Dyer was generally a balanced reviewer who both lauded and criticized Caldwell's work over the course of many years. This was one of his most negative reactions to her work. Robert Baxter, defended her choices in *Opera*, noting that she "revealed the depth of the Faust legend and Berlioz's expansive view of it by merging physical reality with theatrical illusion." As such, he concluded, "If her *Faust* was a failure, then it was a grand failure, extravagant and perhaps undisciplined, but like most of Miss Caldwell's productions, brilliant and filled with flashes of insight that make the work of most other American producers seem pedestrian if not dull."[26]

Caldwell's revision of Berlioz's *The Damnation of Faust* was radical not merely because of the degree of directorial license she took with the drama itself. Rather, it was radical because the process of creating (composing) and recreating (directing), rather than the words or the music, was focus of the stage action. It challenged the hierarchical relationship between what is created (music, drama) and what is recreated (stage production), and raised the latter to an equal—or even higher position. Moreover, creation was not merely the purview of the composer and the librettist, but of the stage director (on stage, no less) as a character in the process of creation. The placement of the director on equal footing with the composer raised that role to the level of *creator*, not merely *interpreter* of a creation. Caldwell had always maintained that in opera neither music nor drama was supreme. With *Faust*, she argued for the equality of the composer and librettist *and stage director* as creators.

The Damnation of Faust was experimental in another way that was both typical of Caldwell and an illustration of the technical difficulties of working in a former vaudeville theater. In order to create the surreal atmosphere of hell, she wanted to use laser lights, and she may, in fact, have been the first director to do so in an opera performance. Caldwell's vision was to enhance the performance throughout with laser effects and for them to be particularly prominent in the *"Dance of the Sylphs"* (Part II, scene 7) and the *"Ride to the Abyss"* (Part IV, scene 18) where multi-colored lights would flicker slowly in order to create a mesmerizing effect of a tunnel to hell. She contracted with a company in New York City that specialized in the research and development of lasers for industry and theater productions. The lasers achieved their desired effects when they did work, but unfortunately, they did not for all the performances. The difficulty centered on the need for the glass laser tube and the gases inside it to remain cool, which was aided by water running through coils that surrounded it. In order to do that effectively, the unit needed not only a certain volume of water per minute, but also a certain amount of water pressure. In the Aquarius Theater, the water supply had to be brought through a hose run from the projection booth in the balcony, where the 300-pound laser unit and a 150-pound transformer were situated, to a sink in the ladies' restroom on the second floor. The system worked well for the first performance, but the glass amplifier tube of the laser unit overheated when a brief test run was conducted just prior to the Sunday matinee. Apparently, the cooling system did not receive a sufficient supply of water because the water pressure was affected by a concurrent peak use of the ladies' restroom at that time. That particular performance proceeded without the laser lights.[27]

In the waning years of the company, as financial struggles and internal conflict arose, Caldwell continued to take artistic and financial risks with her selection of repertoire and experimented even within the operas she chose. In 1988, she produced *Médée*, an *opera-comique*, written by Luigi Cherubini, at the close of the 18th century. Its libretto was based on the ancient Greek myth of Medea, the sorceress who helps Jason win the Golden Fleece and reclaim his father's kingdom of Iolcus. The action of the opera begins years later, after Jason has decided to renounce Médée and marry the daughter of Creon, the King of Corinth. It depicts Médée's struggle to understand her abandonment and her violent response.

Despite the fact that the opera libretto was originally written in French (hence Médée rather than Medea), until a few years before the Opera Company of Boston production, it had been performed almost exclusively in an Italian translation with recitatives replacing the original spoken dialogues. Caldwell was determined to perform the work in the original language and to restore the dialogues as the composer intended. In an effort to achieve greater authenticity in that respect, however, she took license with language on multiple levels. The arias were sung in French, but the spoken passages were translated into ancient Greek, pre-recorded, and then played while actors, costumed in classical attire, pantomimed the action. In addition, the spoken text was accompanied by original music commissioned by Caldwell from a Greek composer, evoking the sparse musical underscoring of ancient Greek plays, and the quality of recitatives.

In *Médée* alternation of singing and pantomime, French and Greek texts, and shifts in the action between the upper and lower levels of the bi-level set, could have slowed down the dramatic pacing. Yet, given the impending tragic conclusion, it served as the equivalent of an ominous swinging dramatic pendulum, heightening the tension by slicing through the flow of action. The overarching path of the pantomime from the upper level of the set in Act I, to the lower level for Acts II and III, served to merge ancient myth with the stage reality of an 18th-century interpretation and brought it closer to the 20th-century audience as the dreadful climax approached.

In the Finale, Médée struggles against her urge to kill her two sons in revenge against Jason. Her psychological turmoil and the intensity of the music were underscored in Caldwell's staging. Médée rushed up the enormous staircase towards the temple (inside of which were her sons), trying to stifle her maternal feelings, and then retreated, overcome with dread. Finally, having resolved to carry out her plan, she charged up the steps again into the temple, leaving the audience to imagine (as they had in ancient Greece) the murders occurring behind the doors. As the chorus fled in horror from the scene, Jason arrived, too late to save their children, and collapsed on the staircase. An enormous winged horse, pulling the chariot of Helios, Médée's grandfather, descended to take to her to safety as fire began to engulf the setting. The staircase to the temple split in two and one of its columns crashed to the ground, perfectly timed to do so on the final chord.[28]

Critics were unsure how to react to the opera or to Caldwell's conception. *The Christian Science Monitor* critic, Jonathan Richmond, seemed to capture their responses. He wrote that she "stood true to her reputation for evoking ever new and more fantastic images, no expense spared." Although he thought that the production was uneven and problematic, his review included a familiar refrain: "Better to be stimulated by an inspired Caldwell experiment that didn't quite make it than to be bored by a traditional production that never elevated the imagination."[29]

In *The Bartered Bride, Don Quichotte, The Damnation of Faust* and *Médée* Caldwell explored oppression, the process of artistic creation, and the interplay of fiction and reality through experiments that radically reconceived the operas. Although her dominant approach was to delve deeply into the musical and dramatic origins of operas and present rediscoveries rather than revisions, the preceding examples illustrate her experiments with directorial supremacy over composers' intentions. This approach was not limited to serious operas, however. One further example illustrates her willingness to change the libretto of an opera, this time merely for comic effect.

Jacques Offenbach's *Orpheus in the Underworld*, entered the Opera Company of Boston repertoire in 1977 and again in 1982, both times staged and conducted by Caldwell. In 1977, it was the fourth opera of the season, following Gluck's sentimental 18th-century treatment of the Orpheus myth that it parodies. In an economy of conception and style, Caldwell used the same sets and costumes for both Gluck's *Orfeo ed Euridice* and Offenbach's *Orpheus in the Underworld*. The performance libretto was an amalgam of the existing libretto, along with improvisations and free translations credited to her and other members of the company. The synopsis in a program for the Opera New England tour that followed the Boston performances included the caveat: "The following is an approximation of the action of this buffoon-opera in which Offenbach indulges in a 'scandalous parody' of the sanctity of antiquity and in which Sarah Caldwell goes a few steps further. If what you see and hear differs from what is hereinafter described,—oh, well!—you're sure to have a grand time anyway."[30]

Caldwell cast celebrities in the opera to heighten its popular appeal. In 1977, Margaret Hamilton performed Public Opinion and Fred Gwynne played Styx, the drunken denizen of Hades. When Caldwell revived the production in 1982, she cast comedians Imogene Coca as Public Opinion and Sid Caesar as Styx. This legendary duo from the early years of television comedy stopped the show (literally) in the second act to do a vaudeville routine. In addition, slapstick comedy, a conga line, and antics in the orchestra pit (including a feigned argument between Caldwell and Orpheus) were part of the performance. One can understand why the *New York Times* critic, Peter G. Davis, reeled from this over-produced presentation filled with "dizzy flights of inventive action."[31]

The productions analyzed in this chapter were unusual in Caldwell's body of work. They are exceptions to her typical approach, which was generally characterized by a strong sense of *Werktreue*, a faithfulness to the score, and a willingness to follow its suggestions in the service of the composer's intentions. The bulk of her work lay in realizing productions dominated by character detail and grounded in psychological realism. She rejected the assumption that operas need updating for modern audiences to comprehend them and respond emotionally. She was convinced that modern audiences (even when unfamiliar with an opera's historical or social context) would be moved by seeing and hearing *more* of what the composer and librettist created, rather than *less*. Hence, she considered cutting operas sacrilegious.

Further, her work was not ego-driven, that is, she did not need to present *her* interpretation. Most often, she was more interested in staging what she thought the composer would have wanted.

Although Caldwell's experiments in director's theater were few, they were part of a body of work characterized by experimentation as it may be more broadly defined. She eagerly incorporated new technologies such as film, recorded sound, laser lights, and supertitles into her work. She also experimented through her selection of operas and in her research-driven approach to presenting well-known operas divested from accepted performance traditions. In the second half of the 20th century, director's theater strayed into egoism and eccentricity. Portraying excesses of sexuality and violence on stage was a common tactic to impress critics and shock audiences out of complacency. Yet, in its fundamental early form, the pioneering *auteur* directors—Walter Felsenstein among them—were radical because of their efforts to join music and theater together. In that way, they attempted to revitalize opera, give it new meaning, and challenge the status quo of stale traditions. Caldwell's explorations as an *auteur* director were examples of that kind of rare and radical approach.

Chapter 7

Final Years

In the 1960s, Caldwell had emerged on the national opera stage as a "Renaissance Woman," who presented captivating productions with the Opera Company of Boston that made her a gem in the cultural crown of the city. Within a decade she had reached the pinnacle of her career. She was profiled in *The New Yorker* and in the *New York Times Magazine*, lauded in multiple publications as a "genius" (*Boston Herald*), "Opera's First Lady" (*Newsweek*), "Music's Wonder Woman" (*Time Magazine* cover), and "The Divine Sarah" (*Opera News*). In 1972, Edward Sullivan, Mayor of Cambridge, Massachusetts, saluted the opening of the OCB's season by proclaiming it "Opera Week in Boston" and toasted her as "Boston's Barnum"[1]; *Musical America* lauded her as "Musician of the Year" in 1974; *Harper's Bazaar* named her one of the 10 most powerful women in America in 1977; and Governor Dukakis declared 1978 "Opera Company of Boston Year in the State of Massachusetts," the same year that Caldwell purchased the Opera House and marked her 20th year as head of the OCB.

By the third decade at the helm of the Opera Company of Boston though, Sarah Caldwell had become a liability. Publicity about her and the OCB focused more on its struggles than on its successes. Headlines such as "Boston Opera's Troubles Are Traced to Caldwell" (*New York Times*), "The Opera Company's Tale of Woe" (*Boston Globe*), and "A Struggle Backstage for Opera Company" (*Boston Globe*) were frequent. There were well-publicized denunciations of her international aspirations, reprimands for her managerial ineptitude, and speculations about whether she still possessed the artistic imagination that had captivated operagoers earlier in her career. Her eccentricities had become tiresome, her chaotic style a frustration to many who worked with her, her fiscal irresponsibility (especially during Making Music Together) an embarrassment to the city. Unions accused her of unfair labor practices, citizen groups reviled her for her involvement with the Philippine government, and her association with the Soviet Union as a frequent guest conduct of the Ural Philharmonic Orchestra (formerly the Sverdlovsk Radio Orchestra) in Yekaterinburg, Russia, may have all contributed to the growing discordance. Subscribers blamed her when the OCB Board did not refund them for the cancellation of the 1985 season. That situation more than any other underscored the fact that Caldwell was the Opera Company of Boston and the Opera Company of Boston was Caldwell. There had been no alternative plan for the company to help it weather her health crisis and there was no succession plan. Without her, the company could not survive. With her, it faced fiscal ruin, artistic unevenness, and personnel crises. After years of uncertainty, audiences and donors shied away from the ongoing drama at the OCB and even from the person who had put Boston on the international opera map.

In January 1991, the deteriorating Opera House closed its doors because it no longer met fire and safety codes. Bay Bank, which held the mortgage, was rumored to be ready to initiate a foreclosure.[2] The Opera Company of Boston owed back taxes to the city and it owed money to Boston Edison, which had shut off power for non-payment of bills.[3] When operas were announced then cancelled, subscribers again demanded their money back, but they did so in vain. There were a number of legal claims made for restitution, and Caldwell and her company manager, James T. Morgan, received letters from angry patrons. One not only demanded that his money for a subscription be returned, but also chastised Caldwell for neglecting the Opera House, writing that "the recent boarding up of the entrance to the Opera House seems to be symbolic of the contempt the Company has for the stewardship of a fine building."[4]

Only those closest to Caldwell knew the lengths to which she had gone to shore up the Opera House and save the company. An agreement between her and the Opera Company of Boston, Inc. drawn up in 1990 showed that she had made three loans to the OCB totaling over $978,000 and had agreed to loan an additional $60,000 in deferred compensation and salary.[5] In a last ditch effort, she purchased the mortgage back for $250,000, the majority of which she raised by selling a portion of her property in Lincoln, Massachusetts. That effort enabled her to maintain control of the theater and avert any possible plans to sell it without her consent. Years later, she admitted that she had believed that "it would be the greatest godsend for the Opera Company of Boston to own a beautiful theater, but ultimately it wasn't.... Funds after funds after funds had to be poured into the theater—with few visible results."[6]

Despite its derelict condition, the historic Opera House attracted the attention of local businessman and developer (and shortly thereafter the owner of the New England Patriots football team) Robert K. Kraft. In 1993, he made a bid to take it over with the intention of restoring it and renting it out for the production of musicals and operas, including those by the Opera Company of Boston. Such an arrangement would have made Caldwell a tenant once again, rather than an owner of a theater where the company could settle. No deal was reached. Instead, with grants from the Action for Boston Community Development "Summer Works" program, 12 men were employed to clean up the building as the "pre–Phase I" of the planned renovation. After weeks of labor, the Opera House was still not up to code, but Boston Edison turned the power back on and Caldwell celebrated with a special concert performance for an invited audience in September of 1993. There were gifts to contributors for their role in the restoration of the Opera House and to creditors, including Boston Edison, for having forgiven the company's power debt.[7] Despite these poignant attempts to regenerate support for the revival of the Opera Company of Boston, no progress was made for two years.

At that time, lower Washington Avenue, which encompassed the area around the Opera House, was a "red light" district. The area that locals referred to as the "Combat Zone" desperately needed more legitimate use establishments for tax revenues and safety. The problems of the neighborhood became even more apparent when the empty Opera House was vandalized. Robbers broke in and stole everything that could be resold, including historical iron grillwork and a large radiator. They (or possibly successive waves of vandals) destroyed props and costumes, set fires, and irreparably damaged computers, company files, and financial records.[8] Fortunately, the music collection remained intact and stage sets, which were stored off-site, were safe. Still, a wealth of information about the company—opera history—was destroyed.

It was estimated that almost $400,000 would be needed for basic safety work in order to reopen The Opera House to the public, and about $5 million (the original cost of the building) for a full restoration.[9] The cost was high, but in 1995, The National Trust for Historic Preservation had put it on its "11 Most Endangered Historic Places" list. It was designated as an historic property and that spurred local efforts to address its deterioration. The Boston Redevelopment Authority was very interested in returning it to active use as part of its midtown revitalization plan. It recognized that the Opera House contributed to the economic viability and safety of the area by bringing people not only to the theater, but also to downtown shops and restaurants, especially in the evening. Finally, a Texas based development firm, Theater Management Group, purchased the property from Caldwell. It signed an agreement that allowed her to present operas there for no more than 12 weeks a year with rental fees to be negotiated.[10] Caldwell, now over 70 years of age, remained hopeful that she could revive the Opera Company of Boston, even if she had to rent space to do so.

In 1998, Boston Mayor Thomas M. Menino prioritized the Opera House restoration as part of the revitalization of lower Washington Avenue, but financing was delayed because banks that had loaned money to the Opera Company of Boston years earlier had since been acquired by other banks. Meanwhile, the Theater Management Group began investing money on feasibility studies and planning the theater's renovation. The most difficult and controversial part of the restoration had to do with the shallow stage. It had always been a challenge for Caldwell and without significant changes, it would remain so for the touring shows that the Theater Management Group hoped to book. Therefore, TMG filed papers with the Boston Redevelopment Authority and the city zoning board to expand the stage to a viable depth for modern production needs. The rear of the building came up to Mason Street, across from which was the loading area for Tremont on the Common, a 26-story condominium on Tremont Street. The proposal included closing Mason Street entirely, which would have added to the restoration cost because of the need to relocate utilities, and raised concerns for the condominium residents about access in cases of emergency.[11]

A court challenge initiated by the residents was unsuccessful. In 2002, a Superior Court judge gave the developers the go ahead, allowing the city of Boston to use its power of eminent domain to seize 2,000 square feet of sidewalk and road to facilitate the $30 million renovation. The city defended its action as one for the greater good: "The only way you can get a theater back in the building is to have the stage expanded," said Albert Rex, executive director of the Boston Preservation Alliance. "[The city is] bringing this incredible theater back for generations of Bostonians to enjoy, so we thought [the seizure] was a reasonable response."[12] The restoration took 18 months during which time the stage and backstage areas were completely demolished and rebuilt and historically significant interior elements such as the sculptural plasters and chandeliers were painstakingly restored. In June 2004, the theater re-opened with a vaudeville benefit show commemorating the restoration, and the following month it hosted an extended run of Disney's *The Lion King*.

* * *

At the same time that the doors of the Opera House were closing, Caldwell was in the midst of planning the second phase of the Making Music

Together festival. Whereas in 1988 Russian artists had come to Boston, in its second iteration, American artists travelled to Russia. Originally, she had scheduled the second event to take place in 1989, but given fundraising obstacles, the outbreak of the First Gulf War, and political uncertainty in the fragmenting Soviet Union, it had to be delayed. When it did finally take place in early 1991, it was even larger than it had been in Boston. Instead of three weeks of events in one city, the Soviet portion extended over three months in several cities. There were profile concerts of music by Leon Kirchner, Lukas Foss, Mario Davidovsky, Joan Tower, and Elliott Carter. A Bernstein festival (Leonard Bernstein had died the previous autumn) in Moscow featured films, videos, songs, and piano music. Most notably, the Opera Company of Boston made history by becoming the first American company to perform in the Soviet Union's most prestigious theater, The Bolshoi in Moscow.

The opera that the Caldwell brought to Moscow was Robert Di Domenica's *The Balcony*, the world premiere of which she had given in Boston the previous summer. Most of the same singers joined the cast, but they performed with a Soviet orchestra, chorus, and dancers. The company also brought with it the set designed by Pond and Senn and costumes from the OCB production. In addition to the familiar visual elements was the chaos, typical of any Caldwell endeavor. For example, although one full week had been scheduled for rehearsals, a conflict with another Bolshoi production decreased the available time for *The Balcony* to three days. The shortened rehearsal period, coupled with the complication of incompatible electrical elements, and the difficulties of coordinating the efforts of people speaking different languages, added to the disarray. Richard Dyer, who travelled with the OCB to observe the performance as part of the Making Music Together festival, reported in the *Boston Globe* that numerous technical glitches were evident during the performances, including an errant drop, missed lighting cues, and missing pieces of scenery. Nevertheless, it was an historical collaboration of two cultures on a common artistic endeavor.

Perhaps not surprisingly, the second iteration of the Making Music Together festival, like the earlier one, was plagued with fund-raising problems and cost over-runs. A major source of revenue for the festival was a $1 million federal grant, obtained through the United States Information Agency, a foreign affairs agency that, among its other activities, sponsored international exchanges for educational and cultural purposes. According to Caldwell, the USIA withheld $100,000 and expected MMT to raise a certain amount itself. Some of the MMT fundraising efforts failed and additional costs were incurred. After the conclusion of the festival, the USIA initiated an investigation into how Caldwell had handled the grant money. As part of its investigation, she was required to explain in detail why MMT had not raised the required funds and how she had spent the grant money provided. In a letter to the USIA, she carefully described the difficulties encountered during the "changing fiscal structure within the Soviet Union" at the time of the festival. In her deposition, she described how the festival added additional cities to the performance itinerary, how it had coincided with the political collapse of the Soviet Union and the uncertainties that had forced the organizers to make expensive changes to their original travel arrangements.[13] The USIA did not find Caldwell guilty of any wrongdoing, but the investigation itself was a public embarrassment and confirmation for her detractors that she could not be trusted with managing such an undertaking.

Years later Caldwell pointed to the stress and negative publicity from the second Making Music Together festival as the reason the Opera Company of Boston was no longer able to continue. Ultimately, however, she felt pride in the accomplishment of having presented two festivals that connected American and Soviet artists: "In a world where technology seems to have overtaken humanity, it's important that we continue to communicate. That was the basis for launching our festival. The exchange worked on a very simple principle: the most important thing one can do in this world is to enable people to keep talking to one another. Even though the performing artists lived in different countries, held vastly different political ideas, and spoke different languages, that didn't matter. Through music they communicated."[14] Her statement of faith in the unifying power of music echoed the sentiment expressed by Serge Koussevitzky at the opening of Tanglewood, almost a half century earlier just after the end of World War II. The Making Music Together festival had brought together artists in unprecedented numbers as part of the first major cultural exchange in the new post–Soviet Union era.

After the closure of the Opera House and the collapse of the Opera Company of Boston, Caldwell took numerous guest conductor assignments with orchestras in the United States and Europe. One orchestra in Russia, however, became her favorite. Through her work on the Making Music Together festivals, she had developed associations with a number of high-profile cultural figures in the Soviet Union/Russia. When she was offered an opportunity to guest conduct the Ural Philharmonic Orchestra, she readily accepted because she had heard that it was well known for its contemporary repertoire. At that time, it was also an orchestra comprised of underpaid, but extremely dedicated musicians, and she relished her opportunities to conduct there.[15] Her association became permanent in 1993 when she was named Principal Guest Conductor and she continued to conduct there regularly (see Appendix A).

After the Opera Company of Boston ceased its activities, Caldwell did not continue stage directing. Of course, it may have been by choice, but given her passion for directing operas, that seems improbable. It is more likely that opera companies were wary of her erratic work habits and did not want to take a chance on her. As a conductor, however, her role was much more constrained and her schedule necessarily regulated, and those remained her only assignments until 1998. That year, James Freeman, who was a music professor at Swarthmore College in Pennsylvania and the Artistic Director and Conductor of Orchestra 2001, sent her a score of *The Black Swan*, a two-act chamber-opera, the first opera by Thomas Whitman, a young composer and faculty member at Swarthmore. The libretto, by Nathalie Anderson (also a Swarthmore faculty member), is based on Thomas Mann's novella *Die Betrogene* (The Black Swan) and a related short story by Richard Selzer, *The Black Swan Revisited: An Homage to Thomas Mann*. The opera intrigued Caldwell, so she took on the project, bringing Helen Pond and Herbert Senn with her to design the set. It was performed in the Lang Performing Arts Center at Swarthmore College. The suggestive scenery consisted of only a few three-dimensional elements, such as a bed or door frame as the action required, and incorporated rear projections that captured seasonal changes referenced in the libretto. Characteristically, she attended to all the details of the production, including the supertitles, carefully ensuring that the appearance of each slide rhythmically matched the stage action and the musical changes. The production received some media attention it may not have otherwise because of Caldwell, but the reviews were lukewarm. The *Boston Herald* praised her for the way she "moved the characters around with utter naturalness and allowed them to advance the story. This was no small accomplishment since only one of the three singers actually looked his part."[16] The *Opera News* reviewer appreciated the "visual magic of the stage."[17] Otherwise, it received limited publicity and did not revive her directing career.

The following year, at the age of 75, Caldwell sold her house in Lincoln, Massachusetts, and returned to Fayetteville, Arkansas. She had accepted an offer from the University of Arkansas to join the music department as a Distinguished Professor and head of the opera program. She had previous attachments to the university. Her stepfather, Dr. Henry Alexander, had taught political science there and after completing high school, she had studied at UA briefly before going to the New England Conservatory of Music. The university hoped that her appointment would add prestige to the music department, attract a high caliber of student, and raise money for the Fayetteville Opera Company. Caldwell retained her commitment to travel to Russia twice a year to conduct the Ural Philharmonic Orchestra and watched developments in Boston, still hoping that she could revive the Opera Company of Boston. When interviewed about her new post, it was clear that she remained connected to Boston: "I would not be sitting here in Fayetteville," she said, "if I though the job would interfere with the work I am planning for Boston."[18]

In December of that same year, the University of Arkansas received a $1.15 million donation that enabled it to develop and enhance its opera program, and to establish an International Center for the Study of Early Asian and Middle Eastern Musics [sic], a research center housed in the department of music. It hired two prominent ethnomusicologists, Rembrandt Wolpert and Elizabeth Markham, members of The Cambridge Group, who had worked with Laurence Picken in studying the music of the Tang court. The Tang dynasty (A.D. 618–907) was a period in Chinese history when music showed widespread influences. Musicians from countries across Eurasia travelled there to perform, to study, and influenced its culture. After the end of the Tang dynasty, however, the music became known only through copies of the original manuscripts that had been made by Japanese musicians. Naturally, over time, the works were modified and the original performance practices obscured. Dr. Picken and his colleagues, including Wolpert and Markham, endeavored to transcribe and interpret the music, in order to discover how it would have been played during the Tang period. Dr. Picken began his research in the 1950s and over the next 40 years, published his findings in seven volumes entitled *Music of the Tang Court*, illuminating not only the music itself, but also the original performance techniques.

Caldwell was instrumental in bringing together The International Center for the Study of Early Asian and Middle Eastern Musics at the University of Arkansas and the Library of Congress to form the Ancient Asian Music Project. A Memorandum of Understanding detailed a number of efforts to preserve ancient music, including fund-raising, archiving, publishing, developing technologies in support of preservation efforts, and academic opportunities for UA students, such as taking master classes from the Juilliard Quartet when it was in residency at the LOC. This arrangement was to enable the continuation of the study and preservation of the work of Dr. Picken and his team of researchers. Caldwell's role was not only to bring the preservation project to fruition, but also to bring to light the music itself. Soon, however, illness impeded her work with the Library of Congress and her goal to record and perform the music.

At the same time that Caldwell was engaged with University of Arkansas researchers on the Asian music project, she was leading the opera program. As might be expected, she delivered the unexpected. In February

2000, she presented *Abstract Opera no. 1* by Boris Blacher, a 35-minute experimental opera written in 1953, in which the characters sing nonsense sounds rather than words, accompanied by an orchestra without any stringed instruments. She conducted the opera, but Patricia Birch, who had worked with her on several productions in Boston, handled the staging. In addition to her conducting contributions, Caldwell lobbied for a new theater to be dedicated to Baroque theater and music. Her vision was for Fayetteville to become the center of an annual Baroque festival that would give it the reputation enjoyed by other popular festival sites such as Charleston, South Carolina and Aspen, Colorado. Unfortunately, Caldwell's time in Arkansas was short-lived as health problems began to curtail her activities. In early 2001, she was admitted to the hospital in serious condition, and remained in a coronary care unit for a month. Her illness forced the postponement of planned productions of Bernstein's *Trouble in Tahiti* and Puccini's *La Bohème* (Act II) at the university. In April, she was able to return to her post and conducted both operas. The following March she conducted Verdi's *La Traviata*, and Benjamin Britten's *Turn of the Screw*. Christopher Lacey, a UA faculty member and assistant conductor to Caldwell, served as the stage director.

By August of that year, Caldwell's health problems returned. She went on extended leave, eventually resigning from the university to return east, ill, exhausted, and alone. Caldwell had no close family members.[19] She and James T. Morgan, her longtime friend and former manager of the Opera Company of Boston, purchased a home in Freeport, Maine, which they shared until her death on March 23, 2006.

Conclusion

After the dissolution of the Opera Company of Boston, Bostonians were left with limited choices to experience live opera. Goldovsky's New England Opera Theater was no longer producing, the Metropolitan Opera had ceased touring, and the Boston Concert Opera had disbanded, deeply in debt. The only company to survive the so-called "opera wars" was the Boston Lyric Opera, founded in 1976 as the result of a merger of the New England Chamber Opera, New England Regional Opera, and the Associate Artists Opera Company of New England. Initially, it utilized the auditorium at Northeastern University for its performance space before moving into the modest 850-seat Majestic Theater belonging to Emerson College, where it mounted three productions a year. It had been formed to provide professional performance opportunities to promising young singers trained at Boston's universities and conservatories, an original ambition of the Opera Company of Boston as well. In contrast to the OCB, where Caldwell's ambitions led her to present large-scale productions and to hire star performers, the Lyric stayed true to its original course and in doing so survived.

In 1991, shortly after the demise of its main rival company, the Lyric joined forces with Robert Canon's Boston Opera Theater. Justin Moss, former director of development for the Baltimore Opera Company, became the general director, and Richard Geddes, formerly of the Opera Theater of St. Louis, the artistic advisor. The new Lyric promised, "To produce intimately scaled operas of diversified repertory and consistently of the highest quality, featuring young American artists.... To provide fiscally responsible and cost-conscious management necessary to achieve these goals."[1] Clearly, it wanted to signal its intention to avoid the tarnished reputation of the Opera Company of Boston. Indeed, the Lyric's responsible management won the confidence of its audiences as evidenced by the growth of its budget from less than $1 million to about $2.5 million by the mid–1990s and to over $6 million just one decade later. Its cost-conscious approach did succeed in building a sustainable company that is still in operation, but opera in Boston has never regained the artistic and critical distinction it had during the era of the Opera Company of Boston. The difference was Sarah Caldwell.

Caldwell is noteworthy first because she was a unique combination of a stage director, conductor, and impresario. Among her contemporaries there were director-designers (Ponnelle, Zefferelli), conductors who staged productions (Karajan), conductors who also served as artistic administrators (Crosby, Patterson), and composers who conducted and staged their own works (Menotti). Caldwell, however, was singular in having a long career as both a stage director and conductor for dozens of operas, acclaimed in both capacities, while at the same time leading her own company. One cannot describe such a career as anything less than an extraordinary, especially given that it began at a time when many women struggled to make their mark in one professional role let alone in three that were then (and remain so today) overwhelmingly dominated by men.

As both director and conductor, Caldwell was able to bring to her productions a level of artistic cohesion not possible when those roles are taken by separate artists, no matter how closely they work together. Her musical abilities enabled her to analyze the scores, to understand how melody, rhythm, orchestration, and a host of other musical elements that were used by composers to suggest dramatic possibilities. Her theatrical imagination and skill enabled her to realize those possibilities for her audiences in works from a wide range of styles and genres. The duality of the director-conductor was not just a practical one for Caldwell, it was a philosophical approach to her work. She was a disciple of Boris Goldovsky and Walter Felsenstein, both of whom endeavored to produce operas that bound together musical values with theatrical values. They created what they called "opera theater" and "music theater," respectively, where the two arts combined and elevated each other. Caldwell tirelessly promoted their philosophical ideals through every one of her productions over the course of her long career.

Although having one person as the central artistic and administrative figure in a company guaranteed cohesiveness of vision, at the Opera Company of Boston it also resulted in an excessive burden under which Caldwell struggled. Other artistic directors of the time, including Kurt Herbert Adler, Rudolf Bing, John Crosby, Carol Fox, David Gockley, Russell Patterson and Glynn Ross functioned in one or two roles, not regularly as artistic director *and* principal conductor *and* stage director. In contrast to her public image as someone who wanted to do it all, Caldwell actually longed to focus her energies. After her life-threatening illness in 1985 she said, "While I'm not angry enough to quit, sometimes I think I am on the verge of that....

I'm a conductor. I'm a stage director. I bring creative people together. I also function as a fund-raiser. That's far too many things for one person to do. I'm angry about that."[2] Her role in the Opera Company of Boston extended well beyond the usual responsibilities of an artistic director and so too did her control over all of the company's endeavors. Of course, though she may have wanted to share responsibilities, she never did. As a consequence, she was inextricably linked to the company and therefore, both its triumphs and shortcomings were placed entirely on her shoulders.

At the helm of the Opera Company of Boston, Caldwell alone determined its repertoire and year after year she delivered an unmatched array of operas that were testaments to her formidable intellectual curiosity and range of theatrical and musical skills. She staged operas ranging from *Hippolyte et Aricie* to *Die Soldaten*. She never shied away from large scale undertakings such as *The Trojans*, *Don Carlos*, *War and Peace*, and *Montezuma*. Yet, she also succeeded with the intimate and refined *Madama Butterfly* on Ming Cho Lee's compact unit set. She staged a stately *Orfeo ed Euridice*, then exploded into buffoonery with *Orpheus in the Underworld* that same season—using the same sets and costumes. From a whimsical presentation of *Voyage to the Moon* that launched the Opera Group/Opera Company of Boston, to the stark and politically charged rendering of *The Balcony* that was its final offering, her stage directing was characterized by versatility and daring.

Caldwell, the director-conductor, was ever present in the way she approached the preparation of an opera. She did so as a music historian first, travelling to libraries and archives throughout the world to seek out the earliest editions of opera scores and in doing so gained a reputation for exposing (quite literally in the case of *Don Carlos*) long-forgotten elements of them. Instead of studying an available edition and devising a directorial concept from that, she approached all operas (even well-known ones) determined to grasp the composer's original intentions before the cuts, before the re-writes, before "tradition" took hold. As a result, she frequently uncovered new musical passages, re-inserted "lost" arias, and discovered new dramatic insights from them. Beverly Sills once said, "She could turn a piece you've done on hundred times into something you felt you were experiencing for the first time."[3] Critics most often agreed, but not always. They accused her of gimmickry and pointed out that even an autograph score did not always represent the composer's definitive artistic statement. It is true that her choices showed an unwillingness to acknowledge that composers sometimes made revisions voluntarily as their artistic conceptions matured or that revisions could improve the artistic merits of a work. Ultimately, the historical significance of her research-based process was that it brought to light numerous musical passages and dramatic aspects of well-known operas that could at least be heard and debated by a new generation of critics and audiences.

Caldwell's process of developing productions through deep analysis of the scores was in contrast to that of many of her contemporaries. Directors such as Herbert Wernicke, Peter Sellars, Ruth Berghaus, Gerard Mortier and others revisioned operas by devising dramatic conceptions—intended to bridge the ever growing historical and sociological divide between operatic works and modern audiences—that often seemed separate from the score. With the exception of a few experiments, Caldwell refused to join in. She asserted that operas did not need to be radically altered to be comprehensible and considered that approach condescending to both the composer and to the audience. As she put it, "Our ancestors were not fools," which is to say that composers and librettists were conscientious artists who created operas for audiences that likewise understood the art form and accepted its conventions. She maintained that there were dramatic and musical qualities in operas from all periods that were accessible to people even across the widest historical and cultural divides. To her, revisionist approaches by stage directors were not merely unnecessary, they were confirmations of directorial hubris. The popularity of her productions of vastly different operas attest to their accessibility.

Throughout the second half of the 20th century the importance of the stage director in opera had risen to equal that of the conductor as interpreter and, at times, even to replace the composer as creator. Critical and popular references to "Zefferelli's 'Bohème,'" "Chereau's 'Ring,'" and "Sellars' Mozart-Da Ponte Trilogy" were evidence of that power shift. Caldwell was unimpressed by what she saw as directors staging works in ways that called attention to themselves. Not surprisingly, a director who labors to uncover the composer's vision is not likely to be linked to the resulting production in a catchy way. Therefore, critics did not write of "Caldwell's 'Barber'" or "Caldwell's 'Mass.'" It is quite likely that she would not have approved if they had. In an era when directors regularly ignored or even suppressed the voice of the composer, she worked to make it heard. She did so through rehearsal process that could be exhausting and exasperating, but which was a rarely practiced co-collaboration with the singers.

Caldwell's rehearsal process was legendary for the successes she achieved with it and equally for the frustration it caused. Inspired by Felsenstein and adhering to the values she had been taught by Goldovsky, she worked methodically with singers through multiple interpretive options until she found one that resonated with her. It was painstakingly slow and it devoured rehearsal time. Most often it resulted in scenes that were insightful and brilliantly executed, but at times it left others muddled or under rehearsed. At her best, Caldwell was an inspiring and inventive leader. At her worst, she was a disorganized, even misguided, perfectionist who could not commit to an idea, leaving singers and other artistic and production staff members bitter and exhausted. Sills and Verrett were among the singers who were able to tolerate her idiosyncrasies and thrived on their explorations of character with her. They were not alone in finding such detailed work rewarding. World class singers regularly came to the Opera Company of Boston precisely because they longed to be more than über-marionettes manipulated by a director bent on executing an ego-driven concept.

The critical and popular success of Caldwell as a director is particularly remarkable because of the spaces in which she worked. She wanted, indeed lobbied for years, for a traditional opera house to replace the one the city had so swiftly demolished, but to no avail. Unlike many other opera stage directors who have at their disposal vast stages, sophisticated technology, and professional crews who can assist in realizing their ideas, Caldwell worked in venues inhospitable to opera performance, lacking space, technology, and even trained production personnel. Out of necessity she staged her operas in movie palaces, vaudeville theaters, concert halls, hockey rinks, gymnasiums, and basketball courts, but her work there became transformative. She transcended even the most awkward spaces with designs and staging that reduced physical and aesthetic distances. She and her designers reshaped the performance area to enable the singers and audiences to experience drama and music together. Audiences were enveloped in the performance (sitting next to the Dutchman's crew, smelling incense in *The Ice Break*, holding up colored placards to create a giant French flag at the end of *The Daughter of the Regiment*). Singers made their entrances and exits through the house, they sang from the side boxes, they interacted with the audience in ways that created an aesthetic as well as a physical connection. The conditions under which she produced opera sparked her imagination and resulted in productions that were not possible in traditional opera houses. She erased the elitism of which opera is often accused; she made it immediate and democratic.

Caldwell's productions were known for their musical and dramatic integrity combined with accessible and captivating visual sensibilities that made her productions popular. Critics sniffed at her "gimmicks," but could not discount her eye for theatrical magic. The use of children to represent Greek soldiers emerging from the Trojan horse in *The Trojans* was a highlight of her career. So, too, was the climax of *Benvenuto Cellini*, when Cellini suddenly struck a 25-foot-high mold that broke away to reveal the smoldering golden statue of Perseus. And audiences gasped when the title character in

Don Quichotte appeared to get swept up by the blades of the windmill. She always understood that she was staging opera not for her own satisfaction, but for an audience and she believed that audiences deserved a good show.

The social and artistic experience of an opera performance by the Opera Company of Boston was, however, frequently at odds with the economic realities of the business of opera. By all accounts Caldwell was an inventive stage director, but managing a company requires its own skill set that she clearly did not have. Therefore, at the same time that she was developing an international reputation as a critically acclaimed director, she was developing local reputation as a careless and fiscally irresponsible impresario. She may have been angry about fulfilling multiple roles in her company, and may even have tried to share them with others, but she continued to dominate the company to its detriment. As Susan Larson, the Boston soprano who sang in Caldwell's production of Di Domenica's *The Balcony*, reflected in 1996, "She left a certain amount of carnage in her wake. Unable in this most collaborative of art forms to relinquish artistic, organizational or fund-raising control to others, she never built a company that could function without her."[4]

Over the years, Bostonians became increasingly frustrated by productions that Caldwell promised, but never delivered. The Opera Company of Boston's history includes unexpected changes in seasons that pointed to shortcomings in preparation and organization: in 1976 Sessions' *Montezuma* came to fruition only seven years after it was originally scheduled; in 1977 Verdi's *Rigoletto* replaced the originally scheduled Bellini's *La Sonnambula*; in 1978 plans for Tchaikovsky's *Mazeppa* were scrapped and never revived; in 1984 Rossini's *Barber of Seville* was added to the season because Peter Maxwell Davies's *Taverner* could not be performed until 1986; in 1988 Cherubini's *Médée* was performed after two postponements, one because Caldwell needed more time to prepare, another because the sets were unable to be shipped to Boston in time. Whatever the reason for these changes, her critics pointed to managerial ineffectiveness on Caldwell's part and concluded that she was entirely to blame.[5] The most damaging cancellation was that of an entire season, owing to Caldwell's serious illness. While her patrons may have forgiven her for that reason, they never forgave the suggestion made by the Board that they make a donation to the Company of the money they had paid for their subscriptions.

As the financial situation of the Opera Company of Boston worsened in its waning years, there was speculation about how it might have taken advantage of new technologies to increase its earned income. Television was an early possibility that seemed to hold great promise for opera companies, particularly given the excitement generated by Menotti's *Amahl and the*

Night Visitors, commissioned by NBC and broadcast live in 1951. However, unlike professional sports, where earnings from television broadcasts are much greater than ticket revenues, opera never rose to a sufficient level of popularity on network television or on cable television to make it a viable option.[6] More recently, but too late for the Opera Company of Boston, another wave of technology has generated promise for increasing the earned income of opera companies. The transmission of opera productions in high definition into movie theaters has become a marketing and financial windfall for the Metropolitan Opera, which began the practice in 2006. In one weekend that year, an audience of 97,000 watched Gounod's *Roméo et Juliette* and the company grossed $1.65 million.[7] Other opera companies have followed suit, confirming that there is a potential market to be tapped and money to be made (although possibly at the cost of fewer people attending live performances[8]). Yet, it is likely that there will always remain a chronic deficit, an "income gap," that precludes opera organizations from being able to survive without generous patronage.

The Opera Company of Boston, like other arts organizations, was dependent upon a combination of ticket sales, private and corporate donations, and grants at the national, state and local levels. At the national level, direct federal support in the United States lags far behind Canada and much of western Europe. The National Endowment for the Arts was created as a federal source of support, but it could never contribute more than 5 percent of the income of any opera company, and when compared to amounts set aside in European budgets for the arts, that is almost insignificant.[9] State spending on arts increased in the 1970s and the 1980s, but it was never more than 3 percent of the total revenue of any opera company. By the end of the 1980s, state spending slowed due to an economic recession that led to devastating cuts. The Commonwealth of Massachusetts, for instance, dropped its arts funding from $21 million in 1988 to $18 million in 1990, and by 1992 to only $3.6 million,[10] a most critical period for the Opera Company of Boston.

It is local governments that have the greatest interest in funding artistic activity because of its positive impact on the local economies. Since the 1970s, interest in the economic impact of the arts sector has become the subject of studies by economists in publications such as the *Journal of Cultural Economics*, founded in 1973 in response to this new area of inquiry. Numerous studies have examined the extent to which a thriving arts community strengthens local economies, reduces crime, and increases quality of life for city residents and have found their impact to be overwhelmingly positive. In *The Rise of the Creative Class: and how it's transforming work, leisure, community and everyday life* Richard Florida estimated that 30 percent of the entire U.S. workforce—up from just 10 percent at the turn of the 20th century and less than 20 percent as recently as 1980—is linked directly or indirectly to the creative arts, and interested in living in cities that support them.[11] Boston recognized that cultural institutions were key to bringing people to the city and included theater development in its plans for revitalizing its downtown core. As early as 1974 a proposal was put forward by the Boston Redevelopment Authority (a municipal entity founded in 1957 and charged with revitalizing the city core) for the conversion of the Music Hall into a performing arts complex, which included a rental option for the Opera Company of Boston for 40 performances a year.[12] In 1989, it put forward a Midtown Cultural District Plan that included a request for a state grant to renovate the Opera House so that it could be made available to the Opera Company of Boston.[13] However, neither of these proposals came to fruition.

In the decades since the original Boston Opera House was razed, the city has helped to restore and renovate several theaters, recognizing what it may not have in 1958, that a vibrant and sophisticated city needs appropriate arts facilities. Within a few years of the demise of the Opera Company of Boston, it undertook several key renovations. The Boston Music Hall/Orpheum/Aquarius, the original home of the Boston Symphony Orchestra, which Caldwell used for several years, remains a concert hall. The Emerson Cutler Majestic Theatre, an intimate 850 seat theater was the home of the Lyric Opera until it was able to move to the 1680 seat Schubert Theater in 1998, shortly after its $3 million renovation, for its three operas a year. Moreover the renovation of the huge Metropolitan Theatre, known for years as the Wang Center for the Performing Arts (later the Citi Performing Arts Center and now the Wang Theatre, which along with the Schubert is part of The Boch Center), also functions as a road house. Even Jordan Hall, the performance venue of the New England Conservatory of Music underwent a renovation in 1995. While each of these can be used for opera, none was built or renovated specifically for opera.

Although the funding situation during the existence of the Opera Company of Boston was perpetually precarious, it was no more so than it was for other companies begun at the same time and with similar budgets and similar obstacles to artistic success and financial stability. Yet, many of those companies did manage to survive and even thrive. Some did so through savvy management and marketing, and others by acknowledging that catering to their audiences' tastes, as they often needed to do, was not necessarily an artistic compromise. Kevin Smith, president of Minnesota Opera, a regional company formed in 1963, argued that it is good to "prove yourself in the community on a daily basis. Tough as it is, the American system is good in a lot of ways ... you have to demonstrate your value."[14] Caldwell did present a number of new and relatively unknown operas to her audiences. Yet, ticket sales were most often strong, which demonstrated interest and support by the opera community for her selected repertoire. Nevertheless, those sales could, at best, contribute to only about half of the cost of producing opera.

Caldwell's operatic community was Boston, a city settled by Puritans with a reputation for conservative theatrical tastes and a skepticism about opera. Yet, Bostonians have supported many arts organizations and musical societies. Moreover, in the early 20th century it was home to the Little Theatre Movement, which contributed to the emergence of a new generation of American playwrights and a distinctly American dramatic voice. Still, it has remained arguably ambivalent about opera, as evident, at least in part, by its inability to secure funding to build a suitable opera house to replace the one it torn down so quickly. Perhaps Caldwell's mistake in producing world class performances on what seemed, at times, like no more than her sheer determination to do so, was that the result appeared to affirm that the company did not need a proper opera house or even more funding. Her own resourcefulness may have worked against her, because if an artist can do so much with so little support, why give more? "This is not the sort of city where you can make a few calls and get civic leadership behind you," one Bostonian said, reflecting on opera funding. "St. Louis, Houston, Tulsa all want to prove something to the world. Boston is smug."[15]

Caldwell invigorated opera in Boston by creating numerous critically acclaimed opera productions, but the by the time the Opera Company of Boston closed its doors, her tattered reputation as an irresponsible impresario had long over-shadowed her work as a director or conductor. She was a polarizing figure throughout her career, defended by adamant supporters and dismissed by bitter detractors. In the years since her death, her work has languished in near obscurity and her contributions to opera stage directing in America—until this monograph—have been unexamined and almost forgotten. As an example, in August 2018, Tanglewood celebrated the life and career of Leonard Bernstein, a great American composer, conductor, friend and fellow Tanglewood alum of Caldwell. The Bernstein Centennial Celebration brochure listed other famous Tanglewood alumni, apologizing for being unable to include all the distinguished musicians who had studied there. The 28 artists listed were indeed distinguished,[16] but 23 were men. The five women listed (Stephanie Blythe, Phyllis Curtin, Leontyne Price, Cheryl Studer, and Shirley Verrett) were singers. Caldwell—a student and teacher at Tanglewood for 10 seasons, a stage director and conductor, who established and led an internationally renowned opera company in Boston for over 30 years—was not on the list.

Appendix A:
The Conductor

This monograph has focused on the work of Sarah Caldwell as a stage director, but as noted throughout, that role inevitably intertwined with her work as a conductor. At times, it was difficult to discern how she balanced choices of staging or musical interpretation or how she weighted each. She underscored musical passages with stage movement and visual "moments" that synchronized music and drama perfectly (see Chapter 6 for an example from the climactic final scene of *Médée*). Yet, she also inserted restored music into opera scenes regardless of its impact on dramatic pacing (see Chapter 3 for an example from her production of *The Barber of Seville* at the New York City Opera). In theory, she maintained that opera was a combination of theater and music and was equally adamant that a good director, therefore, must be a trained musician.[1] In practice, she embodied that ideal, exhibiting a keen musicianship and an ability to analyze scores as dramatic texts in a way that many stage directors of opera, especially those trained in spoken theater, cannot.

During the off-season of the Opera Company of Boston and after it ceased producing, she served regularly as a guest conductor with major orchestras, and earned numerous accolades. Yet, her conducting career and her place within the canon of American conductors of the 20th century remains unexamined. It is beyond the scope of this book and this author's area of expertise to analyze her conducting skills or her historical importance of as a conductor. However, a brief overview and a sample of reviews from leading critics of the day serves as a fitting companion piece to the main portion of this book and an introduction to this aspect of her career. It is hoped that the information provided will prompt a more thorough study.

Caldwell never intended to become a conductor. When she enrolled at the New England Conservatory of Music, she did so as a violinist. Only after she had watched Boris Goldovsky working with students on opera scenes did she begin to seek out training. She took only two classes in Opera Conducting while a student at the NEC,[2] but at Tanglewood and later with the New England Opera Theater under the tutelage of Goldovsky, she received coaching and opportunities to conduct selections from a variety of operatic works, some of which she later produced with the Opera Company of Boston. Those experiences, combined with her training in stage direction, enabled her to become both the primary stage director and conductor of her own company. There were only a few occasions during her career when she served in a single role. Significantly, she gave up the baton more often than she relinquished stage directing. She produced 131 operas with the OCB, conducted 88 of them, but staged 127. When faced with a choice, she opted to direct operas rather than to conduct them. Colleagues have observed that she did not conduct her own productions because she particularly liked conducting. Rather, she did it because she believed that the embodiment of a stage director and conductor in one individual was the surest way to achieve the unity between music and drama that was her goal.

As noted above, Caldwell's conducting career was not limited to the Opera Company of Boston. Regularly throughout her career, she served as a guest conductor with orchestras in Canada, China, Israel, Mexico, South Africa, Sweden, Russia, Venezuela, and in the United States with the American Symphony Orchestra at Carnegie Hall, Boston Symphony Orchestra, Dallas Symphony, Metropolitan Opera Orchestra, New York City Opera Orchestra, the United States Marine Corps Band and others. In 1975, she became only the second woman to conduct the New York Philharmonic since Nadia Boulanger (1939 and 1962), doing so for a pension fund benefit concert that featured compositions by women. In 1978, she was one of three conductors who led the New York Philharmonic in a series of summer concerts in New York City parks that included Symphony No. 2 in B minor by Borodin and the *Symphonie fantastique* by Berlioz. The other two conductors that year were Zubin Mehta and Andre Kostelanetz,[3] a testament to the high regard in which she was held as a conductor.

There are very few reviews of Caldwell conducting performances in the 1940s when she was at Tanglewood, at Boston University, or even during the first few years of the Opera Group/Opera Company of Boston. One of the earliest is from the summer of 1950 when she both directed and conducted Mozart's *La Finta Giardiniera* at Tanglewood. Jay Rosenfeld, the reviewer for the local paper, *The Berkshire Eagle*, wrote: "Miss Caldwell held the alert orchestra and the whole production in complete control and gave it an over-all youthful vivacity, which made it not only one of the center's highlights in its short career, but one of which it could be proud under any circumstances."[4] *La Finta Giardiniera* became one of Caldwell's early triumphs and a production that Goldovsky took on tour with the New England Opera Theater (albeit with himself on the podium).

Most of Caldwell's conducting repertoire consisted of opera music, but occasionally she led a non-vocal concert as well. In 1977, she led the Boston Symphony Orchestra in an evening of symphonic music including. Haydn's Symphony No. 8, Stravinsky's *Petrushka*, and Carter's Symphony No. 1. Richard Dyer reviewed her positively for the *Boston Globe*, and also noted that "Caldwell prepared everything with her usual thoroughness. She discussed the Haydn Symphony with Haydn scholar, H.C. Robbins Landon" and studied the *Petrushka* manuscripts in preparation for her assignment.[5] In 1978, she led the Brooklyn Philharmonia in an all-Berlioz program that included his *Symphonie Fantastique*, excerpts from his song cycle *Les Nuits d'été*, and his opera *Les Troyens*. Joseph Horowitz wrote in the *New York Times* how delighted he was with her choice to place the oboist offstage to echo the English horn solo at the beginning of the third movement of the *Symphonie Fantastique*. Moreover, he said that her tempos "permitted her to explore details of phrasing and instrumentation that are often lost" described the second movement as "gorgeously expansive" and overall approved of an interpretation that "elevated the music rather than exploited it."[6]

One of Caldwell's overseas guest conducting assignments was a production of Verdi's *La Traviata* with the Central Opera Institute in Peking. The performances took place in 1981, less than a decade after American President Richard Nixon made an historic visit to China, which led to agreements between the two countries to engage in scientific and educational exchanges. During the Cultural Revolution the performance of western opera in China would have been considered decadent, if not subversive, and therefore listening or playing it had been suppressed. Consequently, *La Traviata*, a staple of the opera canon in the west, was a new experience for most members of the Chinese audiences. So, too, apparently, was Caldwell's work ethic, which took the musicians by surprise. According to John Ardoin, who traveled with her for an *Opera News* report, when she was asked whether she preferred to rehearse in the morning, afternoon or evening, her response was "Morning, afternoon, and evening."[7] As a result, the Chinese musicians nicknamed her "Miss All Weather" for her indefatigable approach to rehearsing.[8]

Caldwell's most enduring association with an orchestra was with the Ural Philharmonic Orchestra in Yekaterinburg, Russia, a city about 1,000 miles east of Moscow. She was invited to conduct the orchestra while in

Leningrad and soon formed an ongoing partnership with it. In 1993, she was named Principal Guest Conductor and continued to conduct there regularly, often bringing with her a wide variety of Western repertoire ranging from Bach, to Verdi's *Requiem*, Debussy's *Pelléas et Mélisande* and Gershwin's *Porgy and Bess*. She discovered that Sergei Prokofiev had written incidental music for an adaptation of Pushkin's poem by Sigizmund Krzhizhanovsky (a Soviet writer whose work remained mostly unpublished and unknown until the late 20th century) and was determined to present it. In 1996, while working on the world premiere, she called her friend and frequent collaborator Richard Leacock to join her in Yekaterinburg and film a documentary of the rehearsals. The film, entitled *A Musical Adventure in Siberia*, became part of a collection entitled *The Paris Years 1989–2009*, and is the only extensive video documentation of Caldwell at work as a conductor. Leacock followed the progress of the rehearsals over the course of the final few days, using his signature *cinéma vérité* technique, filming without special lighting or body microphones. The result is a rare and unfiltered glimpse into the rehearsal process itself and one that underscored how similar Caldwell the conductor was to Caldwell the stage director.

Caldwell had found Prokofiev's autograph score in the archives of the Tairov Theatre.[9] "It was not terribly obscure," she says in the film, "but people just don't bother." Not surprisingly, she complains bitterly about the stage director for using only the text as his reference, rather than the score: "Everything I know about what Prokofiev said about this is in that score that he's had for weeks. He's never looked at it. He looks at his text. And the text doesn't have what Prokofiev said." The director, too, had his complaints about her, and they were familiar ones: "There are certain things we have to shift—but that's ok. But if she starts making changes again today, then I cannot guarantee—Even I can no longer keep track. It's all mixed up in my head."[10] Their disagreements and confusion about cues and the order of the individual selections of music (Waltz, Mazurka, etc.) that made up the whole were likely compounded by the difficulties of working entirely in translation. Nevertheless, it points to a chaos that characterized Caldwell's rehearsals over the years, whether as a conductor or director or both.

While *A Musical Adventure in Siberia* captured Caldwell during a particularly frustrating rehearsal period, her work at other times with the Ural Philharmonic Orchestra appears to have given her great pleasure. She admired the orchestra members who often worked without steady pay, and often brought music for them with her. It was, perhaps, a setting more conducive to her own bohemian style. In that cold climate and isolated location, she seemed to find a sense of purpose and satisfaction: "There was warmth and a sense of appreciation, not only from the players and the administration of the orchestra, but from the townspeople of Yekaterinburg also. It is very unusual, very special, and I have never felt that kind of warmth anyplace else."[11]

Although no English language reviews of Caldwell's work with the Ural Philharmonic Orchestra are available, critical assessments of her conducting with the Opera Company of Boston and other orchestras are numerous. They range from enthusiastic to derogatory, suggesting that, as with her directorial endeavors, there were times when she excelled, but others when she succumbed to indecision and imprecision. One of her most ardent admirers was *The New Yorker*'s Winthrop Sargeant. This prominent music critic wrote glowingly of her emergence as a conductor with Verdi's *Falstaff* in 1967 when Caldwell's short-lived American National Opera Company brought its touring production of that opera to the Brooklyn Academy of Music. Sargeant's reaction is worth quoting at length because it is the first detailed description of her work at the podium: "There is no keener test of a conductor's abilities than *Falstaff*. Those delicate ensembles in Act I, scene 2, are apt to get muddled, and the grand design of each act is something that does not always come through convincingly. Under Miss Caldwell's baton, everything was as light as sunshine and technically close to perfect. Not only is she a great director; one must also place her among the finest operatic conductors currently before the public."[12] Caldwell conducted in New York City again in December of 1974, this time leading the American Symphony Orchestra at Carnegie Hall in excerpts from Prokofiev's *War and Peace*. John Rockwell wrote in the *New York Times* that "her feeling for the music was apparent in every bar, and she led a performance of compelling sweep and sensitivity. [A]fter yesterday's effort, one can only hope that she will appear here soon again as a conductor, and often."[13]

In 1975, it was Andrew Porter who championed her interpretation of Bellini's *I Capuleti e i Montecchi*, the composer's operatic treatment of the Romeo and Juliet story, for which Caldwell famously cast mezzo-soprano Tatiana Troyanos in the role of Romeo opposite Beverly Sills as Giulietta: "Does it need stressing that Miss Caldwell's baton is a more subtle, trenchant, and precise musicological instrument than the most learned of thematic and harmonic analyses? ... Miss Caldwell was fiery and fearless in her employment of Bellini's heavy brass.... Consistently impressive was Miss Caldwell's musical direction. Who, since Tullio Serafin died, has been able to shape a Bellini score so surely and so sensitively?"[14] Porter praised Caldwell again when she made history as the first woman to conduct the Metropolitan Opera Orchestra in 1976. He wrote in *The New Yorker* that the evening confirmed Caldwell's significance: "Until 'La Traviata' the Met season lacked first-rate conductors. Miss Caldwell's arrival there ... brought a triumph for her and consummation of her great power to animate a score and reveal its composer's intentions.... When a phrase needed to expand, or a syllable to be on, or an attack to be delayed for an instant, Miss Caldwell was there. She showed an uncommon command of dramatically striking timbres and of instrumental balances in support of, not in competition with, the individual voices."[15] In contrast, Harold C. Schonberg, who was generally not a fan of Caldwell's productions, took a more reserved tone in the *New York Times*. He conceded that "everybody seemed to like her conducting, as well they should. It was well-organized, it was brisk, but not pell-mell in tempo, it was accurate in rhythm..." And while he maintained that conducting *La Traviata* was not the most severe test of a conductor, he acknowledged that "whatever problems it poses were expertly handled by Miss Caldwell."[16]

Criticisms of Caldwell's conducting pointed to her tendency to become distracted by the stage action. Although serving as both director and conductor enabled her to achieve unity in theory, in practice, it divided her preparation time and caused her attention to split, even during the performance. Richard Dyer, critic for the *Boston Globe* who covered most Caldwell's productions with the Opera Company of Boston, wrote about her conducting of Verdi's *Falstaff* in 1975 and noted shortcomings that Porter did not: "She has very little of the baton technique conventionally expected of a conductor and is also apt to get rattled. At the very beginning of a performance of 'Falstaff' last season, for example, she neglected to give the anacrusis which prepares the players for the initial downbeat—only about half of them began and not all of them together."[17] There were musicians who complained about Caldwell because she could be so unreliable, but Dyer also found ones who liked to play for her and were energized by her vision if not her technique: "She has a marvelous face ... and watching that is often enough. It doesn't tell you what bar you are in but it tells you what the music's about, what the music means; she makes you feel like playing better than you ever have in your life."[18]

There were clearly times when her conducting was lacking as evidenced in reviews of her productions. Critics have written that "she led with little impetus, nose glued to the score" (*The Barber of Seville*, 1974, Jacobson, *Opera News*[19]); "Miss Caldwell had a noticeable power shortage in her conducting; at times she lost her orchestra altogether" (*Stiffelio*, 1978, Eckert Jr., *Opera News*[20]); "She continually misjudged tempos.... There was a disturbing number of false entries and a disconcerting lack of co-ordination between pit and stage" (*Fidelio*, 1976, Baxter, *Opera*[21]); "Miss Caldwell has had better evenings.... [T]here were instances of nontogetherness [sic] between singers and orchestra and the lack of precision was matched ... by a somewhat lackluster reading of the score" (*L'Elisir d'Amore*, 1978, Hughes, *New York Times*[22]); "she pummeled the work into listless submission" (*Die Fledermaus*, 1980, Eckert Jr., *Opera News*[23]); "unimaginative, square, and at times slack conducting" (*Rigoletto*, 1981, Schwartz, *Boston Phoenix*[24]).

Reviews of Caldwell's conducting provide a wealth of information. They are invaluable to understand her individual strengths and weaknesses, to give insight into operatic interpretations and critical expectations during the second half of the 20th century. Yet, they also provide an opportunity to consider critical reactions within the broader social and historical contexts of a woman in a male-dominated profession, being reviewed exclusively by men. Take, for instance, the review of the 1975 New York Philharmonic Pension Fund concert, by *New York Times* critic Donal Henahan. The concert consisted of five works by women: "Quartet for Strings" by Ruth Crawford, "Faust et Hélène" by Lili Boulanger, "Overture for Orchestra" by Grazyna Bacewicz, "Sands" by Pozzi Escot, and "Concerto for Clarinet and Orchestra" by Thea Musgrave. The selections, he wrote, were interesting, but not arresting. Caldwell's conducting was assured, but not inspired, and the highlight of the evening, ironically, was the performance of the male clarinet soloist.[25] A comprehensive qualitative analysis of each of the critical responses to this concert and other reviews of Caldwell's conducting (compared with other female and male conductors of the time) would help to determine whether they show systemic evidence of gender bias.

When Caldwell began her professional career in the 1950s, there were few women playing in orchestras, and fewer anywhere in the world leading them. In the 1990s, when her career was coming to a close, a few women held associate positions with major orchestras, but only four were principal conductors, and none of them held posts with the so-called "big five": Boston, Chicago, Cleveland, New York, Philadelphia.[26] Remarkably, Caldwell achieved a number of "firsts," including being the first woman to conduct at the Worcester Festival in 1949, the first woman to conduct at the Ravinia Festival in 1976, and as noted above, the first woman to conduct the Metropolitan Opera Orchestra. Yet, she never flaunted these accomplishments, nor promoted herself as a "woman conductor." In fact, when she made her debut with the Met in 1976, she dismissed the historical significance of that feat. "I don't think of myself as a 'woman conductor,' but as a conductor," she said at the time, "and I hope my abilities will speak for themselves."[27]

While critical descriptions and reactions to Caldwell's conducting can provide important insights, audio and video records are more immediate first hand sources to examine. Unfortunately, these records are more limited in scope and availability. The film *A Musical Adventure in Siberia* is an important resource as is the filmed performance of *The Barber of Seville* that she staged and conducted for the New York City Opera in 1976. Only four operas that she conducted are readily available as audio recordings. In 2002, EMI Classics released a digitally remastered version of a recording from 1978 of Donizetti's *Don Pasquale*, starring Beverly Sills, with the London Symphony. In 2003, VAI Audio released Berlioz' *Benvenuto Cellini*, starring Jon Vickers, recorded during a live performance in 1975 with the Opera Company of Boston. The following year VAI Audio released Bellini's *I Capuleti e i Montecchi*, starring Beverly Sills and Tatiana Troyanos. That recording was made from two performances of the OCB in 1975 and both Caldwell and William Fred Scott are credited as conductors, but with no indication of which one conducted which acts. Also in 2004, VAI Audio released Beethoven's *Fidelio*, starring Jon Vickers, in a live performance recording made in 1976.[28] There is a 1997 recording entitled *Cello and Piano Concertos of Shostakovich* (Cello Concerto no. 1 in E flat, Op. 107 and Piano Concerto no. 1 in C Minor available through Audiofon that she made with the Yekaterinburg Philharmonic Orchestra and soloists William De Rosa [cello] and Valentina Lisitsa [piano]). A 1976 recording of the bicentennial opera *Be Glad Then, America* with the Pittsburgh Symphony is not commercially available, but the Special Collections Library of Penn State University includes numerous related items including audio and visual materials.[29] References to recordings of Tang dynasty music from her work at the University of Arkansas can be found,[30] but to date, these are not available commercially. Finally, a recent search of Worldcat catalogs turned up a recording of *The Balcony* that is not licensed for sale or broadcast, but is available in the Blumenthal Family Library at the New England Conservatory of Music in Boston.

Audio and video archival recordings of Opera Company of Boston performances that would be essential to a researcher analyzing her conducting choices are in the Sarah Caldwell collection at the Howard Gottlieb Archival Research Center at Boston University. Unfortunately, many of the recordings are on cassette, so the quality is not ideal and some video recordings would require transfer to new formats for examination. Nevertheless, the collection is extensive. It also includes several boxes of scores that belonged to Caldwell, but careful cross-referencing between the scores, audio, and video sources would have to be done in order for any markings in the scores to be attributed to Caldwell with certainty.

The Opera Stage of Sarah Caldwell has focused on the work of Caldwell as a stage director and argued that her importance to 20th-century opera production in that role has been underestimated. It remains for another writer to take up the challenge of examining her career as a conductor and to determine whether history has judged her fairly in that role.

Appendix B:
Operas Staged by Caldwell

Opera Company of Boston

1958	*Voyage to the Moon***	Offenbach
1959	*La Bohème*	Puccini
	The Barber of Seville	Rossini
	The Beggar's Opera	Gay
	Tosca	Puccini
	Voyage to the Moon	Offenbach
	Hansel and Gretel	Humperdinck
1960	*Carmen*	Bizet
	La Traviata	Verdi
	Otello	Verdi
1961	*Hansel and Gretel*	Humperdinck
	Falstaff	Verdi
	La Bohème	Puccini
	Die Fledermaus	Strauss
	Command Performance*	Middleton
1962	*Manon*	Massenet
	Die Meistersinger von Nürnburg	Wagner
	Rigoletto	Verdi
	Madama Butterfly	Puccini
1963	*The Barber of Seville*	Rossini
	Faust	Gounod
1964	*Lulu*	Berg
	The Magic Flute	Mozart
	I Puritani	Donizetti
	Madama Butterfly	Puccini
	L'Elisir d'Amore	Donizetti
1965	*The Abduction from the Seraglio*	Mozart

Operas Staged by Caldwell

	Semiramide	Rossini
	Intolleranza 1960**	Nono
	The Tales of Hoffmann	Offenbach
	Boris Godunov**	Mussorgsky
1966	*Don Giovanni*	Mozart
	Boris Godunov	Mussorgsky
	Hippolyte et Aricie**	Rameau
	La Bohème	Puccini
	Moses and Aaron**	Schönberg
1967	*Don Giovanni*	Mozart
	Otello	Verdi
	The Rake's Progress	Stravinsky
	Bluebeard's Castle and *The Miraculous Mandarin*	Bartók
	Tosca	Puccini
1968	*Tosca*	Puccini
	Lulu	Berg
	Carmen	Bizet
	La Traviata	Verdi
	Falstaff	Verdi
1969	*Bluebeard's Castle, The Miraculous Mandarin* and *The Wooden Prince*	Bartók
	Lucia di Lammermoor	Donizetti
	Macbeth	Verdi
	The Marriage of Figaro	Mozart
1970	*The Flying Dutchman*	Wagner
	The Daughter of the Regiment	Donizetti
	The Good Soldier Schweik	Kurka
	The Fisherman and His Wife*	Schuller
	Rigoletto	Verdi
1971	*Louise*	Charpentier
	La Finta Giardiniera	Mozart
	Norma	Bellini
1972	*The Trojans***	Berlioz
	Tosca	Puccini
	La Traviata	Verdi
1973	*The Bartered Bride*	Smetana
	The Daughter of the Regiment	Donizetti
	Rise and Fall of the City of Mahagonny	Weill
	Don Carlos	Verdi
1974	*Don Quichotte*	Massenet

	Madama Butterfly	Puccini
	*War and Peace***	Prokofiev
	The Barber of Seville	Rossini
1975	*Falstaff*	Verdi
	Così fan tutte	Mozart
	*Benvenuto Cellini***	Berlioz
	I Capuleti e i Montecchi	Bellini
1976	*Fidelio*	Beethoven
	*Montezuma***	Sessions
	Girl of the Golden West	Puccini
	Macbeth	Verdi
1977	*Russlan and Ludmilla*	Glinka
	La Bohème	Puccini
	Rigoletto	Verdi
	Orfeo ed Euridice	Gluck
	Orpheus in the Underworld	Offenbach
1978	*Stiffelio***	Verdi
	The Damnation of Faust	Berlioz
	Don Pasquale	Donizetti
	Tosca	Puccini
1979	*Falstaff*	Verdi
	La Vida Breve/El Retablo de Maese Pedro	Falla
	The Barber of Seville	Rossini
	*The Ice Break***	Tippet
	Hansel and Gretel	Humperdinck
1980	*Die Fledermaus*	Strauss
	The Flying Dutchman	Wagner
	War and Peace	Prokofiev
	Aida	Verdi
	Hansel and Gretel	Humperdinck
1981	*Faust*	Gounod
	Der Rosenkavalier	Strauss
	Rigoletto	Verdi
	Otello	Verdi
	Hansel and Gretel	Humperdinck
1982	*Die Soldaten***	Zimmermann
	Aida	Verdi
	La Bohème	Puccini
	Orpheus in the Underworld	Offenbach
1983	*Carmen*	Bizet
	The Invisible City of Kitezh	Rimsky-Korsakov

	Norma	Bellini
	Turandot	Puccini
1984	*Der Freischütz*	Weber
	Madama Butterfly	Puccini
	The Barber of Seville	Rossini
	Don Giovanni	Mozart
	The Tales of Hoffmann	Offenbach
1985	*Hansel and Gretel*	Humperdinck
1986	*Turandot*	Puccini
	*Taverner***	Davies
	The Makropulos Case	Janáček
	Tosca	Puccini
1987	*Il Trovatore*	Verdi
	Madama Butterfly	Puccini
	Don Pasquale	Donizetti
1988	*Médée*	Cherubini
	The Threepenny Opera	Weill
	La Traviata	Verdi
1989	*Mass*	Bernstein
	Aida	Verdi
	Der Rosencavalier	Strauss
	La Bohème	Puccini
1990	*Madama Butterfly*	Puccini
	The Magic Flute	Mozart
	*The Balcony**	Di Domenica

New York City Opera

1973	*The Young Lord*	Henze
	Ariadne auf Naxos	Strauss
1976	*The Barber of Seville*	Rossini
1979	*Falstaff*	Verdi

American National Opera Company

1967	*Falstaff*	Verdi
	Lulu	Berg
	Tosca	Puccini

Pennsylvania State University

1976	*Be Glad Then, America**	La Montaine

Swarthmore College

1998	*The Black Swan**	Whitman

Opera New England (ONE)

Often, Caldwell presented operas with ONE that she had already staged for the Opera Company of Boston. The following are operas that she presented at least once with ONE, but which were never part of the OCB repertoire. The year indicates the first time ONE performed the opera. Many ONE operas were performed multiple times and at different locations in different years.

1974	*The Jumping Frog of Calaveras County*	Foss
1976	*The Triumph of Honor*	Scarlatti
1977	*The Second Hurricane*	Copland
1978	*The Impresario*	Mozart
1980	*The Vampire*	Marschner
	The Princess and the Pea	Toch
1982	*The Frog Who Becomes a Prince* and *Zetabet*	Barnes
1985	*The Pearl Fishers*	Bizet

* *World premiere*
** *American premiere*

Chapter Notes

Preface

1. Charles Osgood, *CBS Evening News with Walter Cronkite*, Vanderbilt News Archive, November 12, 1975.

Introduction

1. Stuart Barr, "Laurence Picken, Polymath Equally at Home in Biology and the Musicology of Both East and West," *The Guardian*, June 6, 2007.
2. Siegfried Schoenbaum staged a Felsenstein inspired *The Tales of Hoffmann* in 1965.
3. Sarah Caldwell, *Challenges: A Memoir of My Life in Opera* (Middletown, Connecticut: Wesleyan University Press, 2008) 100.
4. Stuart Barr, "Laurence Picken," *The Guardian*.
5. Sarah Caldwell, *Challenges*, 25.
6. *Sarah Caldwell tells anecdotes about her conducting and production experience and answers questions from National Press Club*. Broadcast on National Public Radio, May 14, 1976. Sound recording. Library of Congress. Washington, D.C.
7. Ellen Pfeiffer, "City Salutes Sarah, launches Opera Week," *Boston Globe*, January 26, 1972. The Mayor of Cambridge, Edward Sullivan, presented Caldwell with a plaque and during a public ceremony described her as "Boston's Barnum."
8. Winthrop Sargeant, "Musical Events: Brava!" review of *Falstaff* by Verdi and *Lulu* by Berg, *The New Yorker* (October 14, 1967): 154.
9. The recording is a combination of two performances, June 5 and June 7, 1975. Caldwell conducted one performance and William Fred Scott the other. The CD does not indicate which tracks are attributable to which conductor.
10. *Central Opera Service Bulletin* 20: 1 (Winter 1977/78): 9.
11. Lynn Gilbert and Gaylen Moore, *Particular Passions, Talks with Women Who Have Shaped Our Times* (New York: C.N. Potter, 1981) 243.
12. "U.S. Female Opera Leader Caldwell Dead at 82," *Today.com*. http://www.today.com/id/11994402/ns/today-today_entertainment/t/us-female-opera-leader-caldwell-dead/#.VXYsWNJViko.
13. Gilbert and Moore, *Particular Passions*, 241.
14. *Camera Three*. May 6, 1973. Film of Caldwell in rehearsal with the Opera Company of Boston for Donizetti's *The Daughter of the Regiment*. Caldwell was adamant about this point in an interview on *Speaking Freely*. She insisted that she cares about theatrical value, but "pays equal attention to theater and music," a clear echo of the values of her mentor, Boris Goldovsky. Also, *Speaking Freely*. Hosted by Edwin Newman. Audio interview with Sarah Caldwell. November 29, 1975. Sound recording. Recorded Sound Reference Center. Library of Congress. Washington, D.C.
15. "Miss Kellogg and English Opera," *New York Times*, February 20, 1874.
16. http://www.bruceduffie.com/massenet7x.html.
17. https://www.nytimes.com/1981/07/23/obituaries/carol-fox-head-of-chicago-lyric-opera-dies.html.
18. https://operaamerica.org/content/about/WON/WomenInLeadershipPositions1990Present.pdf.

19. Karin Pendle, ed., *Women and Music: A History* (Bloomington: Indiana University Press, 1991), 244.

20. https://www.carnegiehall.org/About/History/Performance-History Search?q=ethel%20leginska&dex=prod_PHS.

21. Judy Collins, and Jill Godmilow, "Antonia: A Portrait of the Woman." Public Library of Cincinnati and Hamilton County Collection (Library of Congress). United States: Pyramid Films, 1974.

22. https://archives.nyphil.org/. The distinction of being the first woman to lead the New York Philharmonic has also been given to Nadia Boulanger. Boulanger was listed as a guest conductor in 1939 and conductor in 1941. Brico led the NYP in a stadium concert, rather than at Carnegie Hall. See also, Allan Kozinn, "Antonia Broco, 87, Fought Barriers to Women in 30s," *New York Times*, August 5, 1989.

23. Christine Ammer, *Unsung: A History of Women in American Music* (Westport: Greenwood Press, 1980), 168.

24. www.nadiaboulanger.com.

25. Carol Ann Feather, "Women Band Directors in American Higher Education," in *The Musical Woman 1984–1985*, vol. II, ed. Judith Lang Zaimont (New York: Greenwood Press, 1987), 389.

26. Pendle, ed., *Women & Music*, 244.

27. Bernard Holland, "Judith Somogi, 47, a Conductor; Among First Women on Podium," *New York Times*, March 26, 1988.

28. Pendle, ed., *Women and Music*, 247.

29. John Mason Potter, "Frowns on Female Symphony Leaders," *Boston Massachusetts Post*, August 3, 1952.

30. Kay D. Lawson, "A Woman's Place Is at the Podium," *Music Educator's Journal* (1984): 47.

31. Allan Kozinn, "At Juilliard Gains are Recounted," *New York Times*, October 22, 1988.

32. Milly S. Barranger, *Margaret Webster: A Life in the Theater* (Ann Arbor: University of Michigan Press, 2004), 193. Also, Rudolf Bing, *5,000 Nights at the Opera* (Garden City, New York: Doubleday, 1972), 149.

33. Barranger, *Margaret Webster: A Life in the Theater*, 193. Also, Bing, *5,000 Nights at the Opera*, 149.

34. Herbert Kupferberg, "Women of the Baton—The New Music Masters," *Parade* (May 14, 1975): 4.

35. Dora Jane Hamblin, "She Puts the Oomph in the Opera," *Life* (March 5, 1965): 85.

36. "Opera: The Persistent One," *Time Magazine* (February 21, 1964): 58.

37. Quaintance Eaton, "Renaissance Woman," *Opera News* (April 18, 1964): 26.

38. Robert Jacobson, "The Unsinkable Sarah Caldwell," *After Dark* (May 1972): 52.

39. Winthrop Sargeant, "Profiles: Infinite Pains," *The New Yorker* (December 24, 1973):44.

40. Donal Henahan, "Prodigious Sarah," *New York Times Magazine* (October 5, 1975): 93.

41. Robert Jones, "Walking into the Fire," *Opera News* (February 14, 1976): 12.

42. No author, "Barber of Boston," *Time Magazine* (June 17, 1974): n.p.

43. Jones, "Walking into the Fire," 13.

44. "Music's Wonder Woman," *Time Magazine* (November 1975): 54.

45. Kate Millet, *Sexual Politics* (Garden City, NY: Doubleday, 1970), 46.

46. Lawson, "A Woman's Place Is at the Podium," 49.

47. Lawson, "A Woman's Place Is at the Podium," 47. Also, Carol Ann Feather, "Women Band Directors in American Higher Education," in *The Musical Woman 1984–1985*, vol. II, ed. Judith Lang Zaimont (New York: Greenwood Press, 1987), 238.

48. Mark Swed, "A Maestro and City in Concert; L.A. Has Left Its Mark on Salonen. And He's Made It a Musical Capital," *Los Angeles Times*, April 12, 2009.

49. Robert Jones, "Walking into the Fire," *Opera News* (February 14, 1976): 12.

50. Richard Dyer, "Sarah Caldwell—Her Genius Is Her Gimmick," *New York Times*, January 11, 1976.

Chapter 1

1. Boris Goldovsky, *My Road to Opera: The Recollections of Boris Goldovsky* (Boston: Houghton Mifflin, 1979), 24.

2. Goldovsky, *My Road to Opera*, 344.

3. Boris Goldovsky, *Bringing Opera to Life* (New York: Appleton-Century-Crofts, 1968), 9.

4. Lorraine Thebodeau, "Young Arkansan Stirs Staid Massachusetts Music Circle," *Little Rock Arkansas Gazette*, June 5, 1949.

5. NEC Opera Collection, Box 1, Folder 8, New England Conservatory Archives, Blumenthal Family Library, Boston, MA.

6. Jennifer Hansen, "Sarah Caldwell," *Arkansas Democrat Gazette*, December 5, 1999.

7. Now the Tanglewood Music Center.

8. Herbert Kupferberg, *Tanglewood* (New York: McGraw-Hill, 1976), 41.

9. Hugo Leichentritt, *Serge Koussevitzky, the Boston Symphony Orchestra and the New American Music* (Cambridge: Cambridge University Press, 1947), 173.

10. Philip Hamburger, "Musical Events: In the Hills," *The New Yorker* (August 13, 1949): 49.

11. Information about the Berkshire Music Center comes from yearbooks and other documentation in the Boston Symphony Orchestra Archives, Symphony Hall, Boston, MA, as well as from *My Road to Opera, the Recollections of Boris Goldovsky*.

12. Leichentritt, 189.

13. Sarah Caldwell, *Challenges: A Memoir of My Life in Opera* (Middletown, Connecticut: Wesleyan University Press, 2008), 89.

14. Tanglewood Yearbooks, From the Boston Symphony Orchestra Archives, Symphony Hall, Boston, MA.

15. All titles appear as they did in the Berkshire Music Center Program.

16. Goldovsky, *My Road to Opera*, 346.

17. Tanglewood Yearbook, 1948, from the Boston Symphony Orchestra Archives, Symphony Hall, Boston, MA.

18. Henry Krehbiel, "Chapters of Opera," 1908, BiblioLife. http://www.myilibrary.com?id=183281, 2006, quoted in Joseph Horowitz, *Classical Music in America: A History of its Rise and Fall* (New York: W.W. Norton & Company, 2005), 145.

19. Jane Noria, "A Plea for the Development of a National Opera," *New York Times*, August 28, 1910.

20. Olin Downes, "The Language of Opera—Encores in Symphony Hall," *New York Times*, November 9, 1924.

21. Olin Downes, "More Views on Opera in English," *New York Times*, January 27, 1946.

22. Herbert Graf, *Producing Opera for America* (New York: Atlantis Books, 1961), 156.

23. Olin Downes, "Britten's 'Grimes' Unveiled at Lenox," review of *Peter Grimes* by Britten, *New York Times*, August 7, 1946.

24. Julian Rushton, *W.A. Mozart: Idomeneo* (Cambridge: Cambridge University Press, 1993), 84.

25. Goldovsky, *My Road to Opera*, 355.

26. Goldovsky, *My Road to Opera*, 350.

27. Jay Rosenfeld, "Tanglewood Opera Unit Scores Another Triumph," review of *La Clemenza di Tito* by Mozart, *New York Herald Tribune*, August 9, 1947.

28. This has been cited as her debut as a conductor/director. Caldwell corrects the record in *Challenges*. Her conducting/directing debut was at the Peabody Playhouse in the Settlement House, Boston with Smetana's *The Bartered Bride*. She notes that the staging actually consisted of recreating Goldovsky's staging. Her professional debut as a conductor was at the original Boston Opera House with Mozart's *La Finta Giardiniera* (*Challenges*, 96).

29. Program Note, *La Finta Giardiniera* by Mozart, Performed at the Berkshire Music Center, July 25, 1950, from the Boston Symphony Orchestra Archives, Symphony Hall, Boston, MA.

30. Jay Rosenfeld, "Music Center Opera Students Present '*La Finta Giardiniera*,'" review of *La Finta Giardiniera* by Mozart, *Berkshire Eagle*, July 26, 1950.

31. Kupferberg, *Tanglewood*, 123.

32. Howard Taubman, "'Titus' by Mozart Presented at Fete," review of *La Clemenza di Tito* by Mozart, *New York Times*, August 5, 1952.

33. Howard Taubman, "Opera by Grétry Staged at Lenox," review of *Richard the Lion-hearted* by Grétry, *New York Times*, August 11, 1953.

34. *Boris Goldovsky Collection*, Box 1, Folder 1, New England Conservatory Archives, Blumenthal Family Library, Boston, MA.

35. Boris Goldovsky, *The Story of the Opera Institute*. Pamphlet from the Boris Goldovsky Collection, Box 1, Folder 2, New England Conservatory Archives, Blumenthal Family Library, Boston, MA.

36. Caldwell, *Challenges*, 97.

37. Cyrus Dergin, "Berlioz Opera in American Premiere," review of *The Trojans* by Berlioz, *Musical America* (April 1955): 3.
38. Wallace Dace, "Opera Production and the American Educational Theater," *Educational Theater Journal* 9:3 (October 1957):232.
39. Quaintance Eaton, "Renaissance Woman," *Opera News* (April 18, 1964): 26.
40. "Proposal to Establish an Opera Company." From the Sarah Caldwell Collection, Howard Gottlieb Archival Research Center at Boston University, Boston, MA.

Chapter 2

1. Elliott Norton, *Broadway Down East: An Informal Account of the Plays, Players and Playhouses of Boston from Puritan Times to the Present* (Boston: Trustees of the Public Library of the City of Boston, 1978), 1.
2. Norton, *Broadway Down East*, 4.
3. Joseph Horowitz, *Classical Music in America: A History of Its Rise and Fall* (New York: W.W. Norton & Company, 2005), 11.
4. The New England Conservatory was founded in 1867. Jordan Hall opened in 1903.
5. No author, "Opera House for Boston," *New York Times*, March 22, 1908.
6. Quaintance Eaton, *The Boston Opera Company* (New York: Appleton-Century, 1965), 41. Images of the theater can be viewed at https://www.bostonoperahouse.com/history/.
7. *Aida, La Bohème, I Pagliacci, Lakmé, Cavalleria Rusticana, Rigoletto, Don Pasquale, Madama Butterfly, Faust* (Gounod), *La Traviata, Il Trovatore, Carmen, Lucia di Lammermoor, Mefistofele, Les Huguenots, Tosca, The Barber of Seville,* and *Lohengrin*.
8. Eaton, *The Boston Opera Company*, 52.
9. John Dizikes, *Opera in America* (New Haven: Yale University Press, 1993), 368.
10. Rosanne Martorella, *The Sociology of Opera* (South Hadley, Massachusetts: J.F. Bergin, 1982), 48.
11. Martorella, *The Sociology of Opera*, 49. This data is also in the Central Opera Service Bulletins.
12. Virgil Thomson, "Opera: It Is Everywhere in America," *New York Times*, September 23, 1962.
13. No author, "Opera Group, Inc.," *Boston Globe*, April 5, 1958.
14. No author, "Events in Music, Theater: Opera Group, Inc. to Be Permanent Opera Company," *Boston Herald*, April 6, 1958.
15. Harold Rogers, "The Money, the Time and the Place: Sarah Caldwell's Operatic Aims," *Christian Science Monitor*, March 8, 1963.
16. The American National Theater and Academy Collection, Robert and Wilva Breen Collection, 1933–1980, George Mason University. Information available at http://ead.lib.virginia.edu/vivaxtf/view?docId=gmu/vifgm00039.xml.
17. Lawrence W. Levine, *Highbrow/Lowbrow: The Emergence of Cultural Hierarchy in America* (Cambridge: Harvard University Press, 1988), 145.
18. *Treemonisha* by Scott Joplin was published in 1911, but only received its world premiere in 1972.
19. The libretto has since been deconstructed and reconstructed, but still contain extensive renderings of the original costumes and sets. Courtesy of the Boston Public Library.
20. Sarah Caldwell, *Challenges: A Memoir of My Life in Opera* (Middletown, Connecticut: Wesleyan University Press, 2008), 8.
21. Kevin Kelly, "The Light Side of the Moon," review of *Voyage to the Moon* by Offenbach, *Boston Globe*, June 19, 1958. Also, Robert Taylor, "Music, 'The Voyage to Moon,'" review of *Voyage to the Moon* by Offenbach, *Boston Herald*, June 19, 1958.
22. No author, *Boston Globe*, January 30, 1958.
23. Martorella, *The Sociology of Opera*, 48.
24. Alan Rich, "Opera All Over the Map," *New York Herald Tribune*, February 28, 1965.
25. The reason for the name change was due to its similarity to the Boston Opera Association, a citizen group formed in 1923 to promote and sponsor opera performances in the city. The OCB Board of Trustees approved the change on July 2, 1964.
26. Herbert Kupferberg, "America Sings: Sarah Caldwell's National Opera," *Atlantic Monthly* (September 1967): 120.
27. No author, "Reports: U.S. Indianap-

olis," review of *Falstaff* by Verdi, *Opera News* (October 14, 1967): 22.

28. Winthrop Sargeant, "Musical Events: Brava!" review of *Falstaff* by Verdi and *Lulu* by Berg, *The New Yorker* (October 14, 1967): 154.

29. See Chapter 5 for more on their collaboration.

30. https://edie.pink/lulu-ricky-leacock/.

31. Allen Hughes, "National Opera's 'Falstaff' and 'Tosca' in Brooklyn," review of *Falstaff* by Verdi and *Tosca* by Puccini, *New York Times*, October 9, 1967.

32. Arthur Darack, "The American National Opera Company," review of *Falstaff* by Verdi, *Lulu* by Berg, and *Tosca* by Puccini, *Musical America* (December 1967): 21.

33. Margery Silberman, "Sarah Caldwell's New National Opera in Strong Road Start at Indianapolis," review of *Falstaff* by Verdi, *Lulu* by Berg, and *Tosca* by Puccini, *Variety* (September 20, 1967): 64.

34. Donal Henahan, "Conducting Becomes Sarah Caldwell," *New York Times*, December 22, 1974.

35. Harvey E. Phillips, "Sarah Caldwell's New Idea," *Musical America* (September 1977): 17–19.

36. Harold Rogers, "The Money, the Time and the Place: Sarah Caldwell's Operatic Aims," *Christian Science Monitor*, March 8, 1963.

37. The full amount had been given by a single benefactor, Mrs. Cabot, the first "Chairman of the Friends of the Opera Group." See Caldwell, *Challenges*, 7.

38. Caldwell, *Challenges*, 8.

39. Dora Jane Hamblin, "She puts the Oomph in the Opera," *Life* (March 5, 1965): 83.

40. No author, Untitled notice in the *Boston Herald*, January 30, 1959.

41. The report by the *Boston Herald* suggests a figure closer to $80,000 than the $90,000 that Caldwell references in *Challenges* (see below).

42. Caldwell, *Challenges*, 19.

43. Beverly Sills, *Bubbles: A Self-Portrait* (Indianapolis: Bobbs-Merrill, 1976), 94.

44. Letter from the Ford Foundation to the Opera Company of Boston, September 21, 1964. From the Sarah Caldwell Collection, Howard Gottlieb Archival Research Center at Boston University, Boston, MA.

45. Grant title "Stabilization of The Company's Performance Activities," 1966–68 for $195,000. Grant Number 06600451. From the Ford Foundation Archives.

46. No author, "Boston Opera to Open Late," *New York Times*, January 19, 1982.

47. John Rockwell, "Boston Opera's Troubles are Traced to Caldwell—Union Conflict," *New York Times*, January 20, 1982.

48. Rockwell, "Boston Opera's Troubles."

49. Richard Dyer, "The Question of Caldwell's Link to Manilla," *Boston Globe*, August 1, 1982.

50. Margo Miller, "Caldwell Cuts Manilla Tie," *Boston Globe*, October 18, 1983.

51. No author, "Caldwell Doubling as Israeli Opera Chief," *Variety* (March 23, 1983): 89. Also, *Central Opera Service Bulletin* 24:3 (Spring/Summer, 1983):10.

52. Bernard Holland, "Sarah Caldwell, After Illness, Plans New Projects," *New York Times*, May 5, 1985.

53. Holland, "Sarah Caldwell, After Illness."

54. Holland, "Sarah Caldwell, After Illness."

55. "Background Information: The Opera House." From the Sarah Caldwell Collection, Howard Gottlieb Archival Research Center at Boston University, Boston Massachusetts.

56. Michael Walsh, "High Spirits, Dead Souls," review of *Dead Souls* by Shchedrin, *Time Magazine* (March 28, 1988): 76. Also, Bernard Holland, "U.S.-Soviet Portrayal of Gogol's 'Dead Souls,'" review of *Dead Souls* by Shchedrin, *New York Times*, March 14, 1988.

57. Richard Dyer, "Shchedrin Work is a Triumph," review of *Dead Souls* by Shchedrin, *Boston Globe*, March 14, 1988.

58. William H. Honan, "Constructive Chaos at a Big-Power Arts Feast," *New York Times*, April 2, 1988.

59. Richard Dyer. "Homey Touch," *Boston Globe*, March 15, 1988.

60. William H. Honan, "A U.S.-Soviet Cultural Rapprochement," *New York Times*, February 17, 1988.

61. Will Crutchfield, "Boston and Soviet Plan Music Trade," *New York Times*, September 18, 1987.

62. Alan R. Gold, "Cultural Festival with Soviet Saved," *New York Times*, March 6, 1988.

63. Allan Kozinn, "New York Philharmonic Prepares for Soviet Tour," *New York Times*, May 26, 1988.
64. Richard Dyer, and Jess McLaughlin, "A Struggle Backstage for Opera Company," *Boston Globe*, March 25, 1989.
65. Dyer and McLaughlin, "A Struggle Backstage."
66. Richard Dyer, "The Opera Company's Tale of Woe," *Boston Globe*, April 3, 1989.
67. Julius Novick, "Interlopers in the Opera House," *American Theatre*, May 1986.
68. Richard Dyer, "Opera Company Suspends Canon," *Boston Globe*, March 28, 1989.
69. Desiree French, "Opera Company Gets Management Review Panel's Report," *Boston Globe*, April 21, 1989.
70. Desiree French, "More Resignations at OCB," *Boston Globe*, May 6, 1989.
71. Desiree French, "Opera Company Reinstates Canon," *Boston Globe*, March 29, 1989.
72. Richard Dyer, "Canon Quietly Sets Stage for Opera," *Boston Globe*, July 14, 1989.
73. Richard Dyer, "The Lights Dim for Boston Opera," *Boston Globe*, May 12, 1991.
74. Caldwell, *Challenges*, 211.
75. Richard Dyer, "Four's a Crowd," *Boston Globe*, April 15, 1990.
76. Oestreich, James R. "Review/Music; Jean Genet's 'Balcony' Makes Debut as Opera," review of *The Balcony* by Di Domenica, *New York Times*, June 17, 1990.
77. Richard Dyer, "A Compelling 'Balcony,'" review of *The Balcony* by Di Domenica, *Boston Globe*, June 15, 1990.
78. Richard Dyer, "A Dream Fulfilled," *Boston Globe*, June 10, 1990.

Chapter 3

1. Richard Dyer, "The Divine Sarah," *Opera News* (December 2003): 43.
2. Several operas that she produced with the Opera Company of Boston were ones she had presented on tour with the American National Opera Company.
3. Harold C. Schonberg, "Opera Hits a High Note Across America," *New York Times*, October 9, 1978.
4. Sir Rudolf Bing, *5,000 Nights at the Opera: The Memoirs of Sir Rudolf Bing* (London: H. Hamilton, 1972), 212.
5. James Heilbrun and Charles M. Gray, *The Economics of Art and Culture: An American Perspective* (Cambridge: Cambridge University Press, 2001), 232.
6. *Aida*, by Giuseppe Verdi. Italian libretto by Antonio Ghislanzoni. http://opera.stanford.edu/Verdi/Aida/libretto_ie.html. Notes on the text and translation http://opera.stanford.edu/Verdi/Aida/libnotes.html.
7. Susan Larson, "Homeless in Boston," *Opera News* (September 1996): 16.
8. Everett Helm, "Bedlam in Venice," *New York Times*, May 7, 1961. Also, no author, "Rioters Disrupt Opera Premiere," *New York Times*, April 14, 1961.
9. Dean Wilcox, "Political Allegory or Multimedia Extravaganza? A Historical Reconstruction of the Opera Company of Boston's 'Intolleranza,'" *Theater Survey* 37:2 (November 1996): 119.
10. Video of *Intolleranza 1960* by Nono, conducted by Bruno Maderna, directed by Sarah Caldwell, Opera Company of Boston, 1965. Film by WGBH. Sarah Caldwell Collection, Howard Gottlieb Archival Research Center at Boston University, Boston, MA.
11. Wilcox, "Political Allegory," 127.
12. Beverly Sills, *Bubbles: A Self-Portrait* (Indianapolis: Bobbs-Merrill, 1976), 100.
13. Wilcox, "Political Allegory," 127.
14. Harold C. Schonberg, "Opera: Luigi Nono's 'Intolleranza 1960,'" review of *Intolleranza 1960* by Nono, *New York Times*, February 22, 1965.
15. Sills, *Bubbles: A Self-Portrait*, 100.
16. Wilcox, "Political Allegory," 115.
17. Robert Jacobson, "Musical Masterwork with a 12-Tone Orgy," review of *Moses and Aaron* by Schönberg, *Life* (January 20, 1967): n.p.
18. Winthrop Sargeant, "Musical Events: The Prophets," review of *Moses and Aaron* by Schönberg, *The New Yorker* (December 10, 1966): 198.
19. Harold C. Schonberg, "Opera: 'Moses and Aaron,'" review of *Moses and Aaron* by Schönberg, *New York Times*, December 1, 1966.
20. Peter G. Davis, "General Caldwell Goes to War," review of *War and Peace* by Prokofiev, *New York Times*, May 19, 1974.

21. Paul Hume, "Caldwell's 'War and Peace,'" review of *War and Peace* by Prokofiev, *The Saturday Review*, August 31, 1974.
22. Charles Jahani, "Washington," review of *War and Peace* by Prokofiev, *Opera* (November 1974): 997.
23. Jahani, "Washington," 997.
24. Donal Henahan, "Boston Opera 'Capuletti' Is a Screaming Success," review of *I Capuleti e i Montecchi* by Bellini, *New York Times*, June 4, 1975.
25. Andrew Porter, "Musical Events: Star-cross'd in Boston," review of *I Capuleti e i Montecchi* by Bellini, *The New Yorker* (June 16, 1975): 97.
26. *The Barber of Seville* by Gioacchino Rossini. Produced by John Goberman, conducted by Sarah Caldwell, directed by Kirk Browning. Hollywood: Paramount Home Video, 1988.
27. Arthur Jacobs, "America: Bizarre 'Barber,'" review of *The Barber of Seville* by Rossini, *Opera* (September 1977): 807.
28. Robert Jacobson, "Boston," review of *The Barber of Seville* by Rossini, *Opera News* (September 1974): 54.
29. Robert Jacobson, "Triple Play USA: Montezuma, Ines de Castro, Ashmedai," review of *Montezuma* by Sessions, *Opera News* (June 1976): 33.
30. Andrew Porter, "The Matter of Mexico," *The New Yorker* (April 19, 1976): 120.
31. Donal Henahan, "Opera: Juilliard Gives Sessions Montezuma," review of *Montezuma* by Sessions, *New York Times*, February 21, 1982.
32. Carey Winfrey, "Papp Quits Lincoln Center Citing Artistic-Fiscal Trap," *New York Times*, June 10, 1977.
33. Mel Gussow, "Can a Committee Revive the Beaumont?" *New York Times*, January 21, 1979.
34. Kevin Kelly, "Caldwell Directs Her First Play," *Boston Globe*, January 13, 1981.
35. Richard Dyer and Kevin Kelly, "Caldwell in Bid to Revive NYC's Beaumont Theater," *Boston Globe*, December 14, 1978.
36. Mel Gussow, "Can a Committee Revive the Beaumont?" *New York Times*, January 21, 1979.
37. Mel Gussow, "Can a Committee Revive the Beaumont?" *New York Times*, January 21, 1979.
38. Mel Gussow, "Can a Committee Revive the Beaumont?" *New York Times*, January 21, 1979.
39. Video of Shakespeare's *Macbeth*, Vivian Beaumont Theater. Sarah Caldwell, director. A Lincoln Center Theater Company Production. Princeton: Films for the Humanities, 1988.
40. Frank Rich, "Stage: Macbeth Returns," review of *Macbeth* by Shakespeare, *New York Times*, January 24, 1981.
41. Bernd Alois Zimmermann, and Jakob Michael Reinhold Lenz. *Die Soldaten = The Soldiers: Oper in 4 Akten Nach Dem Gleichnamigen Schauspiel Von = Opera in Four Acts After the Play of the Same Name by Jakob Michael/Reinhold Lenz*. Mainz: B. Schott's Söhne, 1975.
42. John Rockwell, "Boston Opera: 'Die Soldaten' Has U.S. Premiere," *New York Times*, February 8, 1982.
43. Thor Eckert, Jr., "Boston Opera Jousts with a Challenging "Die Soldaten," review of *Die Soldaten* by Zimmermann, *Christian Science Monitor*, March 9, 1982.
44. Harold C. Schonberg, "Bernstein's New Work Reflects His Background on Broadway," review of *Mass* by Bernstein, *New York Times*, September 9, 1971.
45. Leonard Bernstein, *Mass*, Baltimore Symphony Orchestra, Marin Alsop, Naxos, 2009. Translation by the author.
46. Leighton Kerner, "Mass Hysteria," review of *Mass* by Bernstein, *Village Voice* (February 7, 1989): 80.
47. Richard Dyer, "Boston," review of *Mass* by Bernstein, *Opera* (June 1989): 688.
48. Shirley Verrett had been scheduled to sing the role of Santuzza in *Cavalleria Rusticana*.
49. Jeff McLaughlin, "Concert Opera in Red, Ends Season," *Boston Globe*, March 24, 1989.
50. Marian Christy, "As Life Gets Tough, She Gets Motivated," *Boston Globe*, June 13, 1990.
51. Harold Rogers, "The Money, the Time and the Place: Sarah Caldwell's Operatic Aims," *Christian Science Monitor*, March 8, 1963.

Chapter 4

1. Lynn Gilbert and Gaylen Moore, *Particular Passions, Talks with Women Who*

Have Shaped Our Times (New York: C.N. Potter, 1981), 242.

2. John Rockwell, "Donald Gramm Is Dead at 56; Bass-Baritone at Met Opera," *New York Times*, June 3, 1983.

3. Beverly Sills and Lawrence Linderman. *Beverly: An Autobiography* (New York: Bantam Books, 1987), 207.

4. Plácido Domingo, *My First Forty Years* (New York: Alfred A. Knopf, 1985), 55.

5. Michael Cooper, "An 'Otello' Without Blackface Highlights an Enduring Tradition in Opera," *New York Times*, September 17, 2015.

6. No author, "Negro Singer Hailed: Grace Bumbry Is Praised by Prove for Bayreuth Role," *New York Times*, July 26, 1961.

7. Anthony Tommasini, "Colorblind Casting Widens Opera's Options," *New York Times*, December 21, 2012.

8. Dora Jane Hamblin, "She Puts the Oomph in the Opera," *Life* (March 5, 1965): 78.

9. Winthrop Sargeant, "Profiles: Infinite Pains," *The New Yorker* (December 24, 1973): 44.

10. Sarah Caldwell, "What Time Is the Next Swan?" New York: Phoenix films, 1975.

11. Sills and Linderman, *Beverly: An Autobiography*, 280.

12. Alan Rich, "Sarah Caldwell," *Sky* (November 1977): 67.

13. James Neufeld, *Lois Marshall: A Biography* (Toronto: Dundurn Press, 2010), 152.

14. Richard Dyer, "Sarah Caldwell's 20th Anniversary Year: She'll Come Up with Something Special," *Boston Sunday Globe*, February 12, 1978.

15. "Elliot Norton Reviews, Donald Gramm," in *Elliot Norton Reviews* (Boston: WGBH Boston, 1981). https://search.alexanderstreet.com/preview/work/bibliographic_entity%7Cvideo_work%7C2204325.

16. Shirley Verrett, *I Never Walked Alone* (Hoboken: John Wiley & Sons, 2003), 195.

17. Freda Herseth, interview by the author, December 10, 2014.

18. Toby Cole, and Helen Krich Chinoy, *Directors on Directing: A Sourcebook of the Modern Theater* (Indianapolis: Bobbs-Merrill, 1963), 282–284.

19. Sarah Caldwell, *What Time Is the Next Swan?* New York: Phoenix Films, 1975.

20. Boris Goldovsky, *Bringing Opera to Life* (New York: Appleton-Century-Crofts, 1968), 277.

21. Thomas Whitman, interview by the author, November 11, 2014. *The Black Swan* by Thomas Whitman. Libretto by Nathalie Anderson. Conducted by James Freeman. Directed by Sarah Caldwell. Swarthmore College, Swarthmore, PA.

22. Sills and Linderman. *Beverly: An Autobiography*, 152.

23. Verrett, *I Never Walked Alone*, 205.

24. Verrett, *I Never Walked Alone*, 206.

25. Peter Paul Fuchs, *The Music Theater of Walter Felsenstein* (New York: W.W. Norton, 1975), 49.

26. Gilbert and Moore, *Particular Passions, Talks with Women Who Have Shaped Our Times*, 243.

27. Beverly Sills, *Bubbles: A Self-Portrait* (Indianapolis: Bobbs-Merrill, 1976), 20.

28. Phyllis Curtin, quoted in Caldwell memorial service booklet.

29. Donal Henahan, "Prodigious Sarah," *New York Times Magazine* (October 5, 1975): 94.

30. Margo Miller, "New Work, 650 Voices at War Memorial," *The Boston Evening Globe*, January 25, 1965.

31. Andrew Porter, "Musical Events: Caldwell in Command," *The New Yorker* (January 6, 1975): 61.

32. Robert Baxter, "Boston," review of *Falstaff* by Verdi, *Opera* (1975): 383.

33. Alan Rich, "Profile: Sarah Caldwell," *Sky* (November 1977): 67.

34. Verrett, *I Never Walked Alone*, 252.

35. Margo Miller, "Ex-Bass Bonis Inherits the Opera," *Boston Morning Globe*, January 29, 1967.

36. Deborah Trustman, "Opera from the Heart of Texas," *New York Times*, May 3, 1981.

37. Sarah Caldwell Collection, Howard Gottlieb Archival Research Center at Boston University, Boston, MA.

38. 1981 Season Report from the Technical Staff. Sarah Caldwell Collection, Howard Gottlieb Archival Research Center at Boston University, Boston, MA.

39. Lisi Oliver, interview by the author, August 12, 2013.

Chapter 5

1. The original cost to build it was $700,000.
2. Harlow Robinson, "Operatic Intrigue: The Comic, Tragic, True Tale of Opera on Huntington Avenue," *N.U. Magazine Online* (November 1999): 4.
3. Sarah Caldwell, *Challenges: A Memoir of My Life in Opera* (Middletown, Connecticut: Wesleyan University Press, 2008), 55.
4. Caldwell, *Challenges*, 19.
5. http://richardleacock.com/Projections-for-Lulu.
6. Caldwell, *Challenges*, 32.
7. No author, "A Boston Lincoln Center," *Boston Globe*, January 20, 1967.
8. Michael Steinberg, "Opera in Boston Needs a Permanent Home," *Boston Globe*, October 23, 1966.
9. Project Grant Application to the National Foundation on the Arts and Humanities, Nation Endowment for the Arts, September 3, 1970. Sarah Caldwell Collection, Howard Gottlieb Archival Research Center at Boston University, Boston, MA.
10. Caldwell, *Challenges*, 216.
11. Robert Baxter, "America: Caldwell's Bold 'Holländer,'" review of *The Flying Dutchman* by Wagner, *Opera* (May 1970): 419.
12. Lynn Gilbert, and Gaylen Moore, *Particular Passions, Talks with Women Who Have Shaped Our Times* (New York: C.N. Potter, 1981), 241.
13. Beverly Sills, and Lawrence Linderman, *Beverly: An Autobiography* (New York: Bantam Books, 1987), 208.
14. Sills and Linderman, *Beverly: An Autobiography*, 208.
15. Gilbert and Moore, *Particular Passions*, 243.
16. Wallace Dace, "Opera Production and the American Educational Theater," *Educational Theater Journal* 9:3 (October 1957): 232.
17. Sarah Caldwell, "Sarah Caldwell Comments," *The Trojans* Program Notes. Production of *The Trojans* by Berlioz. Opera Company of Boston, April 1972.
18. This production took place before the advent of supertitles.
19. George Movshon, "America 'Trojans' at Boston," review of *The Trojans* by Berlioz, *Opera* (April 1972): 323.
20. Peter Knapp, "'Trojans': The Epic Spectacle Overwhelmed All," review of *The Trojans* by Berlioz, *Patriot Ledger*, February 8, 1972.
21. Louis Snyder, "Berlioz' Complete, two-evening 'Trojans' in U.S. Premiere," review of *The Trojans* by Berlioz, *Christian Science Monitor*, February 9, 1972.
22. Barbara Amiel, "Bravissimo," *Macleans Magazine* (June 12, 2006): 61.
23. Martin Green, *The Problem of Boston: Some Readings in Cultural History* (New York: W.W. Norton, 1966).
24. Robert Jacobson, "The Unsinkable Sarah Caldwell," *After Dark* (May 1972): 51.
25. Alan Rich, "Sarah Caldwell," *Sky* (November 1977): 67.
26. *Camera Three: Sarah Caldwell and the Opera Company of Boston*. Directed by Thomas Knott. Video of rehearsal for *The Daughter of the Regiment* by Donizetti, starring Beverly Sills. May 6, 1973. Twenty minutes. United States: CBS-TV. Motion Picture Reading Room. Library of Congress. Washington, D.C.
27. Richard Dyer, "Opera House Encore: Plans to Restore Boston Landmark to Be Announced Today," *Boston Globe*, April 22, 1999.
28. https://www.loc.gov/resource/hhh.ma0460.photos/?sp=1.
29. Richard Dyer, "Sarah Caldwell Gets a Dream House," *Boston Globe*, December 10, 1978.
30. Charles Osgood, *CBS Evening News with Walter Cronkite*, Vanderbilt News Archive, November 12, 1975.

Chapter 6

1. No author, "Events in Music, Theater: Opera Group, Inc. to be Permanent Opera Company," *Boston Herald*, April 6, 1958.
2. Raymond Ericson, "How Not to Do 'Boris,'" *New York Times*, April 4, 1965.

3. Sarah Caldwell, *Challenges: A Memoir of My Life in Opera* (Middletown, Connecticut: Wesleyan University Press, 2008), 45.

4. Letter from Sarah Caldwell to Laurence Picken. From the Sarah Caldwell Collection, Howard Gottlieb Archival Research Center at Boston University, Boston, MA.

5. Raymond Ericson, "Sarah Caldwell Leads Original 4½ hour 'Don Carlo,'" review of *Don Carlos* by Verdi, *New York Times*, May 24, 1973.

6. Gundula Kreuzer, "Voices from Beyond: Verdi's *'Don Carlos'* and the Modern Stage," *Cambridge Opera Journal* (July 2006): 160. The first was a 1931 production in which director Alexander Schum had the monk lead Don Carlos on stage for the final duet with Elizabet to set him up as his guardian angel. In a 1932 production, Don Carlos stabbed himself to death in an ending reworked by Franz Werfel and stage director Lothar Wallerstein.

7. *Don Carlos*: opéra en cinq actes / paroles de Méry et Camille du Locle; musique de G. Verdi. UR Research, Eastman School of Music, Sibley Music Library http://hdl.handle.net/1802/14328. Translation by the author.

8. Andrew Porter, "Musical Events," *The New Yorker* (June 2, 1973): 104.

9. Program notes for Gounod's *Faust*, presented by the Opera Company of Boston, February 20, 22, 26, and March 1, 1981, at The Opera House, Boston. Staged and Conducted by Sarah Caldwell. From the Sarah Caldwell Collection, Howard Gottlieb Archival Research Center at Boston University, Boston, MA. The final two paragraphs of the notes are the following:

> A completely definitive performing version cannot be prepared until certain significant missing sections of the manuscript are found. An aria for Valentin which stood in the midst of the original Soldier's Chorus, a mad scene for Marguerite, and an aria for Mephistopheles in the Kermesse (replacing the more familiar "Veau d'or" rondo) are the major missing links. The Mephisto aria has been located—but too late for inclusion in these performances. The well-known Soldier's Chorus was a last-minute addition by Gounod, using the material he had written for an earlier project. Stylistically it is so different from the rest of the piece that we decided to exclude it from these performances.
>
> We would like to thank especially M. Francois Lesure, the director of the Bibliothèque Nationale; Gilles Daziano, the director of the Cultural Section of the American Embassy in Paris; musicologist Robert Cohen; the directors of Choudens et Fils in Paris; as well as the librarians, research personnel and archivists of the libraries of Lincoln Center and Stanford University, the Pierpont Morgan Library and the Library of Congress. And, of course, no small debt of gratitude goes to "Maitre" McConathy who first conducted *Faust* for our company in 1963 and whose untiring efforts to fashion a "first version" have led to brilliant, exciting and surprising discoveries. To be sure, the accepted version of *Faust* that has filtered down to us through the years is a masterwork, but we hope that you will find these original thoughts as fascinating as we have.

10. Joseph Kerman, *Contemplating Music: Challenges to Musicology* (Cambridge: Harvard University Press, 1986), 192.

11. https://www.opera-arias.com/mozart/don-giovanni/libretto/. Translation by the author.

12. http://opera.stanford.edu/iu/libretti/figaro.htm. Translation by the author.

13. Richard Wagner, "Remarks on Performing the Opera 'Der Fliegende Holländer,'" in *Wagner on Music and Drama: A Compendium of Wagner's Prose Works*, ed. Albert Geldman and Evert Sprinchorn, trans. H. Ashton Ellis (New York: E.P. Dutton, 1964).

14. Wieland Wagner, "Tradition and Innovation," *Opera News* (December 31, 1951): 5.

15. Neil Genzlinger, "Frank Corsaro, Director Who Shook Up Opera World, Dies at 92," *New York Times*, November 13, 2017.

16. Sarah Caldwell, *Challenges: A Memoir of My Life in Opera* (Middletown, Connecticut: Wesleyan University Press, 2008), 211.

17. Theodore Strongin, "Boston Goes Mod over Stravinsky," review of *The Rake's Progress* by Stravinsky, *New York Times*, March 31, 1967.

18. Smetana composed and revised the opera between 1863 and 1870, a period that overlapped the formation of the Austro-

Hungarian Empire in 1867. The Czech people had previously been under Hapsburg control for more than two centuries.

19. Peter Paul Fuchs, *The Music Theater of Walter Felsenstein* (New York: W.W. Norton, 1975), 51.

20. Program for *The Bartered Bride* by Smetana. Opera Company of Boston, 1973. From the Sarah Caldwell Collection, Howard Gottlieb Archival Research Center at Boston University, Boston, MA.

21. Raymond Ericson, "Opera: 'Bartered Bride' Fascinates and Maddens," review of *The Bartered Bride* by Smetana, *New York Times*, January 28, 1973.

22. Speight Jenkins, "America: Caldwell's 'Bride,'" review of *The Bartered Bride* by Smetana, *Opera* (April 1973): 321.

23. Harold C. Schonberg, "Music: A Rare Performance of 'Don Quichotte' is Staged by Sarah Caldwell in Boston," review of *Don Quichotte* by Massenet, *New York Times*, February 22, 1974. Also, Harold C. Schonberg, "On an Ego Trip with Don Quichotte," review of *Don Quichotte* by Massenet, *New York Times*, March 3, 1974.

24. Robert Baxter, "American: Boston," review of *Don Quichotte* by Massenet, *Opera* (August 1974): 692.

25. Richard Dyer, "'Faust'—Did the Devil Make Caldwell Do It?" review of *The Damnation of Faust* by Berlioz, *Boston Globe*, March 23, 1978.

26. Robert Baxter, "Boston," review of *The Damnation of Faust* by Berlioz, *Opera* (August 1972): 783.

27. Terry Helbing, "The Use of Lasers in 'The Damnation of Faust,'" *Theatre Design and Technology* (Fall 1978): 15–16. A photo of the production is on the cover of this issue, which is archived online at http://www.nxtbook.com/nxtbooks/hickmanbrady/tdt_1978fall/index.php#/1.

28. Archival Video of *Médée* by Cherubini, conducted and directed by Sarah Caldwell, Opera Company of Boston, January 1988. From the Sarah Caldwell Collection, Howard Gottlieb Archival Research Center at Boston University, Boston, MA.

29. Jonathan Richmond, "Bolder if not Wiser, Sarah Caldwell Returns," *Christian Science Monitor*, February 11, 1988.

30. Program note in the Program for *Orpheus in the Underworld*, Opera New England. Performance at Westhill High School Auditorium, Stamford, Connecticut, October 28, 1983. Courtesy Lisi Oliver.

31. Peter G. Davis, "Opera: A Too Lavish 'Orfeo' and a Zesty 'Orpheus,'" review of *Orfeo ed Euridice* by Gluck and *Orpheus in the Underworld* by Offenbach, *New York Times*, June 10, 1977.

Chapter 7

1. Ellen Pfeiffer, "City Salutes Sarah, launches Opera Week," *Boston Globe*, January 26, 1972. The Mayor of Cambridge, Edward Sullivan, presented Caldwell with a plaque and described her during a public ceremony as "Boston's Barnum."

2. Richard Dyer, "Fate of the Opera House Remains Uncertain," *Boston Globe*, February 1, 1992.

3. Richard Dyer, "Caldwell Purchases Mortgage on Opera House," *Boston Globe*, November 11, 1992.

4. Letter addressed to James T. Morgan, Opera Company of Boston, 1991. From the Sarah Caldwell Collection, Howard Gottlieb Archival Research Center at Boston University, Boston, MA.

5. Agreement between Sarah Caldwell and the Opera Company of Boston, Inc. and The Opera House, Inc. Unsigned copy. Dated June 1990. From the Sarah Caldwell Collection, Howard Gottlieb Archival Research Center at Boston University, Boston, MA.

6. Sarah Caldwell, *Challenges: A Memoir of My Life in Opera* (Middletown, Connecticut: Wesleyan University Press, 2008), 209.

7. Dyer, "Opening Act at the Opera House," *Boston Globe*, September 2, 1994.

8. Dyer, "Opening Act at the Opera House."

9. Richard Dyer, "Opening Act at the Opera House."

10. M.R. Montgomery, "Opera House Restoration Plans Move Forward," *Boston Globe*, April 23, 1999.

11. Montgomery, "Opera House Restoration Plans Move Forward."

12. Margaret Forster, "Boston's Opera House Expansion Approved," September

26, 2002. Online at http://findarticles.com/p/articles/mi_kmpre/is_200209/ai_n6889636/

13. Letter from Sarah Caldwell to the United States Information Agency. February 20, 1991. From the Sarah Caldwell Collection, Howard Gottlieb Archival Research Center at Boston University, Boston, MA.

14. Caldwell, *Challenges*, 183.

15. Caldwell, *Challenges*, 185.

16. Ellen Pfeiffer, "'Black Swan' Brings Sarah Caldwell Back to America," review of *The Black Swan* by Whitman, *Boston Herald*, September 15, 1998.

17. Robert Baxter, "In Review: Swarthmore, PA," review of *The Black Swan* by Whitman, *Opera News* (December 1998): 101.

18. Richard Dyer, "Caldwell will go to Arkansas for Academic Post," *Boston Globe*, July 29, 1999.

19. Her stepfather, Henry Alexander, had died in 1969. http://www.encyclopediaofarkansas.net/encyclopedia/entry-detail.aspx?entryID=2598. Her mother, Margaret Baker Alexander, had died in 1983. "Margaret Alexander, 82; was Opera Patron and Sarah Caldwell's Mother," *Boston Globe*, September 10, 1983. Caldwell's only sibling, George Baker Alexander, had predeceased her (2001).

Conclusion

1. Richard Dyer, "The Opera Wars: A Truce," *Boston Globe*, October 20, 1991

2. Marion Christy, "As Life Gets Tough, She Gets Motivated," *Boston Globe*, June 13, 1990.

3. Richard Dyer, "Impresario of Boston Opera, dead at 82," *Boston Globe*, March 25, 2006.

4. Susan Larson, "Homeless in Boston," *Opera News* (September 1996): 14.

5. Richard Dyer, "Sarah Caldwell: At the Crossroads," *Los Angeles Times*, June 26, 1983. A reprint of the *Boston Globe* article entitled "Has Sarah Lost It?"

6. James Heilbrun, "Baumol's Cost Disease," in *A Handbook of Cultural Economics*, ed. Ruth Towse (Northampton, MA: Edward Elgar, 2003), 91.

7. Daniel J. Wakin, "Met Has New Rival in Operas at Movies," *New York Times*, December 19, 2007.

8. Anthony Tommasini, "A Success in HD, but at What Cost?" *New York Times*, March 14, 2013.

9. The U.S. devotes about .13 percent of its total spending to the arts, compared to Australia .82 percent, Canada .93 percent, France 1.13 percent, Germany 1.79 percent, Finland 2.10 percent. It lags well behind all other industrialized nations. *Canada Council for the Arts: Comparisons of Arts Funding in Selected Countries: Preliminary Findings*, October 2005. http://www.ronbashford.com/Comparisonsofartsfunding27Oct2005.pdf?attredirects=0.

10. James Heilbrun, and Charles M. Gray, *The economics of art and culture, An American Perspective* (Cambridge: Cambridge University Press, 2001), 254.

11. Richard L. Florida, *The Rise of the Creative Class: And How It's Transforming Work, Leisure, Community and Everyday Life* (New York: Basic Books, 2004), 74.

12. "The Return of the Boston Opera House: A Proposal for Converting the Music Hall Theatre to a Performing Arts Complex." Proposal by the Boston Redevelopment Authority, Robert T. Kenney, Director, 1974.

13. "Midtown Cultural District Plan: A Framework for Discussion." Boston Redevelopment Authority and City under Mayor Raymond L. Flynn. February 1989.

14. Jonathan Leaf, "America's Opera Boom," *The American* (July/August 2007): 51. http://www.american.com/archive/2007/july-august-magazine-contents/america2019s-opera-boom.

15. Susan Larson, "Homeless in Boston," *Opera News* (September 1996): 16.

16. Concert program booklet for The Bernstein Centennial Celebration at Tanglewood, Saturday, August 25, 2018. The artists listed were Claudio Abbado, Luciano Berio. Leonard Bernstein, Stephanie Blythe, William Bolcom, Phyllis Curtin, David Del Tredici, Christoph von Dohnányi, Jacob Druckman, Lukas Foss, Michael Gandolfi, Osvaldo Golijov, John Harbison, Gilbert Kalish, Oliver Knussen, Lorin Maazel, Wynton Marsalis, Zubin Mehta, Sherrill Milnes, Seiji Ozawa, Leontyne Price, Ned Rorem, Cheryl Studer, Sanford Sylvan, Michael Tilson Thomas, Dawn Upshaw, Shirley Verrett, and David Zinman.

Appendix A

1. Lynn Gilbert and Gaylen Moore, *Particular Passions: Talks with Women Who Have Shaped Our Times* (New York: C.N. Potter, 1981), 241.
2. New England Conservatory Archives, Blumenthal Family Library, Boston, MA.
3. https://archives.nyphil.org/index.php/artifact/7e544e4f-4c3a-405f-b127-b291f47c9bec-0.1?search-type=singleFilter&search-text=caldwell&search-dates-from=05%2F01%2F1978&search-dates-to=09%2F01%2F1978.
4. Jay Rosenfeld, "Music Center Opera Students Present 'La Finta Giardiniera,'" review of *La Finta Giardiniera* by Mozart, *Berkshire Eagle*, July 26, 1950.
5. Richard Dyer, "Guest Caldwell Does Well," review of concert performance, Symphony Hall, *Boston Globe*, January 21, 1977.
6. Joseph Horowitz, "Miss Caldwell, Philharmonia in All Berlioz," review of concert performance, Brooklyn Academy of Music, *New York Times*, March 5, 1978.
7. John Ardoin, "Making Contact," *Opera News* (March 6, 1982): 28.
8. Takashi Oka, "Peking Cheers Sarah Caldwell's 'Traviata,'" *The Christian Science Monitor*, July 17, 1981.
9. The music was performed in the United States in 2012 by the Princeton Symphony Orchestra, a performance which the reviewer suggests may have been its first complete performance. No mention of Caldwell's premiere is made. James R. Oestreich, "Prokofiev Version of 'Eugene Onegin' in a Russian Weekend at Princeton," *New York Times*, February 13, 2012.
10. Richard Leacock and Valerie Lalonde, "A Musical Adventure in Siberia," in *Richard Leacock & Valerie Lalonde: The Paris Years, 1989 to 2009*, Watertown, MA. Documentary Educational Resources, 2013.
11. Sarah Caldwell, *Challenges: A Memoir of My Life in Opera* (Middletown, Connecticut: Wesleyan University Press, 2008), 194.
12. Winthrop Sargeant, "Musical Events: Brava!" review of *Falstaff* by Verdi and *Lulu* by Berg, *The New Yorker* (October 14, 1967): 154.
13. John Rockwell, "Opera: Rich Sample of 'War and Peace,'" review of *War and Peace* by Prokofiev, *New York Times*, December 23, 1974.
14. Andrew Porter, "Musical Events: Star-crossed in Boston," *The New Yorker* (June 16, 1975): 97.
15. Andrew Porter, "Musical Events: Verdi and Violettas," review of *La Traviata* by Verdi, *The New Yorker* (Jan 26, 1976): 90.
16. Harold C. Schonberg, "Opera: Caldwell at Met," review of *La Traviata* by Verdi, *New York Times*, January 15, 1976.
17. Richard Dyer, "Sarah Caldwell—Her Genius Is Her Gimmick," *New York Times*, January 11, 1976.
18. Richard Dyer, "Sarah Caldwell—Her Genius Is Her Gimmick."
19. Robert Jacobson, "Boston," review of *The Barber of Seville* by Rossini, *Opera News* (September 1974): 54.
20. Thor Eckert, Jr., "Boston," review of *Stiffelio* by Verdi, *Opera News* (April 8, 1978): 62.
21. Robert Baxter, "Boston," review of *Fidelio* by Beethoven, *Opera* (May 1976): 464.
22. Allen Hughes, "Descent in Balloon Enlivens 'L'Elisir' at the Met," review of *L'Elisir d'Amore* by Donizetti, *New York Times*, March 4, 1978.
23. Thor Eckert, Jr., "Boston," review of *Die Fledermaus* by Strauss, *Opera News* (March 29, 1980): 35.
24. Lloyd Schwartz, "Exhuming Rigoletto," review of *Rigoletto* by Verdi, *Boston Phoenix*, May 12, 1981.
25. Donal Henehan, "Music: Sarah Caldwell," review of New York Philharmonic concert, *New York Times*, November 11, 1975.
26. Karen Pendle, ed., *Women & Music: A History* (Bloomington: Indiana University Press, 1991), 244.
27. Robert Jones, "Walking into the Fire," *Opera News* (February 14, 1976): 13.
28. Readers may also find a CD of the Opera Company of Boston production of *Semiramide* (1965) starring Joan Sutherland is also available, but that was conducted by Richard Bonynge.
29. https://www.libraries.psu.edu/findingaids/95.htm. From the collection webpage: "In 1976, the Institute for the Arts and Humanistic Studies sponsored the production of the original opera *Be Glad Then, America* to commemorate Ameri-

ca's bicentennial. The opera incorporated a chorus of two hundred Penn State choir students, professional opera singers from the Metropolitan Opera, popular folk singer Odetta, and Penn State's ROTC students as soldiers. The production was planned by Stanley Weintraub and William Allison, the Institute's Director and Associate Director at that time, respectively. Composers from across the country sent applications; Weintraub and Allison selected the work of Pulitzer Prize winner John La Montaine. The opera was conducted by the Boston Opera's Sarah Caldwell, and was performed in the newly-completed Eisenhower Auditorium.... Production records for the opera, 'Be Glad Then, America,' include correspondence, financial and legal materials, music scores, minutes, schedules, cast and crew information, 82 posters, publicity, 142 audiotapes, 3 scrapbooks, and 40 video recordings."

30. Melissa Blouin, "Voices of the Past," *University of Arkansas Research Frontiers* (Fall 2001): 13.

Bibliography

Archives and Collections

The American National Theater and Academy Collection, Robert and Wilva Breen Collection, 1933–1980, George Mason University. Information available at http://ead.lib.virginia.edu/vivaxtf/view?docId=gmu/vifgm00039.xml.
Boris Goldovsky Collection, New England Conservatory Archives, Blumenthal Family Library, Boston, MA.
Boston Symphony Orchestra Archives, Boston, MA.
Central Opera Service Bulletins, 1959–1990.
Cultural Policy and the Arts National Data Archive (CPANDA).
Ford Foundation Archives.
Harvard Theater Collection, Cambridge, MA.
Library of Congress, Audio-Visual Collection, Washington, D.C.
New York Public Library, Performing Arts Research Collections, Music Division, New York, NY.
Sarah Caldwell Collection, Howard Gottlieb Archival Research Center at Boston University, Boston, MA.

Video Sources

"Antonia, a Portrait of the Woman." Judy Collins and Jill Godmilow, Public Library of Cincinnati and Hamilton County Collection (Library of Congress). United States: Pyramid Films, 1974.
The Balcony by Di Domenica. Conducted and directed by Sarah Caldwell. Opera Company of Boston. Archival video, June 17, 1988. From the Sarah Caldwell Collection, Howard Gottlieb Archival Research Center at Boston University, Boston, MA.
The Barber of Seville by Rossini. Conducted and Directed by Sarah Caldwell. New York City Opera. Hollywood: Paramount Home Video, 1988.
The Black Swan by Whitman. Conducted by James Freeman. Directed by Sarah Caldwell. Archival video, September 11, 1998. Courtesy of Swarthmore College, Swarthmore, PA.
Camera Three: Sarah Caldwell and the Opera Company of Boston. Directed by Thomas Knott. Rehearsal for Donizetti's *Daughter of the Regiment* starring Beverly Sills. May 6, 1973. United States: CBS-TV. Motion Picture Reading Room. Library of Congress. Washington, D.C.
CBS Evening News with Walter Cronkite. Report by Charles Osgood. Vanderbilt News Archive, November 12, 1975.
Great Performances: The Opera House. Great Performances: Directed and Produced by Susan Froemke, 2018. The PBS Great Performances series is produced by THIRTEEN PRODUCTIONS LLC for WNET.
Intolleranza 1960 by Nono. Conducted by Bruno Maderna. Directed by Sarah Caldwell. Opera Company of Boston. Filmed for television broadcast by WGBH Boston, 1965. From the

Sarah Caldwell Collection, Howard Gottlieb Archival Research Center at Boston University, Boston, MA.
Macbeth by Shakespeare. Directed by Sarah Caldwell. Directed for video by Kirk Browning. Princeton: Films for the Humanities, 1981.
Madama Butterfly by Puccini. Conducted and directed by Sarah Caldwell. Opera Company of Boston. Archival video, January 28, 1990. From the Sarah Caldwell Collection, Howard Gottlieb Archival Research Center at Boston University, Boston, MA.
The Makropulos Case by Janáček. Conducted and directed by Sarah Caldwell. Opera Company of Boston. Archival video, No exact given, May1986. From the Sarah Caldwell Collection, Howard Gottlieb Archival Research Center at Boston University, Boston, MA.
Mass by Bernstein. Conducted and Directed by Sarah Caldwell. Opera Company of Boston. Archival video, January 29, 1989. From the Sarah Caldwell Collection, Howard Gottlieb Archival Research Center at Boston University, Boston, MA.
Médée by Cherubini. Conducted and Directed by Sarah Caldwell. Opera Company of Boston. Archival video, January 27,1988. From the Sarah Caldwell Collection, Howard Gottlieb Archival Research Center at Boston University, Boston, MA.
"A Musical Adventure in Siberia," in *Richard Leacock & Valerie Lalonde: The Paris Years, 1989 to 2009*. Richard Leacock and Valerie Lalonde. Watertown, MA: Documentary Educational Resources, 2013.
On the Road to Tang. Jon Newsom, Jan Lauridsen, and Thomas A. Knott, 2003. Laurence Ernest Roland Picken Collection, Library of Congress, Washington, D.C.
Orpheus in the Underworld by Offenbach. Conducted and Directed by Sarah Caldwell. Opera Company of Boston. Archival video, June 1982. From the Sarah Caldwell Collection, Howard Gottlieb Archival Research Center at Boston University, Boston, MA.
What Time Is the Next Swan? Uncredited. Rehearsal for *Benvenuto Cellini* by Berlioz. Opera Company of Boston, May 1975. New York: Phoenix Films.

Audio Sources

Beethoven, Ludwig von. *Fidelio*, VAI Audio, 2004. Chorus and Orchestra of the Opera Company of Boston. Conducted by Sarah Caldwell. Starring Teresa Kubiak and Jon Vickers.
Bellini, Vincenzo. *I Capuleti e i Montecchi*, VAI Audio, 2004. Chorus and Orchestra of the Opera Company of Boston. Conducted by Sarah Caldwell and William Fred Scott. Starring Tatiana Troyanos and Beverly Sills.
Berlioz, Hector. *Benvenuto Cellini*, VAI Audio, 2003. Chorus and Orchestra of the Opera Company of Boston. Conducted by Sarah Caldwell. Starring Jon Vickers.
Bernstein, Leonard. *Mass*, Naxos, 2009. Baltimore Symphony Orchestra. Conducted by Marin Alsop. Starring Jubilant Sykes.
Donizetti, Gaetano. *Don Pasquale*, EMI Classics, 2002. London Symphony. Conducted by Sarah Caldwell. Starring Beverly Sills and Donald Gramm.
Interview with Sarah Caldwell and Beverly Sills. Hosted by Bob Sherman. 1st National Bank Great Artists Series, November 9, 1975. Sound recording. Recorded Sound Reference Center. Library of Congress. Washington, D.C.
Sarah Caldwell Tells Anecdotes About Her Conducting and Production Experiences and Answers Questions from National Press Club. Broadcast on National Public Radio, May 13, 1976. Sound recording. Recorded Sound Reference Center. Library of Congress. Washington, D.C.
Shostakovich, Dimitri. *Cello and Piano Concertos of Shostakovich* (Cello Concerto no. 1 in E flat, Op. 107 and Piano Concerto no. 1 in C Minor), Audiofon, 1997. Yekaterinburg Philharmonic Orchestra. Conducted by Sarah Caldwell. William De Rosa (cello) and Valentina Lisitsa (piano).
Speaking Freely. Hosted by Edwin Newman. Audio interview with Sarah Caldwell, November 29, 1975. Sound recording. Recorded Sound Reference Center. Library of Congress. Washington, D.C.

Books

Ammer, Christine. *Unsung: A History of Women in American Music.* Westport: Greenwood Press, 1980.
Barranger, Milly S. *Margaret Webster: A Life in the Theater.* Ann Arbor: University of Michigan Press, 2004.
Bing, Rudolf. *5000 Nights at the Opera: The Memoirs of Sir Rudolf Bing.* New York: Doubleday, 1972.
Caldwell, Sarah. *Challenges: A Memoir of My Life in Opera.* Middletown, Connecticut: Wesleyan University Press, 2008.
Cole, Toby, and Helen Krich Chinoy. *Directors on Directing: a source book of the modern theater.* Indianapolis: Bobbs-Merrill, 1963.
Dizikes, John. *Opera in America.* New Haven: Yale University Press, 1993.
Domingo, Plácido. *My First Forty Years.* New York: Alfred A. Knopf, 1983.
Eaton, Quaintance. *The Boston Opera Company.* New York: Appleton-Century, 1965.
Feather, Carol Ann. "Women Band Directors in American Higher Education," in *The Musical Woman 1984–1985*, vol. II, ed. Judith Lang Zaimont. New York: Greenwood Press, 1987.
Florida, Richard L. *The Rise of the Creative Class: and how it's transforming work, leisure, Community and everyday life.* New York: Basic Books, 2002.
Fuchs, Peter Paul. *The Music Theater of Walter Felsenstein.* New York: W.W. Norton, 1975.
Gilbert, Lynn, and Gaylen Moore. *Particular Passions, Talks with Women Who Have Shaped Our Times.* New York: C.N. Potter, 1981.
Goldovsky, Boris. *Bringing Opera to Life.* New York: Appleton-Century-Crofts, 1968.
Goldovsky, Boris. *My Road to Opera: The Recollections of Boris Goldovsky.* Boston: Houghton Mifflin, 1979.
Green, Martin. *The Problem of Boston: Some Readings in Cultural History.* New York: W.W. Norton, 1966.
Heilbrun, James, and Charles M. Gray. *The Economics of Art and Culture: An American Perspective.* Cambridge: Cambridge University Press, 2001.
Horowitz, Joseph. *Classical Music in America: A History of Its Rise and Fall.* New York and London: W.W. Norton, 2005.
Kerman, Joseph. *Contemplating Music: Challenges to Musicology.* Cambridge: Harvard University Press, 1985.
Kessler, Daniel. *Sarah Caldwell: The First Woman of Opera.* Lanham, MD: Scarecrow Press, 2008.
Kufrin, Joan. *Uncommon Women.* Piscataway: New Century, 1981.
Kupferberg, Herbert. *Tanglewood.* New York: McGraw-Hill, 1976.
Leichentritt, Hugo. *Serge Koussevitzky The Boston Symphony Orchestra and the New American Music.* Cambridge: Cambridge University Press, 1947.
Martorella, Rosanne. *The Sociology of Opera.* South Hadley, MA: J.F. Bergin, 1982.
Millet, Kate. *Sexual Politics.* Garden City, NY: Doubleday, 1970.
Neufeld, James. *Lois Marshall: A Biography.* Toronto: Dundurn Press, 2010.
Norton, Elliot. *Broadway Down East: An Informal Account of the Plays, Players and Playhouses of Boston from Puritan Times to the Present.* Boston: Trustees of the Public Library of the City of Boston, 1978.
Parker, Roger, ed. *The Oxford Illustrated History of Opera.* New York: Oxford University Press, 1994.
Pendle, Karin, ed. *Women and Music: A History.* Bloomington: Indiana University Press, 1991.
Rushton, Julian. *W.A. Mozart: Idomeneo.* Cambridge: Cambridge University Press, 1993.
Sills, Beverly. *Bubbles: A Self-Portrait.* Indianapolis: Bobbs-Merrill, 1976.
Sills, Beverly, and Lawrence Linderman. *Beverly: An Autobiography.* New York: Bantam Books, 1987.
Sutherland, Joan. *The Autobiography of Joan Sutherland: A Prima Donna's Progress.* Milsons Point: Random House Australia, 1997.

Verrett, Shirley. *I Never Walked Alone*. Hoboken: John Wiley & Sons, 2003.
Williams, Jeannie. *Jon Vickers: A Hero's Life*. Boston: Northeastern University Press, 1999.

Articles

Amiel, Barbara. "Bravissimo." *Macleans Magazine* (June 12, 2006): 61–64.
Ardoin, John. "Making Contact." *Opera News* (March 6, 1982): 28–29.
Barr, Stuart. "Laurence Picken, Polymath Equally at Home in Biology and the Musicology of Both East and West." *The Guardian,* June 6, 2007.
Blouin, Melissa. "Voices of the Past." *University of Arkansas Research Frontiers* (Fall 2001): 8–15.
Boston Redevelopment Authority and City under Mayor Raymond L. Flynn. "Midtown Cultural District Plan: A Framework for Discussion." February 1989.
Caldwell, Sarah. "The Dedicated Artist's Cry: Send Money." *New York Times*, June 4, 1967.
_____. "The Future of Opera in the United States." *Music Educator's Journal* 54 (February 1968): 56–57.
_____. "An Opera Company for Boston." *Music Journal* 12 (May 1964): 23–25.
_____. Program notes for Gounod's *Faust*, presented by the Opera Company of Boston, 1981 at The Opera House, Boston. Conducted and Directed by Sarah Caldwell. From the Sarah Caldwell Collection, Howard Gottlieb Archival Research Center at Boston University, Boston, MA.
_____. "Sarah Caldwell Comments." Program note for *The Trojans* by Berlioz. Presented by the Opera Company of Boston, 1972, at the Aquarius Theater. Conducted and Directed by Sarah Caldwell. From the Sarah Caldwell Collection, Howard Gottlieb Archival Research Center at Boston University, Boston, MA.
Christy, Marian. "As Life Gets Tough, She Gets Motivated." *Boston Globe,* June 13, 1990.
Cooper, Michael. "An 'Otello' Without Blackface Highlights an Enduring Tradition in Opera." *New York Times,* September 17, 2015.
Crutchfield, Will. "Boston and Soviet Plan Music Trade." *New York Times*, September 18, 1987.
Dace, Wallace. "Opera Production and the American Educational Theater." *Educational Theater Journal* 9:3 (October 1957): 231–235.
Downes, Olin. "The Language of Opera—Encores in Symphony Hall." *New York Times*, November 9, 1924.
_____. "More Views on Opera in English." *New York Times*, January 27, 1946.
Duffie, Bruce. "Conversation Piece: Sarah Caldwell." *The Opera Journal* (1994): 41–51.
Dyer, Richard. "Caldwell Purchases Mortgage on Opera House." *Boston Globe*, November 11, 1992.
_____. "Caldwell Will Go to Arkansas for Academic Post." *Boston Globe*, July 29, 1999.
_____. "Canon Quietly Sets Stage for Opera." *Boston Globe*, July 14, 1989.
_____. "The Divine Sarah." *Opera News* (December 2003): 43–45.
_____. "A Dream Fulfilled." *Boston Globe*, June 10, 1990.
_____. "Fate of the Opera House Remains Uncertain." *Boston Globe*, February 1, 1992.
_____. "Four's a Crowd." *Boston Globe*, April 15, 1990.
_____. "Homey Touch." *Boston Globe*, March 15, 1988.
_____. "Impresario of Boston Opera, dead at 82." *Boston Globe*, March 25, 2006.
_____. "The Lights Dim for Boston Opera." *Boston Globe*, May 12, 1991.
_____. "Opening Act at the Opera House." *Boston Globe*, September 2, 1994.
_____. "Opera Company Suspends Canon." *Boston Globe*, March 28, 1989.
_____. "The Opera Company's Tale of Woe." *Boston Globe*, April 3, 1989.
_____. "Opera House Encore Plans to Restore Boston Landmark to Be Announced Today." *Boston Globe*, April 22, 1999.
_____. "The Opera Wars: A Truce." *Boston Globe*, October 20, 1991.

———. "The Question of Caldwell's Link to Manila." *Boston Globe*, August 1, 1982.
———. "Sarah Caldwell Gets a Dream House." *Boston Globe*, December 10, 1978.
———. "Sarah Caldwell's 20th Anniversary Year: She'll Come Up with Something Special." *Boston Sunday Globe*, February 12, 1978.
Dyer, Richard, and Jess McLaughlin. "A Struggle Backstage for Opera Company." *Boston Globe*, March 25, 1989.
Eaton, Quaintance. "Renaissance Woman." *Opera News* (April 18,1964): 26–29.
Ericson, Raymond. "How not to do 'Boris.'" *New York Times*, April 4, 1965.
Forster, Margaret. "Boston's Opera House Expansion Approved." September 26, 2002. http://findarticles.com/p/articles/mi_kmpre/is_200209/ai_n6889636/.
French, Desiree. "More Resignations at OCB." *Boston Globe*, May 6, 1989.
———. "Opera Company Gets Management Review Panel's Report." *Boston Globe*, April 21, 1989.
———. "Opera Company Reinstates Canon." *Boston Globe*, March 29, 1989.
Genzlinger, Neil. "Frank Corsaro, Director Who Shook up Opera World, Dies at 92." *New York Times*, November 13, 2017.
Gold, Alan R. "Cultural Festival with Soviet Saved." *New York Times*, March 6, 1988.
Gussow, Mel. "Can a Committee Revive the Beaumont?" *New York Times*, January 21, 1979.
Hamblin, Dora Jane. "She Puts the Oomph in the Opera." *Life* (March 5, 1965): 77–85.
Hamburger, Philip. "Musical Events: In the Hills." *The New Yorker* (August 13, 1949): 48–49.
Hansen, Jennifer. "Sarah Caldwell." *Arkansas Democrat Gazette*, December 5, 1999.
Heilbrun, James. "Baumol's Cost Disease," in *A Handbook of Cultural Economics*, ed. Ruth Towse (Northhampton, MA: Edward Elgar, 2003): 91–101.
Helbing, Terry. "The Use of Lasers in 'The Damnation of Faust.'" *Theatre Design and Technology* (Fall 1978): 15–16.
Hemann, Shannon. "Renowned Opera Conductor to Offer Music Department 'a little boost' in Stint at UA." *Arkansas Democrat-Gazette*, July 29, 1999.
Henahan, Donal. "Conducting Becomes Sarah Caldwell." *New York Times*, December 22, 1974.
———. "Prodigious Sarah." *New York Times Magazine* (October 5, 1975): 21–98.
Holland, Bernard. "Judith Somogi, 47, a Conductor; Among First Women on Podium." *New York Times*, March 26, 1988.
———. "Musicians Come In from the Cold War." *New York Times*, March 13, 1988.
———. "Sarah Caldwell, After Illness, Plans New Projects." *New York Times*, May 5, 1985.
Honan, William H. "A U.S.-Soviet Cultural Rapprochement." *New York Times*, February 17, 1988.
Jacobson, Robert. "The Unsinkable Sarah Caldwell." *After Dark* (May 1972): 51–52.
Jones, Robert. "Walking into the Fire." *Opera News* (February 14, 1976): 11–13.
Kelly, Kevin. "Caldwell Directs Her First Play." *Boston Globe*, January 13, 1981.
Kozinn, Allan. "At Juilliard Gains Are Recounted." *New York Times*, October 22, 1988.
———. "New York Philharmonic Prepares for Soviet Tour." *New York Times*, May 26, 1988.
Kreuzer, Gundula. "Voices from Beyond: Verdi's *'Don Carlos'* and the Modern Stage." *Cambridge Opera Journal* (July 2006): 151–179.
Kupferberg, Herbert. "America Sings: Sarah Caldwell's National Opera." *Atlantic Monthly* (September 1967): 120–122.
———. "Women of the Baton—The New Music Masters." *Parade* (May 14, 1975): 4–5.
Larson, Susan. "Homeless in Boston." *Opera News* (September 1996): 12–17.
Lawson, Kay D. "A Woman's Place Is at the Podium." *Music Educator's Journal* (1984): 46–49.
Leaf, Jonathan. "America's Opera Boom." *The American* (July/August 2007). http://www.american.com/archive/2007/july-august-magazine-contents/america2019s-opera-boom.
Leedom, Joanne. "Consortium Ensures Opera for New England." *The Christian Science Monitor*, June 4, 1970.

McLaughlin, Jeff. "Concert Opera in Red, Ends Season." *Boston Globe*, March 24, 1989.
Miller, Margo. "Caldwell Cuts Manilla Tie." *Boston Globe*, October 18, 1983.
———. "Ex-Bass Bonis Inherits the Opera." *Boston Morning Globe*, January 29, 1967.
Montgomery, M.R. "Opera House Restoration Plans Move Forward." *Boston Globe*, April 23, 1999.
Noria, Jane. "A Plea for the Development of a National Opera." *New York Times*, August 28, 1910.
Novick, Julius. "Interlopers in the Opera House." *American Theatre* (May 1986): 10–17.
Oka, Takashi. "Peking Cheers Sarah Caldwell's 'Traviata.'" *The Christian Science Monitor*, July 17, 1981.
Pfeiffer, Ellen. "City Salutes Sarah, Launches Opera Week." *Boston Globe*, January 26, 1972.
Phillips, Harvey E. "Sarah Caldwell's New Idea." *Musical America* (September 1977): 17–19.
Porter, Andrew. "Musical Events: Proper Bostonian." *The New Yorker* (June 2, 1973): 102–108.
Potter, John Mason. "Frowns on Female Symphony Leaders." *Boston Massachusetts Post*, August 3, 1952.
Rich, Alan. "Sarah Caldwell." *Sky* (November 1977): 66–67.
Rich, Frank. "Stage: 'Macbeth' Returns." *New York Times*, January 24, 1981.
Richmond, Jonathan. "Bolder If Not Wiser, Sarah Caldwell Returns." *Christian Science Monitor*, February 11, 1988.
Robinson, Harlow. "Operatic Intrigue, the Comic, Tragic, True Tale of Opera on Huntington Avenue." *N.U. Magazine Online* (November 1997): 1–8.
Rockwell, John. "Boston Opera's Troubles Are Traced to Caldwell—Union Conflict." *New York Times*, January 20, 1982.
———. "Donald Gramm Is Dead at 56; Bass-Baritone At Met Opera." *New York Times*, June 3, 1983.
Rogers, Harold. "The Money, the Time and the Place." *Christian Science Monitor*, March 18, 1963.
Sargeant, Winthrop. "Profiles: Infinite Pains." *The New Yorker* (December 24, 1973): 43–49.
Schonberg, Harold C. "Opera Hits a High Note Across America." *New York Times*, October 9, 1977.
Steinberg, Michael. "Opera in Boston Needs a Permanent Home." *Boston Globe*, October 23, 1966.
Swed, Mark. "A Maestro and City in Concert; L.A. Has Left Its Mark on Salonen. And he's Made It a Musical Capital." *Los Angeles Times*, April 12, 2009.
Thebodeau, Lorraine. "Young Arkansan Stirs Staid Massachusetts Music Circle." *Little Rock Arkansas Gazette*, June 5, 1949.
Thomson, Virgil. "Opera: It Is Everywhere in America." *New York Times*, September 23, 1962.
Tommasini, Anthony. "Colorblind Casting Widens Opera's Options." *New York Times*, December 21, 2012.
Trustman, Deborah. "Opera from the Heart of Texas." *New York Times*, May 3, 1981.
Wagner, Richard. "Remarks on Performing the Opera 'Der Fliegende Holländer,'" in *Wagner on Music and Drama: A Compendium of Wagner's Prose Works*, ed. Albert Geldman and Evert Sprinchorn, trans. H. Ashton Ellis (New York: E.P. Dutton, 1964).
Wakin, Daniel J. "Met Has New Rival in Operas at Movies." *New York Times*, December 19, 2007.
Wilcox, Dean. "Political Allegory of Multimedia Extravaganza? A Historical Reconstruction of the Opera Company of Boston's 'Intolleranza.'" *Theater Survey* 37:2 (November 1996): 115–134.
Winfrey, Carey. "Papp Quits Lincoln Center, Citing Artistic-Fiscal 'Trap.'" *New York Times*, June 10, 1977.

Reviews

Baxter, Robert. "*America:* Caldwell's Bold 'Hollander.'" Review of *The Flying Dutchman* by Wagner. *Opera* (May 10, 1970): 418–420.

———. "American: Boston." Review of *Don Quichotte* by Massenet. *Opera* (August 1974): 692–693.

———. "Boston." Review of *Falstaff* by Verdi. *Opera* (1975): 382–384.

———. "Boston." Review of *Fidelio* by Beethoven. *Opera* (May 1976): 463–464.

———. "Boston." Review of *The Damnation of Faust* by Berlioz. *Opera* (August 1978): 782–784.

———. "In Review: Swarthmore, PA." Review of *The Black Swan* by Whitman. *Opera News* (December 1998): 101–102.

Darack, Arthur. "The American National Opera Company." Review of *Lulu* by Berg, *Falstaff* by Verdi, and *Tosca* by Puccini. *HI FI/Musical America* (December 1967): 20–21.

Davis, Peter G. "General Caldwell Goes to War." Review of *War and Peace* by Prokofiev. *New York Times*, May 19, 1974.

———. "Opera: A Too Lavish 'Orfeo' and a Zesty 'Orpheus.'" Review of *Orfeo ed Euridice* by Gluck and *Orpheus in the Underworld* by Offenbach. *New York Times*, June 10, 1977.

Dergin, Cyrus. "Berlioz Opera in American Premiere." Review of *The Trojans* by Berlioz. *Musical America* (April 1955): 3.

Downs, Olin. "Britten's 'Grimes' Unveiled at Lenox." Review of *Peter Grimes* by Britten. *New York Times*, August 7, 1946.

Dyer, Richard. "Boston." Review of *Mass* by Bernstein. *Opera* (June 1989): 688.

———. "A Compelling 'Balcony.'" Review of *The Balcony* by Di Domenica. *Boston Globe*, June 15, 1990.

———. "Faust—Did the Devil Make Caldwell Do It?" Review of *The Damnation of Faust* by Berlioz. *Boston Globe,* March 23, 1978.

———. "Guest Caldwell Does Well." Review of concert performance of *Symphony #8* by Haydn, *Petrushka* by Stravinsky, and *Symphony no. 1* by Carter. Symphony Hall, Boston Symphony Orchestra. *Boston Globe*, January 21, 1977.

———. "Shchedrin Work Is a Triumph." Review of *Dead Souls* by Shchedrin. *Boston Globe*, March 14, 1988.

Eckert, Thor, Jr. "Boston." Review of *Die Fledermaus* by Strauss. *Opera News* (March 29, 1980): 35.

———. "Boston." Review of *Stiffelio* by Verdi. *Opera News* (April 8, 1978): 62.

———. "Boston Opera Jousts with a Challenging "Die Soldaten." Review of *Die Soldaten* by Zimmermann. *Christian Science Monitor*, March 9, 1982.

Ericson, Raymond. "Opera: 'Bartered Bride' Fascinates and Maddens." Review of *The Bartered Bride* by Smetana. *New York Times*, January 28, 1973.

———. "Sarah Caldwell Leads Original 4½ Hour 'Don Carlo.'" Review of *Don Carlos* by Verdi. *New York Times*, May 24, 1973.

Helm, Everett. "Bedlam in Venice." Review of *Intolleranza 1960* by Nono. *New York Times*, May 7, 1961.

Henahan, Donal. "Boston Opera 'Capuleti' Is a Screaming Success." Review of *I Capuleti e i Montecchi* by Bellini. *New York Times*, June 4, 1975.

———. "Music: Sarah Caldwell." Review of New York Philharmonic concert. *New York Times*, November 11, 1975.

———. "Opera: Juilliard Gives Sessions 'Montezuma.'" Review of *Montezuma* by Sessions. *New York Times*, February 21, 1982.

Holland, Bernard. "U.S.-Soviet Portrayal of Gogol's 'Dead Souls.'" Review of *Dead Souls* by Shchedrin. *New York Times*, March 14, 1988.

Horowitz, Joseph. "Miss Caldwell, Philharmonia in All Berlioz." Review of concert performance, Brooklyn Academy of Music. *New York Times*, March 5, 1978.

Hughes, Allen. "Descent in Balloon Enlivens 'L'Elisir' at the Met." Review of *L'Elisir d'Amore* by Donizetti. *New York Times*, March 4, 1978.

_____. "National Opera's 'Falstaff' and 'Tosca' in Brooklyn." Review of *Falstaff* by Verdi and *Tosca* by Puccini. *New York Times*, October 9, 1967.

Hume, Paul. "Caldwell's 'War and Peace.'" Review of *War and Peace* by Prokofiev. *The Saturday Review*, August 31, 1974.

Jacobs, Arthur. "America: Bizarre 'Barbiere.'" Review of *The Barber of Seville* by Rossini. *Opera* (September 1974): 807–808.

Jacobson, Robert. "Boston." Review of *The Barber of Seville* by Rossini. *Opera News* (September 1974): 54.

_____. "Triple Play USA: Montezuma, Ines de Castro, Ashmedai." Review of *Montezuma* by Sessions. *Opera News* (June 1976): 33.

Jahani, Charles. "Washington." Review of *War and Peace* by Prokofiev. *Opera* (November 1974): 997–998.

Jenkins, Speight. "America: Caldwell's 'Bride.'" Review of *The Bartered Bride* by Smetana. *Opera News* (March 10, 1973): 24–25.

Kelly, Kevin. "The Light Side of the Moon." Review of *Voyage to the Moon* by Offenbach. *Boston Globe*, June 19, 1958.

Kerner, Leighton. "Mass Hysteria." Review of *Mass* by Bernstein. *Village Voice* (February 7, 1989): 80.

Knapp Peter M. "'Trojans': The Epic Spectacle Overwhelmed All." Review of *The Trojans* by Berlioz. *Patriot Ledger*, February 8, 1972.

Movshon, George. "America: 'Trojans' at Boston." Review of *The Trojans* by Berlioz. *Opera* (April 1972): 323–325.

Pfeiffer, Ellen. "'Black Swan' Brings Sarah Caldwell Back to America." Review of *The Black Swan* by Whitman. *Boston Herald*, September 15, 1998.

Porter, Andrew. "Musical Events: Caldwell in Command." Review of *War and Peace* by Prokofiev. *The New Yorker* (January 6, 1975): 61–63.

_____. "Musical Events: Star-crossed in Boston." Review of *I Capuleti e i Montecchi* by Bellini. *The New Yorker* (June 16, 1975): 97–98.

_____. "Musical Events: The Matter of Mexico." Review of *Montezuma* by Sessions. *The New Yorker* (April 19, 1976): 115–120.

_____. "Musical Events: Verdi and Violettas." Review of *La Traviata* by Verdi. *The New Yorker* (January 26, 1976): 86–91.

Rich, Frank. "Stage: Macbeth Returns." Review of *Macbeth* by Shakespeare. *New York Times*, January 24, 1981.

Rockwell, John. "Opera: Rich Sample of 'War and Peace.'" Review of *War and Peace* by Prokofiev. *New York Times*, December 23, 1974.

Rosenfeld, Jay C. "Music Center Opera Students Present 'La Finta Giardiniera.'" Review of *La Finta Giardiniera* by Mozart. *Berkshire Eagle*, July 26, 1950.

_____. "Tanglewood Opera Unit Scores Another Triumph." Review of *La Clemenza di Tito* by Mozart. *New York Herald Tribune*, August 9, 1947.

Sargeant, Winthrop. "Musical Events: Brava!" Review of *Falstaff* by Verdi and *Lulu* by Berg. *The New Yorker* (October 14, 1967): 154–155.

Schonberg, Harold C. "Bernstein's New Work Reflects His Background on Broadway." Review of *Mass* by Bernstein. *New York Times*, September 9, 1971.

_____. "Music: A Rare Performance of 'Don Quichotte' is Staged by Sarah Caldwell in Boston." Review of *Don Quichotte* by Massenet. *New York Times*, February 22, 1974.

_____. "On an Ego Trip with Don Quichotte." Review of *Don Quichotte* by Massenet. *New York Times*, March 3, 1974.

_____. "Opera: Caldwell at Met." Review of *La Traviata* by Verdi. *New York Times*, January 15, 1976.

_____. "Opera: Luigi Nono's 'Intolleranza 1960.'" Review of *Intolleranza 1960* by Nono. *New York Times*, February 22, 1965.

_____. "Opera: 'Moses and Aaron.'" Review of *Moses and Aaron* by Schönberg. *New York Times*, December 1, 1966.

Schwartz, Lloyd. "Exhuming 'Rigoletto.'" Review of *Rigoletto* by Verdi. *Boston Phoenix*, May 12, 1981.
Silberman, Margery. "Sarah Caldwell's New National Opera Company in Strong Road Start at Indianapolis." Review of *Lulu* by Berg, *Falstaff* by Verdi, and *Tosca* by Puccini. *Variety* (September 20, 1967): 64.
Snyder, Louis. "Berlioz's Complete, two-evening 'Trojans' in U.S. Premiere." Review of *The Trojans* by Berlioz. *Christian Science Monitor*, February 9, 1972.
Strongin, Theodore. "Boston Goes Mod Over Stravinsky." Review of *The Rake's Progress* by Stravinsky. *New York Times*, March 31, 1967.
Taubman, Howard. "Opera by Grétry Staged at Lenox." Review of *Richard the Lion-Hearted* by Grétry. *New York Times*, August 11, 1953.
_____. "'Titus' by Mozart Presented at Fete." Review of *La Clemenza di Tito* by Mozart. *New York Times*, August 5, 1952.
Taylor, Robert. "Music, 'The Voyage to Moon.'" Review of *Voyage to the Moon* by Offenbach. *Boston Herald*, June 19, 1958.
Walsh, Michael. "High Spirits, Dead Souls." Review of *Dead Souls* by Shchedrin. *Time Magazine* (March 28, 1988): 76.

No author

"A Boston Lincoln Center." *Boston Globe*, January 20, 1967.
"Boston Opera to Open Late." *New York Times*, January 19, 1982.
"Events in Music, Theater: Opera Group, Inc. to Be Permanent Opera Company." *Boston Herald*, April 6, 1958.
"Music's Wonder Woman." *Time Magazine* (November 1975): 52–65.
"Negro Singer Hailed: Grace Bumbry is Praised by Prove for Bayreuth Role." *New York Times*, July 26, 1961.
"Opera Group, Inc." *Boston Globe*, April 5, 1958.
"Opera House for Boston." *New York Times*, March 22, 1908.
"Reports: U.S. Indianapolis." Review of *Falstaff* by Verdi. *Opera News* (October 14, 1967): 22.
"U.S. Female Opera Leader Caldwell Dead at 82." *Today.com*. http://www.today.com/id/11994402/ns/today-today_entertainment/t/us-female-opera-leader-caldwell-dead/#.VXYsWNJViko.

Index

***Bold italics** refers to pages with illustrations*

The Abduction from the Seraglio 68, 103, 166
Aida 18, 31, 33, 68, 69, 88, 168, 169
American National Opera Company (ANOC) 5, 48, 51, 52, 70, 83, 102, 161, 169, 175
Ancient Asian Music Project 6, 145
animals in Caldwell's productions 7, 8, 49, 73, 74, 132
Aquarius Theater 74, 75, 109, 110, 121, 122, 129, 132, 134, 154
Ariadne auf Naxos 36, 67, 169
Auerbach, Cynthia 18

Back Bay Theater 71, 101, 103, 104, 111, 120
The Balcony 9, 64, 65, 67, 83, 142, 149, 152, 164, 169
The Barber of Seville 20, 55, 67, 68, 75–76, 85, 94, 100, 120, 127, 152, 157, 162, 164, 166, 168, 169
Barnes, Edward *see Zetabet*
The Bartered Bride 7, 8, 31, 129, 130, 135, 167
Bartók, Béla *see Bluebeard's Castle; The Miraculous Mandarin; The Wooden Prince*
Baxter, Robert 96, 105, 132, 133, 163
Be Glad Then, America 67, 164, 169, 184n
The Beggar's Opera 68, 89, 100, 166
Bellini, Vincenzo *see I Capuleti e i Montecchi; Norma*
Benvenuto Cellini 8, 67, 91, 151, 164, 168
Berg, Alban *see Lulu*
Berghaus, Ruth 18, 127, 150
Berkshire Music Center 27, 29, 30, 35
Berlioz, Hector *see Benvenuto Cellini; The Damnation of Faust; The Trojans*

Bernstein, Leonard 22, 29, 30, 33, 46, 66, 81, 82, 142, 155, 169; *see also Mass*
B.F. Keith Memorial Theatre 53, 114, 115, **116, 117**
Bing, Rudolf 7, 12, 17, 69, 112, 113, 148
Bizet, Georges *see Carmen; The Pearl Fishers*
The Black Swan 67, 90, 92, 102, 144, 169
Bluebeard's Castle 9, 167
La Bohème 8, 31, 47, 54, 68, 85, 86, 87, 89, 92, 100, 102, 146, 166, 167, 168, 169
Bond, Victoria 21
Boris Godunov 31, 101, 120, 167
Boston Concert Opera 83, 147
Boston Cyclorama 100, 108–109
Boston Lyric Opera 70, 83, 147
The Boston Music Hall *see* Aquarius Theater
Boston Opera Company 43–44, 47, 99
Boston Redevelopment Authority 109, 140, 141, 154
Boulanger, Nadia 15, 158
Brico, Antonia 15, 16
Brook, Peter 12, 95, 118
Brooklyn Academy of Music 49, 50, 51, 161
Brown, Beatrice 16, 17

Canon, Robert 62, 63, 64, 147
I Capuleti e i Montecchi 9, 68, 74, 85, 86, 161, 164, 168
Carmen 33, 36, 39, 119, 166, 167, 168
casting of singers 74, 75, 79, 86–88
celebrities in Caldwell's productions 7, 136
Charpentier, Gustave *see Louise*
Cherubini, Luigi *see Médée*
Command Performance 9, 48, 66, 166
Copland, Aaron *see The Second Hurricane*

Corsaro, Frank 12, 62, 128, 132
Così fan tutte 33, 68, 168
Cousens Gymnasium at Tufts University 106

The Damnation of Faust 8, 33, 115, 132–133, 135, 168
Darack, Arthur 50, 175
The Daughter of the Regiment 7, 67, 68, 105, 106–107, 151, 167
Davies, Peter Maxwell *see Taverner*
De Falla, Manuel *see El Retablo de Maese Pedro*; *La Vida Breve*
Di Domenica, Robert *see The Balcony*
Domingo, Plácido 2, 9, 48, 68, 86
Don Carlos 17, 68, 78, 120, 122–123, 149, 167
Don Giovanni 8, 31, 33, 56, 68, 87, 125, 128, 167, 169
Don Pasquale 68, 85, 97, 115, 164, 168, 169
Don Quichotte 85, 130–132, 135, 152, 167
Donizetti, Gaetano *see The Daughter of the Regiment*; *Don Pasquale*; *L'Elisir d'Amore*
Donnelly Theater *see* Back Bay Theater
Downes, Olin 32, 33
Dyer, Richard 2, 22, 60, 64, 65, 82, 133, 142, 159, 162

Eastern Opera Consortium 10, 104–108
Eben, Jordan, Jr. 42, 113
L'Elisir d'Amore 163, 166
Ericson, Raymond 122, 130

Falstaff 8, 31, 33, 48, 49, 51, 67, 68, 70, 85, 96, 126, 161, 162, 166, 167, 168, 169
Faust 54, 123, **124**, 166, 168, 180
Felsenstein, Walter 5, 9, 10, 12, 84, 88, 98, 127, 128, 129, 137, 148, 150
Fidelio 10, 33, 67, 94, 96, 163, 164, 168
Fine Arts Theater in the Loew's State Theater 47, 100, 101
La Finta Giardiniera 35, **37**, 68, 158, 159, 167
The Fisherman and His Wife 9, 51, 67, 167
Die Fledermaus 7, 8, 85, 163, 166, 168
The Flying Dutchman 82, 103, 105, **106**, 107, 125, 126, 127, 167, 168
Ford Foundation 54
Foss, Lukas *see The Jumping Frog of Calaveras County*
Fox, Carol 13, 14, 148,
Der Freischütz 32, 87, 169
The Frog Who Becomes a Prince 170
funding 55, 113, 127, 153–155

Garden, Mary 13
Gay, John *see The Beggar's Opera*
Gedda, Nicolai 9
Girl of the Golden West 8, 68, 168
Glinka, Mikhail Ivanovich *see Russlan and Ludmilla*
Gluck, Christoph Willibald *see Orfeo ed Euridice*
Gobbi, Tito 9, 48, 85
Goldovsky, Boris 2, 5, 8, 9, 12, 17, 19, 25–26, **27**, 30, 39, 40, 44, 67, 68, 84, 91, 92, 98, 99, 109, 110, 128, 147, 148, 150, 158, 159; *La Clemenza di Tito* at Tanglewood 36; *Idomeneo* at Tanglewood 33–34, 35, 36; *The Trojans* with NEOT 37–38; views on English language translations 31–32
The Good Soldier Schweik 97, 103, 105, 107, **108**, 167
Gounod, Charles *see Faust*
Graf, Herbert 32
Gramm, Donald 9, 30, 47, 68, 73, 75, 85, 89
Green, Martin 112

Hansel and Gretel 15, 26, 51, 55, 57, 166, 168, 169
Heinrich, Rudolf 9, 48, 50, 52, 101
Henahan, Donal 74, 163
Henze, Hans Werner *see The Young Lord*
Hillis, Margaret 16, 17
Hippolyte et Aricie 67, 70, 86, 103–104, 120, 149, 167
Holland, Bernard 2, 60
Horne, Marilyn 9, 48, 68, 85, 86
Humperdinck, Engelbert *see Hansel and Gretel*

The Ice Break 83, 103, 151, 168
The Impresario 52, 170
Intolleranza 1960 8, 70–73, 102, 120, 167
The Invisible City of Kitezh 87, 168

Jacobson, Robert 20, 73, 76, 162
Jahani, Charles 74
Janáček, Leoš *see The Makropulos Case*
The Jumping Frog of Calaveras County 35, 51, 170

Kellogg, Clara Louise 13
Kerner, Leighton 82
Komische Oper 9, 10, 50, 101
Koussevitzky, Serge 17, 27, 28, 29, 30, 32, 33, 35, 143
Krehbiel, Henry 32

Index

Kresge Auditorium, MIT 67, 105, ***106***
Kupfer, Harry 127
Kurka, Robert *see The Good Soldier Schweik*

La Montaine, John *see Be Glad Then, America*
language, performing English translations 31–32, 34, 36, 37, 38, 47, 60, 110
lasers, in Caldwell's productions 133, 134, 137
Laterna Magika 7, 73
Leacock, Richard 49, ***50***, 102–103, 105, 108, 160
Lee, Ming Cho 48, 101, 149
Leginska, Ethel 15
Lert, Ernst 26
Lincoln Center for the Performing Arts 75, 77, 104, 113, 118
The Little Opera House *see* Fine Arts Theater in the Loew's State Theater
Lloyd, David 30, 47
Loew's State Theater 101
Louise 82, 109, 131, 167
Lucia di Lammermoor 67, 68, 104, 167
Lulu 48, 49, ***50***, 51, 70, 101, 102, 103, 166, 167, 169

Macbeth (Shakespeare) 67, 76, 78–80
Macbeth (Verdi) 18, 67, 78, 87, 93, 102, 104, 167, 168
Madama Butterfly 8, 33, 39, 56, 64, 68, 87, 88, 92, 94, 101, 126, 149, 166, 168, 169
The Magic Flute 5, 33, 55, 64, 68, 118, 125, 166, 169
Making Music Together (1988) 5, 58–62, 138
Making Music Together (1991) 5, 142–143
The Makropulos Case ***121***, 169
Manon 85, 166
The Marriage of Figaro 31, 33, 63, 64, 68, 88, 102, 104, 125, 126, 127, 167
Marschner, Heinrich *see The Vampire*
Marshall, Lois 89
Mass 81–82, 169
Massenet, Jules *see Don Quichotte*; *Manon*
Médée 32, 134, 135, 152, 157, 169
Die Meistersinger von Nürnburg 8, 48, 82, 166
Metropolitan Opera 7, 12, 17, 32, 48, 51, 69, 78, 87, 101, 112, 147, 153; Caldwell conducting orchestra 1, 5, 6, 20, 22, 85, 158, 161–162, 163; construction of the "New Met" 113, 114

Middleton, Robert *see Command Performance*
The Miraculous Mandarin 51, 167
Monteux, Pierre 17
Montezuma 66, 76, 149, 152, 168
Morgan, James T. 3, 139, 146
Mortier, Gerard 127, 150
Moses and Aaron 7, 54, 66, 73, 74, 111, 167
Movshon, George 110
Mozart, Wolfgang Amadeus *see The Abduction from the Seraglio*; *Così fan tutte*; *Don Giovanni*; *La Finta Giardiniera*; *The Impresario*; *The Magic Flute*; *The Marriage of Figaro*
Mussorgsky, Modest Petrovich *see Boris Godunov*

New England Conservatory of Music 2, 9, 17, 19, 25, 26, ***27***, 31, 36, 40, 42, 59, 64, 67, 104, 144, 154, 157, 164
New England Opera Theater (NEOT) 2, 9, 36–38, 40, 44, 68, 99, 109, 147, 158, 159; production of *The Trojans* 37–38, 109
New Opera Company of Israel 56
New Opera Company of the Philippines 55–56, 138
New York City Opera 7, 8, 14, 16, 18, 32, 67, 75, 78, 80, 83, 85, 90, 128, 157, 158, 164, 169
Nono, Luigi *see Intolleranza 1960*
Norma 85, ***86***, 87, 92, 96, 114, 167, 169

Oenslager, Donald 122
Offenbach, Jacques *see Orpheus in the Underworld*; *The Tales of Hoffmann*; *Voyage to the Moon*
Olivero, Magda 9, 115
Opera House (formerly the B.F. Keith Memorial Theatre) 53, 54, 58, 60, 62, 64, 81, 92, 97, 101, 114, ***117***, 138, 139–141, 143, 154
Opera House (original 1909) 37, 42, ***43***, 44, 99, 104
Opera New England (ONE) 5, 9, 51–53, 67, 136, 147, 170
Orfeo ed Euridice 68, 87, 136, 149, 168
Orpheum Theater *see* Aquarius Theater
Orpheus in the Underworld 7, 68, 136, 149, 168
Otello 10, 67, 68, 87, 101, 166, 167, 168

The Pearl Fishers 52, 170
Petrides, Frédérique 15
Picken, Laurence 5, 6, 121, 145

Pond, Helen 74, 75, 79, 81, 103, 105, 107, 108, 109, 111, 142, 144
Porter, Andrew 2, 74, 76, 95, 118, 121, 123, 161, 162
The Princess and the Pea 52, 170
Prokofiev, Sergey Sergeyevich *see War and Peace*
Puccini, Giacomo *see La Bohème; Girl of the Golden West; Madama Butterfly; Tosca*
I Puritani 8, 67, 68, 95, 166
Puritanism 112

Queler, Eve 16
Quilico, Louis 9, 85

The Rake's Progress 39, 51, 119, 128, 167
Rameau Jean-Philippe *see Hippolyte et Aricie*
Reese, Sarah 85, 87
Regietheater 12, 126
research on operas by Caldwell 9, 57, 93, 95, 109, 119, 120, *121*, 128, 137, 149
El Retablo de Maese Pedro 168
revision/revisioning operas 5, 11, 12, 35, 62, 126–129, 131, 133, 135, 150
Rich, Alan 48
Rich, Frank 79
Rigoletto 33, 68, 89, 152, 163, 166, 167, 168
Rimsky-Korsakov, Nikolay Andreyevich *see The Invisible City of Kitezh*
Rise and Fall of the City of Mahagonny 167
Rockwell Cage, MIT 97, 107, *108*
Rosenberg, Pamela 18
Der Rosencavalier 33, 96, 169
Rossini, Gioachino *see The Barber of Seville; Semiramide*
Russlan and Ludmilla 168

Sack Savoy Theater *see B.F. Keith Memorial Theatre*
Sarah Stories 10, 20
Sargeant, Winthrop 2, 8, 49, 161
Scarlatti, Alessandro *see The Triumph of Honor*
Schönberg, Arnold *see Moses and Aaron*
Schonberg, Harold C. 2, 68, 72, 74, 81, 132, 162
Schubert Theater 104, 154
Schuller, Gunther *see The Fisherman and his Wife*
Schwartz, Lloyd 163
The Second Hurricane 51, 52, 170
Sellars, Peter 12, 62, 63, 64, 127, 150

Semiramide 7, 8, 67, 68, 70, 86, 167
Senn, Herbert 74, 75, 79, 81, 103, 105, 107, 108, 109, 111, *121*, 142, 144
Sessions, Roger *see Montezuma*
Silja, Anja 9, 85
Sills, Beverly 1, 2, 9, 14, 48, 54, 67, 68, , 74, 75, 76, 78, 85, *86*, 89, 92, 94, 96, 107, 149, 151, 161, 164
Smetana, Bedřich *see The Bartered Bride*
Snyder, Louis 111
Die Soldaten 55, 70, 80, 103, 149, 168
Somogi, Judith 16
Stanislavski, Constantin 17, 25–26, 89, 90
Steiner, Emma R. 15
Stewart, Thomas 30
Stiffelio 68, 115, 162, 168
Strauss, Richard *see Ariadne auf Naxos; Die Fledermaus; Der Rosencavalier*
Stravinsky, Igor 6, 29, 39, 45, 51, 59, 66, 119, 128, 159, 167; *see also The Rake's Progress*
Stroman, Susan 18
Stubblefield, Sally 18
supertitles 5, 32, 60, 110, 137, 144
surtitles 32
Sutherland, Joan 2, 7, 8, 9, 48, 67, 68, 85, 86, 95
Svoboda, Josef 7, 48, 71, 73, 102

The Tales of Hoffmann 10, 87, 101, 167, 169
Tanglewood 2, 8, 9, 12, 16, 17, 27, 28, 29, 30–31, 32, 33, 34, 35, 36, 37, 38, 40, 67, 68, 81, 143, 155, 159
Taverner 152, 169
Taymor, Julie 18
Tebaldi, Renata 9, 48, 68, 85, 86
technology/multi-media in Caldwell's productions 5, 71, 72, 100, 102, 108, 143, 151; *see also* lasers
The Threepenny Opera 169
Thurber, Jeanette 13
Tippet, Michael *see The Ice Break*
Toch, Ernst *see The Princess and the Pea*
Tosca 8, 48, 49, 68, 70, 88, 89, 102, 115, 166, 167, 168, 169
tours/touring opera 5, 8, 13, 37, 40, 44, 48–53, 54, 55, 70, 96, 99, 104, 136, 141, 147, 159, 161
La Traviata 1, 5, 20, 67, 68, 85, 101, 146, 159, 162, 166, 167, 169
The Triumph of Honor 51, 170
The Trojans 32, 54, 109–112,149, 151, 167
Il Trovatore 33, 68, 169
Troyanos, Tatiana 9, 68, 74, 85, 86, 161, 164
Turandot 33, 56, 68, 87, 169

University of Arkansas 144, 145, 164
Ural Philharmonic Orchestra 5, 103, 139, 143, 144, 159, 160–161

The Vampire 52, 170
Van Beethoven, Ludwig *see Fidelio*
Verdi, Giuseppe *see Aida*; *Don Carlos*; *Falstaff*; *Macbeth*; *Otello*; *Rigoletto*; *Stiffelio*; *La Traviata*; *Il Trovatore*
Verrett, Shirley 2, 9, 30, 67, 82, 85, 87–88, 90, 92, 93, 96, 115, 151, 155
Vickers, Jon 2, 9, 67, 85, 164
La Vida Breve 168
Vivian Beaumont Theater 67, 77, 78, 80, 114
Von Weber, Carl Maria *see Der Freischütz*
Voyage to the Moon 46–47, 48, 54, 85, 89, 149, 166

Wagner, Richard *see The Flying Dutchman*; *Die Meistersinger von Nürnburg*

Wallmann, Margarete 18
War and Peace 66, 74, 149, 161, 168
Webster, Margaret 12, 17, 18
Weigel, Helene 18
Weill, Kurt *see Rise and Fall of the City of Mahagonny*; *The Threepenny Opera*
Wernicke, Herbert 127, 150
Whitman, Thomas *see The Black Swan*
The Wooden Prince 167

The Young Lord 7, 67, 90, 69

Zambello, Francesca 14, 18
Zetabet 170
Zimmerman, Mary 18
Zimmermann, Bernd Alois *see Die Soldaten*

www.ingramcontent.com/pod-product-compliance
Lightning Source LLC
Chambersburg PA
CBHW032045300426
44117CB00009B/1195